The Attachment Parenting Book

The Attachment Parenting Book

A Commonsense Guide to Understanding
and Nurturing Your Baby

WILLIAM SEARS, M.D., AND MARTHA SEARS, R.N.

LITTLE, BROWN AND COMPANY

New York ♦ *Boston* ♦ *London*

Dedicated to the
persons we're most
attached to — our children:

James

Robert

Peter

Hayden

Erin

Matthew

Stephen

Lauren

Little, Brown and Company
Hachette Book Group
1290 Avenue of the Americas, New York, NY 10104
littlebrown.com

FIRST EDITION

Little, Brown and Company is a division of Hachette Book Group, Inc.
The Little, Brown name and logo are trademarks of Hachette Book Group, Inc.

The publisher is not responsible for websites (or their content)
that are not owned by the publisher.

LIBRARY OF CONGRESS CATALOGING-IN-PUBLICATION DATA

Sears, William, M.D.
    The attachment parenting book : a commonsense guide to under-
standing and nurturing your baby / by William Sears and Martha Sears.
        p. cm.
    Includes index.
    ISBN 978-0-316-77809-1
    1. Parenting. 2. Parent and child. 3. Child rearing. I. Title: Commonsense guide to understanding and nurturing your baby. II. Sears, Martha. III. Title.
HQ755.8 .S428 2001
649'.1 — dc21   2001029150

20 19 18 17 16 15 14

RRD-C

Designed by Jeanne Abboud

Drawings by Deborah Maze

PRINTED IN THE UNITED STATES OF AMERICA

Contents

A Word from Dr. Bill and Martha

ALL PARENTS WANT their children to grow up to be kind, affectionate, empathic, well disciplined, and, of course, bright and successful. The ways in which parents help their children develop these qualities differ, since every child is born with a unique personality. The first step in learning how to guide your child is to become an expert in your child. To help you to do this, we will introduce you to a style of parenting called attachment parenting (AP) and a list of helpers we call the Baby B's.

Our ideas about attachment parenting are based on thirty-plus years of parenting our own eight children and observing moms and dads whose parenting choices seemed to make sense and whose children we liked. We have witnessed the effects this approach to parenting has on children. There is something wonderfully special about these children: they are compassionate, caring, and responsive, and they trust themselves and the people who are close to them. We believe that attachment parenting immunizes children against many of the social and emotional diseases that plague our society. How you parent your children in the early years really does make a difference when it comes to what kind of adults they become. While certainly we can't promise you that attachment parenting will make you perfect parents of perfect children, we can promise you that your children will turn out better than if you hadn't practiced attachment parenting. In addition, attachment parenting will make you a wiser parent and help you enjoy your children more.

Actually, attachment parenting is what most parents would do anyway if they had the confidence and support they needed to follow their own intuitions. In a way, this book is our attempt to give back to parents the instinctual, high-touch way of caring for their children that decades of detachment advice have robbed them of. We are passionate about attachment parenting because for more than three decades we have seen its effects. It's wonderful! It works! Now let's see how it can work for you.

Becoming Attached — How to Get There

"I can read her so well," a new mother proudly exclaimed as she brought her one-month-old infant in for a checkup. "She loves to nurse, and I love to watch her."

♦ ♦ ♦

"Everyone tells me what a bright baby I have," said the mother of a cheerful six-month-old who caught my eye and smiled as I listened to his mother. "Andrew hardly ever cries. He really doesn't need to."

♦ ♦ ♦

"I saw that look in his eye, and I knew he was headed right for the street," recalled the mother of an almost-two-year-old. "I called out, 'Stop,' and Ben instantly turned and looked at me. Maybe he read the alarm in my voice. It made him stop even before I could get to him and pick him up."

♦ ♦ ♦

"My daughter marched off to kindergarten last week, excited and proud to be going to 'real' school," said the relieved mother of a four-year-old. "I was concerned because we tried preschool last year and she just wasn't happy there. But now she's more confident, and she seems happy to be on her own for part of the day."

♦ ♦ ♦

"Kris's best friend has been having some trouble getting along with the other kids," said the mother of a fourth-grader. "But Kris seems to know how to humor this kid and help him relax and have a good time."

♦ ♦ ♦

"Yes, we trust our daughter with the car on her own (no passengers yet, though)," the mother of a sixteen-year-old told me. "She knows what kind of behavior we expect of her, and she generally lives up to our expectations."

These are the experiences of attached parents, parents who know their children well and whose children trust them. Parenting seems to come naturally to them, yet they also spend time and energy discovering and paying attention to their children's needs. These parents got to be attached parents by working at it. They have been rewarded with warm, open, and trusting relationships with their children. Being attached has made parenting easier and more enjoyable.

The Baby B's of attachment parenting.

WHAT IS ATTACHMENT PARENTING?

Attachment parenting is an approach to raising children rather than a strict set of rules. Certain practices are common to AP parents; they tend to breastfeed, hold their babies in their arms a lot, and practice positive discipline, but these are just tools for attachment, not criteria for being certified as an attached parent. So forget the controversies about breast versus bottle, crying it out or not, and which methods of discipline are acceptable, and go back to the basics. Above all, attachment parenting means opening your mind and heart to the individual needs of your baby and letting your knowledge of your child be your guide to making on-the-spot decisions about what works best for both of you. In a nutshell, AP is learning to read the cues of your baby and responding appropriately to those cues.

As you'll find out, attachment parenting is not an all-or-nothing approach. Realistically, you may not be able to do everything we recommend all of the time, perhaps because you are working outside the home. This does not mean you cannot be an attached mother or that you cannot use the AP tools effectively. In my pediatrics practice I see mothers of all kinds, from stay-at-home moms to moms who work full-time, and they are able to practice AP quite successfully. In fact, attachment parenting is the ideal parenting choice for working mothers. Building a strong attachment can actually make it easier both to work and to parent your baby. In chapter 11, we offer tips for keeping your attachment strong before and after you return to work.

Babyhood, the beginning of attachment.
Raising a child is like taking a trip to a place you've never been. Before your baby's birth, you imagine what the journey will be like. You read guidebooks. You plan your itinerary. You listen to friends who have taken this trip. Once your baby is born and you're on the road together, you recognize some of the sights and know some of the highlights. But you also discover that in many ways the place is nothing like the guidebooks described, and at times you seem to be on an altogether different journey. You encounter good weather one day, unsettling storms the next. Sometimes you have lots of fun; other times you feel like catching the next flight home.

Fortunately there are signs to follow along the way that tell you whether you're on the right path. People you meet share their knowledge of the road ahead. By listening to your baby, you pick up the language. The more you learn about this challenging new place, the more comfortable you become. Eventually you discover that this is a wonderful place to be and that you have learned a lot about yourself here as well as about your baby.

Like any journey, parenting requires adjustments along the way. You can't see everything, and some days you don't go anywhere. You and your baby will devise your own way of covering the miles. But if you are flexible and pay attention, you will arrive together at your destination as a connected parent and child.

Help along the way. "Okay, certainly I want to be attached to my baby," you may feel, "and I want to be able to figure out what's best for her. But how do I get there?"

Your journey to become attached to your child will be different from other parents' journeys, because your child is an individual, and so are you. But at the outset you rely on the same means that other parents use: the tools that will help you be attached to your baby. All these tools are part of the style of parenting we call attachment parenting. Your relationship with your child is the real destination of your journey. Attachment parenting is just a way to get there.

Actually, attachment parenting is the style that many parents use instinctively. When parents open their hearts and minds to their baby's needs and emotions, they use many of the tools that we describe in this book to respond to those needs and emotions and fit them into their own lives. The important point is to get connected to your baby and stay connected as your child grows.

We did what we did just because it seemed natural to us. Only later did we find out there was a name for it, which validated what we did in the first place.

SEVEN ATTACHMENT TOOLS: THE BABY B'S

Attachment parenting, like any job, requires a set of tools. The better your tools are, the more easily and better you can do the job. Notice we use the term *tools* rather than *steps*. With tools you can choose which ones to use to do the job. The term *steps* implies that you have to follow all the steps in order if you want to get the job

---

THE ABC'S OF ATTACHMENT PARENTING

When you practice the Baby B's of AP, your child has a greater chance of growing up with the qualities of the A's and C's:

A's	B's	C's
Accomplished	Birth bonding	Caring
Adaptable	Breastfeeding	Communicative
Adept	Babywearing	Compassionate
Admirable	Bedding close to baby	Confident
Affectionate	Belief in baby's cry	Connected
Anchored	Balance and boundaries	Considerate
Assured	Beware of baby trainers	Cuddly
		Curious

---

done. Think of attachment parenting as *connecting tools,* interactions with your infant that help you and your child get connected. Once you are connected, the whole parent-child relationship (discipline, health care, and just plain day-to-day living with your child) becomes more natural and enjoyable.

Our shorthand name for the tools of attachment parenting is the *Baby B's.* These Baby B's help parents and baby get off to the right start. Use these attachment tools as a starting point for working out your personal parenting style — one that fits the individual needs of your child and your family.

What I learned from attachment parenting is that there is no expert better than me for my baby.

The attachment tools you use with a new baby are based on the biological attachment between mother and baby as well as on the behaviors that help babies to thrive and parents to feel rewarded for their efforts. Take advantage of these tools when your child is a baby, and you'll have a head start on understanding her as a preschooler, as a ten-year-old, and as an adolescent.

Some parents rely more on some tools than on others. Some will use all the tools all the time and use them intensively. Others will use some of the tools some of the time and may not need others, depending on baby's temperament and their own. Sometimes, because of medical or family circumstances, parents can't practice some of the Baby B's. Do the best you can with the resources you have. That's all your child will ever expect of you. And keep your goal in mind: getting — and staying — connected to your child.

Birth bonding. The way baby and parents get started with one another helps the early attachment unfold. The hours and days after birth are a sensitive period when mothers are uniquely primed to care for their newborns, and newborns display their almost magical power over attentive caregivers. Spending lots of time together after birth and beyond allows the natural attachment-promoting behaviors of the infant and the intuitive, biological caregiving qualities of the mother to come together. The infant is needy, and the mother is ready to nurture. Both members of this biological pair get off to the right start if they are constantly together during the first six weeks. Dads also can enjoy birth bonding. While they don't share the physical experience of birth and breastfeeding, in the days and weeks after birth, they can tune in emotionally to their fascinating newborn.

Breastfeeding. Breastfeeding is an excellent exercise in getting to know your baby — something we call *baby reading.* Successful breastfeeding requires a mother to respond to her baby's cues, which is the first step in getting to know your baby and building a trusting relationship. The maternal hormones associated with lactation — prolactin and oxytocin — give intuitive mothering a boost, since they help women feel more relaxed and calm around their babies.

Babywearing. Carried babies fuss less and spend more time in a state of quiet alertness, the behavioral state in which babies learn most about their environment and are nicest to be around. Also, when you "wear" your baby, you become more sensitive as a parent. Because your baby is so close to you, you get to know him better. Baby learns to be content and to trust his caregiver. He also learns a lot about his environment in the arms of a busy caregiver.

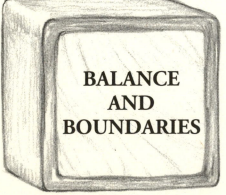

Bed sharing. There is no one right place for all babies to sleep. Wherever all family members get the best night's sleep is the right arrangement for your individual family. Most, but not all, babies sleep best when they are close to their parents. Sleeping close to baby can help some busy parents connect with their babies and care for their babies' needs at night as well as during the day and evening. This is particularly true for mothers who return to work after their maternity leave. Since nighttime is scary for little people, sleeping within close touching and nursing distance minimizes nighttime separation anxiety and helps babies learn that sleep is a pleasant state to enter rather than a fearful one. It is also easier for mothers to do nighttime breastfeeding with baby close at hand. It may work for you some nights and not on other nights.

Belief in baby's cries. A baby's cry is a baby's language. Crying is a valuable signal designed to ensure the baby's survival and to develop the parents' caregiving abilities. Babies, therefore, cry to communicate, not to manipulate. The more sensitively you respond, the more baby learns to trust his parents and his ability to communicate.

Balance and boundaries. In your zeal to give so much to your baby, it's easy to neglect your own needs and those of your marriage. As you will learn in later chapters, the key to putting balance in your parenting is being appropriately responsive to your baby — knowing when to say yes and when to say no, and having the wisdom to say yes to yourself when you need help.

Beware of baby trainers. Once you have a baby, you may become the target of well-meaning advisers who shower you with detachment advice, such as, "Let him cry it out," "Get him on a schedule," and "Don't pick her up so much, you're spoiling her!" This restrained style of baby care, which we dub baby training, is based upon the misguided assumptions that babies cry to manipulate, not to communicate, and that a baby's cry is an inconvenient habit that must be broken to help baby fit more conveniently into an adult environment. As you will learn in chapter 10, baby training, especially if carried to an extreme, can be a lose-lose situation. Baby loses trust in the signal value of his cues, and parents lose trust in their ability to read and respond to their baby's cues. A distance can develop between baby and child — just the opposite of the closeness that happens with attachment parenting. Throughout this book we want to help you learn to evaluate parenting advice. Attachment parenting will give you a sixth sense, so that eventually you'll become so confident about your own style of parenting that you'll be less vulnerable to the advice of baby trainers.

You will learn more about each of these seven attachment tools in later chapters.

How these tools shape your parenting. The Baby B's are about things you do as a parent, yet they will also shape what kind of a parent you will be. Breastfeeding, birth bonding, babywearing, and the other Baby B's will make you more sensitive to the cues of your infant. When his needs are met quickly and his language is listened to, the infant develops trust in his ability to give cues. As baby becomes a better cue giver, parents become even more responsive, and the whole parent-child communication system works better. Attachment parenting is a style of caring for an infant that brings out the best in baby and the best in parents.

This style asks a lot of parents, especially in the first three to six months. You give a lot of yourself to your baby — your time, your en-

ergy, your commitment. But you get back a lot more in return. Parenting is like investing in an IRA. The more you put into your child in the early years, the greater the later returns. If you work hard at the beginning, later on you can relax more and enjoy the fruits of your labors.

I feel emotionally invested in my children. I have spoken to other parents who don't seem to be as emotionally invested in their children, and I think they are missing out on one of the best experiences in life.

Attachment parenting means more than breastfeeding your baby, wearing your baby, or sleeping with your baby. It really means developing the ability to respond sensitively to the needs of your child. These seven attachment tools help that happen.

ATTACHMENT TIP
Mutual Giving

The list of Baby B's may lead you to think that attachment parenting is one big give-a-thon, that you will be constantly giving, giving, giving to your baby. You may wonder how you will survive with so much energy flowing out of you. But as the communication between you and your child becomes more sophisticated, the more connected you will feel. You will find yourself more confident as a parent. The more responsive you are to your infant, the more responsive baby is to you, and the more you both will relax. This may take longer to develop in some mother-infant pairs than in others. Also, you'll notice the carryover effect: you'll become more sensitive, perceptive, and discerning toward other relationships in your family, marriage, and work.

WHAT ATTACHMENT FEELS LIKE

Attachment is a special bond between parent and child, a feeling that draws you magnetlike to your baby. For a mother, it begins with the sense that baby is part of her, a feeling that starts in pregnancy. As the attachment develops after birth, the mother continues to feel complete only when she is with her baby. When separated from her baby, she feels as if part of herself is missing. This level of attachment doesn't grow overnight. Nor is it created in one hour of after-birth bonding. It's more like a weaving that is created over time out of many mother-infant interactions.

AP IS LIBERATING

During the first month, especially if you are a first-time mother, the bond that you read about may feel more like bondage. It's common to feel helpless and worry that you're not a good mother. These feelings may be compounded by circumstances, such as not having the birth you planned to or not getting the dream baby you pictured. Other energy drainers, such as feeding problems, sleepless nights, and the drastic changes in lifestyle that your childbirth educator warned you about (but you may not have been ready to listen to or didn't want to hear), finally occur. Then, after this initial month of high-maintenance problem solving, the attachment switch seems to click on. When and how this occurs will be unique to every mother-infant pair, but it does happen! Then you begin to think less about what you are giving up and more about what you are gaining. Gradually, attachment parenting becomes liberating. You are now free to tap in to some basic instinctual drives, and you find the confidence to follow your gut feelings for caring for your baby. You are now free to be a mother.

He seems influenced by my moods. I'm part of him, just as he's part of me.

Attachment is harmony. Mothers often describe being attached as being *in tune* with their infants. When musicians are in tune, they produce tones that vibrate in harmony with one

---

FATHER ATTACHMENT

In the early months, in most families the mother-infant attachment is more obvious and more intense than that between father and infant. This does not mean that fathers do not become deeply attached to their babies, but it is a different type of attachment. It's neither of a lesser quality than mother's nor better. It's just different. A father can also use the Baby B's to build his attachment to his child. By being responsive to his baby's language and comforting his baby when she cries, a father can build his own strong attachment to his baby. (We discuss father-infant attachment in detail in chapter 12.)

---

another. When you are in harmony with your baby, it's as if something inside of you vibrates in response to your baby's needs. The baby's cue, such as crying, fidgeting, or a certain facial expression, sets the mother's response in motion, and her response is at exactly the right frequency. As you rehearse cues and responses with your infant, you will fine-tune your harmony, and your baby will make adjustments along with you. Eventually the two of you will be singing in tune, and it will feel wonderful.

By being connected to my children I learn their rhythms.

Attachment is a connection. Like love, attachment is wonderful to feel and impossible to describe, but it is always present. There are times when you are happy to be holding your baby, times when you feel ecstatic about your relationship with her. There are also times when

you need to be alone, but even then, the connection continues.

I feel right when we're together and not right when we're separated. When I have one of those days in which my baby's needs are all-consuming, I may take a much-needed break when my husband arrives home from work, but after a short time, I really crave getting back together with my baby.

When we are traveling, Martha keeps her watch on home time. This can make getting places on time a bit complicated. I asked her why she doesn't reset her watch. She explained: "Knowing what time it is in California keeps me connected to the kids. I know what they're likely to be doing from moment to moment."

Attachment is knowledge of a person. When you're attached to your baby, you see her as a little person with distinct needs and preferences. You know exactly what these are, and they add up to a unique little personality. "I can read her so well," a first-time mother confidently said when discussing her toddler's efforts at exploring her environment. When you're attached to your baby, you become an expert on your baby. This knowledge of her behavior will help you know when she is not feeling well, when she needs reassurance, and when she needs to work out something on her own. Because you know your baby so well, you will be able to help your pediatrician provide appropriate health care for her. In years to come, you'll be able to help your child's teachers better facilitate her learning.

My attachment to Jessica empowers me to be a smarter mother.

Attachment is about *fit*. This tiny word beautifully sums up how parents and infants adjust to one another in the early months of life. Fitting together brings a completeness to a relationship, a rightness that brings out the best in parents and baby.

Some babies and parents fit together easily. An easygoing baby fits in well with a mother who may be worried and anxious. Baby's happy nature gives this mother lots of positive reinforcement, and she learns to relax and enjoy her baby. A baby with a more difficult temperament may fit in well with a mother who is very nurturing. Mother responds to baby's high level of needs in a positive way, and baby eventually mellows out. Fitting together is more challenging when baby is fussy and mother is either unsure of herself or has rigid ideas about what babies need. This mother will have to make some alterations in order to fit well with her baby, or she will need to take more baby breaks, but if she changes her approach to her baby, she will find that baby responds by becoming easier to live with.

From baby's viewpoint. To a newborn life is one big puzzle. Mother shows baby how to put the pieces together. Mother interprets the world for baby, demonstrating, for instance, that hunger is satisfied by nourishment, that distress is followed by comfort, that cold is replaced by warmth, that it feels better to relax than to stay tense. To a baby, particularly in the early months, mother provides food, comfort, warmth, sleep, and meaning. She not only fills baby's need for nourishment and security, she helps him make sense of the world. Babies, like adults, naturally cling to the persons who best satisfy their needs.

Whereas attachment for a mother is a desire to stay close to her baby, for a baby, attachment is a need to stay close to her mother. Not all mothers feel an intense desire to stay close to their baby right from the start. You might care for your baby out of a sense of obligation or some other complex set of emotions that you might not necessarily describe as love. This can be a difficult stage to go through, but using the tools of attachment parenting, including taking baby breaks, will help you want to do the things you have to do for your baby. Your desire to be with your baby will grow if you let it, until you will feel that you need your baby as much as he or she needs you.

I like being with my two-year-old. I can't imagine anything that's more fun or more satisfying.

Consider AP a starter style. Attachment parenting means first opening your mind and heart to the individual needs of your baby. If you do this, eventually you will develop the wisdom to make on-the-spot decisions about what works best for both you and your baby. Do the best you can with the resources you have. That's all your child will ever expect of you.

The Benefits of Attachment Parenting

THE GREATEST BENEFITS of attachment parenting come from practicing all of the Baby B's together — using a principle called synergy. For example, babywearing makes breastfeeding work better because proximity fosters frequent feeding, and bedding close to baby also makes breastfeeding easier and facilitates bonding and sensitivity to baby's cries. Because of the behavioral effects of lactation hormones, a breastfeeding mother is often more sensitive to her infant's cries. And the more you practice the first six Baby B's, the more you will be wary of baby trainers. If you feel a bit shaky about the first Baby B — feeling bonded to your baby — intensify the others. They will all help you deepen your relationship with your baby, eliciting the feelings that make mothering so rewarding. While your life circumstances may affect how much you can practice the Baby B's, use as many as you can whenever you can. Once you're convinced of the short- and long-term benefits of attachment parenting, you will find a way to do it. As you learn more about attachment parenting, and as you practice it, you will be amazed to discover what's in it for baby, for parents, and for family.

AP BABIES ARE SMARTER

AP is not only common sense, it's supported by science. Everything scientists know about the way babies learn supports the idea that babies raised in a high-touch, responsive environment turn out smarter. How does this happen? Let's take a look at brain biology, the caretaking environment, and a baby's own viewpoint to see what it is about attachment parenting that boosts a baby's intellectual development.

Better brains. Babies at birth have in their brains miles and miles of tangled "wires" called neurons. Neurons are the cells that conduct thoughts through the brain. Many of the neurons in the infant brain, however, are unconnected, or disorganized, at birth. As baby grows, the brain grows, too. It doubles in size and reaches 60 percent of its adult volume by the end of the first year. As the brain grows, the neurons grow, too, and make connections with one other. These connections are the way baby gets organized and learns, storing patterns and memories in circuits of neurons. How well

MORE TOUCH, LESS STUFF

As we browse through infant-product stores, we wonder how on earth we raised eight kids without all this stuff: plastic infant seats, infant monitors, mechanical swings, oscillating baby beds, and all the high-tech equipment that promises (for a high price) to make babies more convenient to care for — at a distance.

From the moment you announce that you're pregnant, you're bombarded with advice about everything you'll need to raise a happy and very smart baby. Books, classes, and educational toys all hold out the promise of adding a few points to your child's SAT scores seventeen years hence, with Ivy League colleges to follow. The baby market is a big one, and parents who want the very best for their new child are all too ready to open the checkbook or hand over the credit card.

Here's our advice on baby equipment, infant-stimulation materials, and all the other gadgets that line the aisles of stores all over America: Choose "high touch" over "high tech." The absolute best plaything for a baby is another human being. Invest in a baby sling — or even two slings: one for Mom and one for Dad, or one to keep in the house and one to keep in the car. (Remember, though, not to use the sling in the car; baby must be in a car seat in the car at all times.) Then let your baby's enriched environment be the view from your arms, which is constantly changing. Relationships, not things, make brighter babies.

these neurons hook up and how many connections baby makes are directly related to baby's interaction with his environment.

After rehearsing hundreds of cue-response interactions during the early months (I'm hungry, I get fed; I'm frightened, I get held), the infant stores mental pictures of these scenes. Eventually baby has built up a cerebral library of attachment scenes that form the beginning of a sense of self and of what the caregiving world is all about. This library of patterns of association helps the infant anticipate the response to a need, such as getting picked up if he cries. Being able to replay an expected attachment scene and have the expectation fulfilled appropriately by a sensitive caregiver reinforces a sense of well-being that will forever influence future relationships: *the ability to trust.*

Babies raised with limited amounts of interac-

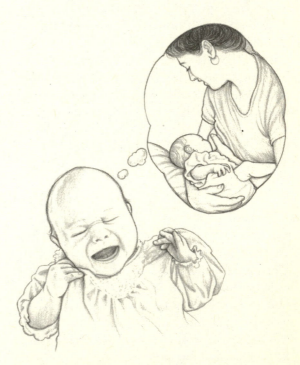

Patterns of association.

tion — which usually means limited contact with loving, caring adults — don't have the same opportunities as infants who are involved in the world of sensitive caregivers to develop connections in their brain. Brain researchers believe that more and better connections make a child smarter in the long run. Attachment parenting promotes brain development by feeding the brain the right kind of stimulation at a time in the child's life when the brain needs it the most.

An enriched caregiving environment. Research into infant development has identified the following four elements in the baby's caregiving environment that most enhance development:

1. sensitivity and responsiveness to infant's cues
2. reinforcement of infant's verbal cues and frequency of interchange during play
3. acceptance of and going with the flow of baby's temperament
4. a stimulating environment with the primary caregiver, and play that encourages decision making and problem solving

A quiet alertness. How does the world look from baby's perspective? To get behind baby's inquisitive eyes, remember that babies learn best when they are in the state of quiet alertness. The tools of attachment parenting help baby spend more time in this state. When his cries get a prompt response, and when he gets to spend lots of time in Mom's and Dad's arms, baby is calm and more open to learning. Not

---

ATTACHMENT TIP

Attachment parenting helps the developing brain make the right connections.

SCIENCE SAYS:
AP babies are likely to become smarter.

Once upon a time, parents worried and baby trainers taught that the more you held, or "spoiled," a baby, the less competent the baby might be in his motor skills. Studies by Dr. Sylvia Bell and Dr. Mary Ainsworth at Johns Hopkins University spoiled the spoiling theory. Their studies showed that infants who were securely attached to their mothers and whose mothers gave appropriate responses to their needs (for example, knowing when to pick up a baby and when to put him down) showed more advanced intellectual and motor development. The studies also showed that "playpen babies" tended to be slower in their intellectual and motor development. They found that the maternal interactions that seemed to affect intellectual and motor development most positively were the sensitivity of the mother's response, the frequency of physical and verbal interactions (this is where babywearing and breastfeeding shine), and the amount of floor freedom (the baby's opportunity to explore his environment with mother acting as a facilitator). The researchers concluded that a harmonious mother-infant attachment correlated with an infant's IQ. They concluded that the nurturing of the parents had a greater impact on their infant's IQ than the education of the parents did. They went on to conclude — as have other researchers after them — that maternal sensitivity to the cues of her infant is the prime influencer of an infant's physical and intellectual development.

only are babies more attentive when they are in the quiet alert state, they are able to hold the attention of their caregivers longer and thus learn more from them.

When baby is worn in a sling, in touch and in motion with his mother, he is intimately involved in her world. At night, in bed with Mom and Dad, baby notices the back-and-forth of sleepy voices in conversation as he himself drifts off to sleep. At the store or at a party, baby studies the faces of strangers and waits to see a smile that looks something like Mom's. Because his own mom or dad is right there, baby feels secure — still quietly alert — even in new places.

Parents as baby's first teachers. You don't have to be rich or highly intelligent to give your infant an enriched environment. You just have to be there and care. Infant intellectual development doesn't depend on superbaby classes, educational toys, or listening to Mozart. More than anything else, infants need loving, responsive human beings around them in order to develop to their fullest potential. In the keynote address at the 1986 annual meeting of the American Academy of Pediatrics, infant-development specialist Dr. Michael Lewis, in response to the overselling of the superbaby phenomenon that emphasized the use of programs and kits rather than the presence of caregivers who were playful companions and sensitive nurturers, reviewed studies of the factors that enhance infant development. He summed up his presentation with this statement: "The single most important influence on a child's intellectual development is the responsiveness of the mother to the cues of her baby."

AP BABIES ARE HEALTHIER

During my thirty years as a pediatrician, I have noticed that attachment-parented babies are

SCIENCE SAYS:
AP babies show enhanced motor development.

Parents may wonder whether carrying their baby so much might delay baby's desire to crawl. Don't worry! Both experience and research show that attachment-parented infants actually show enhanced motor development.

In 1958, Dr. Marcelle Geber studied 308 infants in Uganda who were reared by the attachment style of parenting, as was typical for that culture (babies were worn most of the day in a sling, breastfed very often throughout the day and night, and they slept next to mother). She compared the psychomotor development of the AP-reared infants with European infants who were reared in the more distant, scheduled style of parenting prevalent at the time (babies were bottle-fed on schedule, slept separately in a crib, were not worn in a sling, and were trained in the cry-it-out method). Compared with the European infants, the AP-raised Ugandan infants showed precocious motor and intellectual development throughout the first year. This gives scientific credibility to dispelling the myth that if you carry a baby all the time, you might delay her motor growth.

generally the healthiest babies. Studies back me up on this observation. These babies have fewer sick visits to the doctor, and when they do get sick, they generally get better faster. They are less likely to end up in the hospital with a serious illness, and they have fewer problems with most childhood diseases. AP babies are healthier for several reasons:

APPROPRIATELY PROTECTIVE

AP mothers tend to be very selective about substitute caregivers for their children and are careful about exposing their children to runny-nosed playmates. Their children are also less likely to get hurt, because their mothers and caregivers are so aware of what their child is doing from moment to moment. Because they also know what their child is capable of doing, they can also identify dangers in their child's environment, such as climbable furniture that is placed next to an unsecured window.

As a single mom, when I returned to work, I took great care in screening day-care providers for my child. My antennae were up as I made my rounds from one day-care home to another, and I noticed all kinds of things, from the diaper-changing facilities to how healthy and happy the other kids seemed. I really grilled the day-care providers on their sick-child admission policies.

- They are more likely to be breastfed. Human milk provides significant protection against disease, thanks to the immunities a mother passes on to her baby through her milk.

- Babies with responsive parents have lower levels of stress hormones. High levels of stress hormones compromise one's immunity to disease. (This is why children and adults alike often get sick in response to stressful situations.)

- Because attachment parenting makes babies better organized physically, with less time spent crying and more time in the quiet, alert state, they are more physiologically stable. This means better overall health.

ATTACHMENT TIP

Attachment parenting = nature's earliest immunization.

- AP moms tend to be more conscious of good nutrition. Their own wise food choices model healthy eating habits for their children. They don't let their babies and toddlers eat sugary junk foods that have little nutritional value. These mothers seem to follow what Hippocrates once said: "Let food be thy medicine."

One day I was sharing with some pediatricians my observation that attachment-parented infants are healthier. I quipped, "If all babies were attachment-parented, half of us could go fishing."

AP moms are partners in health. Attachment parenting also makes baby's primary health-care provider — Mom — more observant and better able to work with the medical professionals who care for her baby. Pediatrics calls for a partnership between parents and doctor. The parents' job is to be keen observers and accurate reporters. The pediatrician uses this information to diagnose and treat the baby.

AP moms perceive illness sooner. An attached mother has knowledge about her baby that can't be matched by any diagnostic tests. Sick infants usually change emotionally before they change physically. Because the mother knows her infant so well, she promptly notices any changes in behavior that indicate baby is ill. Baby's body language tells her about tummy aches and gastrointestinal upsets. Baby's mood, or just the look in his eye, tells her when he's getting a cold, and because she holds her baby a lot she is quick to detect a fever. She can bring these

---

SCIENCE SAYS:
· AP parents use medical care more wisely.

A study published in *Pediatrics* in 1989 showed that attachment parents tended to use medical care more wisely during their baby's first year than non-AP parents. Researchers showed that securely attached infants had one-half the number of visits to the emergency room or doctor's office. The researchers discovered that parent-infant pairs with a lesser quality of attachment had a higher frequency of unscheduled acute-care visits. The conclusions of this study were that less attached parents were less able to appropriately read the health and sickness indicators of their children.

---

symptoms to the doctor's attention sooner — before a minor illness has a chance to become worse. Mother may not know *what* is wrong with her baby (that's the doctor's job), but she definitely knows *when* something is wrong.

I can tell she is getting another ear infection by the different way she sucks at the breast.

It is colic or something else? When a young baby cries a lot, parents may be told that it is "just colic," and that baby will grow out of it. Attached mothers, because they are so in tune with their babies, become extremely perceptive about crying, and they may not buy the colic diagnosis. I frequently see parents in my office for a second opinion about a colicky baby. Mothers will often say, "I know there's something wrong. I can tell that he's hurting. This is not his normal cry." Because I so highly value an AP mother's intuition, I investigate thoroughly when Mom thinks something might be hurting her baby. For exam-

ple, when investigating "colicky" babies (we prefer the term *hurting babies*), often we find out that these infants have a medical reason for hurting, such as gastroesophageal reflux or a milk allergy. Mom was right!

Older children are partners in health. I find that a parent's sensitivity to how a child is feeling carries over into the child's own awareness of her body and her health. Attachment-parented children not only seem to be more in tune with their bodies but are also quicker to communicate changes to their parents. Because parents and child trust one another, it's easier to talk about stomachaches and sore throats, about whether they are serious and what to do about them.

My eight-year-old AP child, who turned out to have a serious intestinal disorder, said to me, "Mommy, I'm going to tell you my darkest secret. I've been having tummy aches."

Here's a piece of doctorly and fatherly advice I gave my sons Dr. Jim and Dr. Bob as they joined the Sears Family Pediatric Practice: "Spend the early months teaching new parents attachment tools. Then sit back and listen to what they have to teach you."

AP BABIES GROW BETTER

Not only are AP babies smarter and healthier, they *thrive,* which means more than just getting taller and heavier. It means growing optimally to a child's fullest potential intellectually, emotionally, and physically. AP children can do that because they don't have to waste energy putting on a big show to get what they need. A baby uses up a lot fewer calories if he can get Mom's attention with a look or a nuzzle rather than having to cry for five minutes at full blast. He can use those calories to grow and develop instead.

THE BODY CHEMISTRY OF ATTACHMENT

Hormones affect the physiology and the behavior of both baby and mother, particularly during breastfeeding. When mothers and babies stay in close contact, they are rewarded not just with pleasant emotions but with pleasant feelings from their bodies. Frequent doses of AP act like biological booster shots to keep you in tune with your baby. Believe in your biology. It will work for you.

Babies also respond physiologically when they are securely attached. One example of this involves the hormone cortisol. Produced by the adrenal glands, cortisol has a number of different jobs, including helping a person respond to stressful, even life-threatening situations. For the body to function optimally, it must have the right amount of cortisol — too little and the body shuts down; too much and it becomes distressed. Studies have shown that a secure mother-infant attachment keeps the baby in hormonal balance. Incecurely attached infants may either get used to a low cortisol level, and so become apathetic, or constantly have high levels of stress hormones and become chronically anxious.

Human infants who are deprived of sufficient attachment just do not grow well. They seem sad or even detached. It's as if they've lost their joy of living. Through the years, I have noticed that AP babies look and feel different. While it's difficult to describe, they actually appear to feel connected. These babies seek eye contact, are trusting, and like to be held close. They have a firm feel to their flesh, and their eyes are bright and eager. Simply put, a baby who feels right grows right. Consider attachment parenting to be a thriving tonic for your baby.

AP BABIES BEHAVE BETTER

It's hard being a baby. Going from the quiet, contained atmosphere of the womb into the bright, busy, intensely exciting world outside is quite a challenge, especially when your brain doesn't yet have the wiring to understand concepts like time or even what it means to be a separate person. In the early weeks, babies spend a lot of energy dealing with the basic problem of adjusting to life outside the womb. During this time, mothers and fathers must help them regulate their behavior. When baby signals hunger, Mother needs to step in and say, "Let's nurse." Baby's tummy gets filled, and he thinks, "Ah, that scary feeling is gone. And nursing made it go away." Baby wakes

AP BUILDS LITTLE CONSCIENCES

It's not that attached kids are never naughty and always nice, but they are more likely to try to do right than wrong. They're not constantly angry, and they're not locked in power struggles with their parents, so they don't have to do wrong to get attention. Because attachment-parented children have been treated fairly, they tend to have an inner sense of fairness. When they do something wrong, they want to make it right again and are willing to follow advice from adults they trust, most often their parents.

I was baby-sitting a friend's son who was used to hitting as a technique for problem solving. My AP daughter, Madison, came and told me that he had hit her. She told the boy that in our house we don't hit, we talk about what makes us angry. Madison is three years old.

SCIENCE SAYS:
AP infants thrive.

Experiments on both human infants and infant experimental animals showed these fascinating results:

1. Human infants with the most secure attachment to their mothers had the best cortisol balance.
2. The longer infant animals were separated from their mothers, the higher their cortisol levels, suggesting that these babies could be chronically stressed. The mothers also experienced elevated cortisol levels when separated from their babies.
3. Prolonged cortisol elevations may diminish growth and suppress the immune system.
4. Infant animals separated from their mothers showed imbalances in the autonomic nervous system, the master control system of the body's physiology. They didn't show the usual stable heart rate and body temperatures, had an abnormal heartbeat (called arrhythmia), and showed disturbances in sleep patterns, such as a decrease in REM sleep. Similar physiological changes were measured in preschool children who were separated from their parents.
5. In addition to the agitation caused by prolonged elevation of adrenal hormones, separation sometimes caused the opposite physiological effect: withdrawn, depressed infants who had low cortisol levels.
6. Infant animals who stayed close to their mothers had higher levels of growth hormones and enzymes essential for brain and heart growth. Separation from their mothers, or lack of interaction with their mothers when they were close by, caused the levels of these growth-promoting substances to fall.

Researchers all come to the same conclusion: Mother acts as a regulator of her infant's disorganized physiology.

up alone in his crib, and as he stretches his arms and legs out into space, he feels fear. Dad comes in and picks him up, containing baby's tiny body in his strong hands. Baby thinks, "Yes, Dad will take care of me. I'm safe."

When parents wear their baby around the house or pat his back to calm him down when he fusses, he can feel calm and not waste his energy worrying. Staying "in the groove" is a way of describing what we mean when we talk about babies becoming organized. The more time baby spends in the groove, the more he learns to create this state for himself. He can stay in the "feel-good groove" longer, then move into the "nursing groove" more easily when he is hungry. With Mom sleeping next to him, he can stay in the "sound-asleep groove" through much of the night and slide right back into it after waking to nurse. With all these prompts from Mom and Dad, AP babies get organized more efficiently. This makes them better-behaved babies, babies who are a lot more pleasant to be around.

Better-behaved babies make better-behaved children. You probably never thought of the Baby B's as discipline tools, but they actually are. Babywearing, breastfeeding on cue, bedding close to your baby, and believing in her

AP CHILDREN BECOME "RESPONSE-ABLE"

Naturally all parents want their children to grow up taking responsibility for their actions, and when they are adults, they want them to make responsible contributions to their families and society. Being responsible has its roots in responsiveness. When parents are appropriately responsive to the cues of their children, their children grow up with the ability to respond to the needs of others. They become response-able adults.

ATTACHMENT TIP
The R & R of Discipline

For AP parents and their children, discipline is based more on their relationship than on a set of rules.

cries are powerful ways of shaping your baby's behavior, now and in the future.

Since I attachment-parented my child for the first few years, I now feel I have more margin for error. Because I gave her such a secure foundation, I don't worry so much when I mess up, because I know it's unlikely to undo what I have done.

Six Ways AP Makes Discipline Easier

Discipline may be far from your thoughts when you bring your new baby home from the hospital. It may be a topic you dread having to confront, as you wonder what kind of a disciplinarian you will be. Or you may already have some ideas about discipline, the kind that start with "I will *never* allow *my* child to talk back to me."

Here's the good news about discipline: It is not something you do *to* a child; it is something you do *with* a child and it starts in babyhood. Attachment parenting creates a solid foundation for guiding your child in the years to come by giving you the best starter tools for discipline. Here's how:

1. AP helps you get to know your child. To be a wise disciplinarian, you have to know your child well. This is true no matter what you believe about good discipline. As we often tell new parents, "You don't have to be an expert in parenting or in discipline methods, but you must become an expert in your baby. Nobody else will." When you know your child well, you understand how things look to your child, and with this knowledge you can shape your child's behavior appropriately. For example, our sixth child, Matthew, was a very focused toddler who would become completely engrossed in his play. Because Martha knew this about him, she knew that she couldn't simply scoop him up and carry him away when it was time to stop playing. It was hard for him to let go of his activity and tune in to Mom's agenda. So as a sensitive disciplinarian, Martha developed a routine for leaving playtime behind. A few minutes before it was time to go, she got down to his level and helped him sign off: "Say bye-bye to the trucks, bye-bye to the cars, bye-bye to the boys, bye-bye to the girls," and so on. This helped him close out one activity (even a preferred one) and be ready to transition to the next without protest.

Knowing my child empowers me. This "kid knowledge" becomes like a sixth sense, enabling me to anticipate and control situations to keep my child out of trouble. I know Lea so deeply at every stage of development. Attachment parenting allows me to put myself in her shoes. I imagine how she needs me to act.

ATTACHMENT TIP

Discipline is more about having the right relationship with your child than about having the right techniques.

---

2. AP helps you get behind the eyes of your child. Understanding your child's perspective will help you react appropriately and guide her behavior. On one occasion, our two-year-old, Lauren, impulsively grabbed a carton of milk out of the refrigerator and dropped it on the floor. She burst into howls, and Martha came running. She looked at the situation, and instead of scolding or being angry about the mess, she talked to Lauren calmly and sensitively about what had happened. Later, when I asked her how she managed to handle things so calmly, Martha said, "I asked myself, if I were Lauren, how would I want my mother to respond?"

3. AP promotes trust. If you want someone to follow your directions, you must first earn his or her trust. Trust develops when you meet your child's needs. A child who trusts Mom or Dad to give food and comfort when needed will also trust Mom or Dad when they say, "Don't touch!" or even "Time to pick up your toys and get ready for bed." Authority is vital to discipline, and authority must be based on trust. If an infant can trust his mother to feed him when he's hungry, he will be more likely as a toddler to listen to her for what to do when, for example, he encounters breakable objects on Grandma's coffee table.

4. AP builds better-behaved brains. Children who don't receive responsive parenting are, we believe, at an increased risk for developing behavioral problems later on, such as hyperactivity, distractibility, and impulsivity. These are the be-

havioral characteristics that define attention deficit hyperactivity disorder (ADHD), a condition diagnosed with increasing frequency in children and now also in adults. AP children in general seem to be more focused than others. Could the level of nurturing during those formative years affect the way the behavioral pathways in the brain become organized? Could it be that some behavioral problems that develop later in childhood are actually preventable results of early disorganization? While certainly autism and attention deficit disorder (ADD) are not caused by low-touch parenting (there are biological differences in these children), we have noticed that in children who already have a tendency toward these problems, attachment parenting can lessen their severity and increase the parents' ability to cope and help.

5. AP encourages obedience. *To obey* means to listen attentively. Attachment parenting, besides opening up parents to the needs of their baby, opens the baby up to the wishes of the parent. Attached children want to please their parents. They want to mind their mothers. What does it mean *to mind?* When a parent and a child are closely attached, they frequently find themselves of one mind. This can make it easier for a child to obey. Because your child knows that you can see the world from his perspective, he is more open to accepting your view. He trusts you, so he more easily accepts the boundaries you set. Even strong-willed children can be pulled into following Mom's or Dad's direction when the relationship is strong enough.

All I have to do is look at him disapprovingly, and he stops misbehaving.

6. AP helps you discipline the difficult child. Attachment parenting is especially rewarding when you have a child who challenges your parenting skills at every turn. We call kids with these kinds of personalities high-need children. They seem to need more of everything: more interaction with parents, more frequent feeding as infants, more time in the baby sling, more guidance in play — more of everything but sleep. Sometimes parents don't realize until their child is three or four years of age that they have a child who needs a special kind of discipline (for example, a hyperactive child, a developmentally delayed child, or a temperamentally difficult child). Parents who have worked hard from the beginning to build their attachment to their child find it easier to weather the challenges of having such a child.

The stronger my child's will, the stronger must be my connection.

Connected parents know their child well and are sensitive to their child's personality. Children who feel connected trust their parents to help them control themselves. Studies that have looked at the long-term effects of early parenting styles have found a correlation between attachment parenting in infancy and adaptability later in childhood. A child who is more adaptable can be redirected more easily. Parents may have to keep a close eye on this child, but the child will accept suggestions and correction from the parents. This keeps behavioral problems from escalating into behavioral battles.

RAISING AN INTERDEPENDENT CHILD

If you're like most parents, you want your child to become independent. Historians and social critics say that America's frontier past created a nation that values independence and individuality above all. However, becoming too independent too soon is not good for your child. We take issue with the concept of independence as a quality to shoot for, either for a child or for an adult. Think about it. Emotionally healthy people are never completely independent. We all need people and relationships to complete ourselves. Consider the following stages:

1. Dependence: "*You* do it for me." From birth to one year, infants trust that their parents will be responsive to their needs.
2. Independence: "I do it *myself*." During the second year, with the parents acting as facilitators, the exploring toddler learns to do many things independently.

3. Interdependence: "*We* do it." This is the most mature stage. The term *interdependence* may be new to you, but it's really a healthier trait than either dependence or independence. Interdependent people know how to work with others and get the most out of their relationships while asking the most of themselves as well.

As you parent your child, you help him move through these stages gradually on his way to becoming emotionally mature. You want your child to be comfortable being alone and being with other people. Interdependence teaches a child to be both a leader and a follower. The independent individualist may be so tied up in himself that he misses what the crowd has to offer. The dependent child is so busy following the crowd that he never gets a chance to know his own mind.

AP CHILDREN ARE "FULL"

Going through my gallery of AP testimonials, I have noticed a recurrent theme: AP children seem *filled* with the inner tools that will help them succeed in life. When asked about the payoff, AP parents often volunteer that their children seem care-full, resource-full, respect-full, and thought-full.

As the word no *enters her world, simply changing our tone of voice or giving her a certain look is usually all that it takes to get our message across, because she trusts us and wants to please us.*

◆ ◆ ◆

Nancy, the mother of a high-need baby who is now a strong-willed four-year-old, volunteered, "Initially attachment parenting took more energy and was less convenient. Now caring for Jonathan is easier because discipline flows naturally between us. I'm finally beginning to cash in on my investment."

AP PROMOTES INTIMACY

Attachment-parented kids are comfortable around people because they are comfortable with themselves. They are interested in others and know how to connect appropriately with family members, old friends, and new acquaintances. This ability to engage others may be as simple as knowing how to maintain eye contact. Their gaze is attentive but not intrusive. They have a deep understanding of relationships that stems from their own close relationship with their parents. This ability to be intimate, or emotionally comfortable, with others serves these children well throughout their lives.

THE LONG TERM

Parents, especially mothers, whom we have interviewed express a common feeling about their own involvement in attachment parenting: "I feel emotionally invested in my child." In the short term, they have caring and empathic children who are a joy to be around. In the long term, they are instilling in their children the capacity for forming healthy attachments during childhood and adulthood.

When you attachment-parent your children early, they won't spend their whole lives trying to catch up, and neither will you. Your children, now and in the future, will find comfort in feeling close to other people. They will form appropriate attachments and have the skills that make relationships last. This kind of investment pays off not only for your children but for their friends, for the people they will one day marry, for their children, and for future generations.

Like a sunflower, he turns toward people who light up.

Psychologists and therapists we've known through the years have told us that many of their clients have problems with intimacy, and that much of their therapy is aimed at reparenting their clients. Kids with high-quality connections to their parents get what they need during childhood. The lessons they learn from their very first relationship will ultimately make them better friends and better spouses. Because connected kids grow up learning to bond with people rather than things, they carry this skill into adulthood. Many a night I watched our two-year-old Lauren inch over and snuggle next to Martha in bed.

Even at this young age Lauren was learning a life-long asset: the capacity for intimacy.

When going from oneness to separateness (a process called individuation or hatching), the securely attached toddler establishes a balance between his desire to explore and encounter new situations and his continued need for the safety and contentment provided by Mother. During an unfamiliar play situation, the mother gives a sort of "go ahead" message, providing the toddler with the confidence to explore and handle the new situation. The next time the toddler encounters a similar situation, he has more confidence to handle it by himself or by enlisting less help from his caregivers. The consistent emotional availability of the mother provides security, which helps the child develop a very important quality: the capacity to enjoy being alone at times.

AP PARENTS AND CHILDREN WORK TOGETHER BETTER

Attachment parenting teaches parents and other caregivers to become facilitators of their child's development. Facilitators don't tell the child what to do, they help the child learn what to do. When parents facilitate, they don't give commands or follow their own agenda. Instead, they take their cues from their child.

The best kind of learning happens spontaneously, as a child's interest is awakened by the world around her. Teachable moments arise throughout the day, and a parent/facilitator takes advantage of them. A child notices something new, and sensitive parents gently help the child stretch and grow. As the toddler reaches for the neighbor's puppy, Mom holds his hand and shows him how to pet the dog gently. The preschooler's tower tumbles over, so Dad offers an engineering tip and lets his daughter experi-

ment some more. Attached parents know how to respond appropriately. They know when to say, "Yes, you can do it yourself!" and when to provide some help. Because the child trusts the parent, he listens.

Facilitators ease frustrations. Parent/facilitators also provide emotional refueling when learning is frustrating, while at the same time realizing that it's important to allow children to experience some frustrations and learn how to handle them.

Facilitators promote discipline. Facilitating is also an important element in how attached parents discipline their children. They create an atmosphere in their home that makes it easier for a child to obey. Toys are stored in such a way that cleaning up is easy and fun to do. Helping Mom or Dad with chores is a fun way to learn about housework. When parents need their child's cooperation in getting ready for an outing or for bed, they gently steer their child's attention from his play to the next activity. They can do this effectively because they know their child so well. Ultimately, these children learn to be self-disciplined, because the rules of the parent, whom they trust, become a part of themselves.

Facilitators promote independence. Being on standby helps your child find the right level of independence. Becoming independent is a two-steps-forward, one-step-back process. When you know your toddler well, you'll be able to anticipate in which direction you should be moving to keep in step with his progress. Learn the dance now, and it will feel familiar when you visit independence issues again in the teenage years.

In most homes, at first the facilitator is the mother, though she may work in tandem with a caregiver or her husband. As children grow, they latch on to additional facilitators: grandparents, teachers, coaches, Scout leaders, and other persons of significance. The connected child latches on to other facilitators easily because attachment parents have built into their developing child the capacity to get connected.

Learning interdependence prepares a child for life, especially for relationships at work. Management consultants teach the concept of interdependence to increase productivity. Stephen Covey, author of the bestselling *Seven Habits of Highly Effective People,* stresses that interdependence is characteristic of the most successful people. Even a two-year-old learns interdependence: "I can do it myself, but I can do it better with help." This is how your child learns to become "resource-full." So, when your child asks you to help him with a project, don't immediately shut him down by informing him that he'll learn more if he does it by himself. Consider that you may be raising a future executive — one who knows how to work well with people.

AP PROMOTES EMPATHY

Attachment parenting builds kids who care. Because these children are on the receiving end of sensitive parenting, they become sensitive. Caring, giving, listening, and responding to needs are family norms, and these qualities become part of the child. One day a mother brought her newborn into my office for a checkup accompanied by her attachment-parented almost-three-year-old daughter, Tiffany. As soon as the new baby started to fuss, Tiffany pulled at her mother's skirt and pleaded, "Mommy, baby is crying. Pick up, rock-rock, nurse!"

I often watch AP children in play groups. They are concerned about the needs and rights of their peers because this has been their model. When friends are hurting, these children, like good Samaritans, rush to help.

My five-year-old was in an AP play group at a park when she fell and cut her head. She was ter-

ribly shaken and crying. I sat her on my lap and tried to calm her. Meanwhile, her AP friends, ages three to eleven, stopped everything and gathered around her. They came close and stroked her head, held her hand, and looked upon her with faces expressing such compassion. A couple of children left the circle in order to locate ointment and bandages. Providing a striking contrast to this touching scene of compassion was the neighborhood girl who was not part of the AP group. She stood next to my daughter with a twisted look on her face. Unlike the other children, she fixated on what Jasmine was doing rather than on how she was feeling. The difference between her reaction and the extremely heartfelt responses from the other children was striking. How lucky Jasmine is to be surrounded by friends capable of such compassion.

◆ ◆ ◆

She is very compassionate, kissing everyone she thinks may have a boo-boo.

◆ ◆ ◆

My nineteen-month-old's little friend was visiting, and they were jockeying for toys, as all toddlers do. When the other child cried after my son took her toy, he handed it back to her and gave her a kiss. If that doesn't make a mom's heart swell! He is so gentle-spirited around other kids.

Attachment-parented children learn empathy, so they are able to get behind the eyes of another child. They can imagine the effect of their behavior on another child — before they act. In essence, they think before they act. They also have a well-developed conscience, feeling guilty when they act badly and good when they should. Contrast these children with troubled teens, who feel no remorse for what they do. Studies have shown that these young people share one abnormal feature: a lack of empathy. They act without considering the effect of their behavior on others.

I once found my three-year-old son petting a very sick grasshopper on our patio. The insect was obviously on its way out. Sitting next to the grasshopper, Lloyd put his head down to grasshopper eyeball level and told the poor thing, "You're okay, you're okay," while stroking the little body very gently. I felt proud that I had a child (especially a boy!) who cared about a sick little creature rather than chasing it or tormenting it.

◆ ◆ ◆

Our two-year-old already shows a sophisticated level of empathy and compassion toward others. He and his friend were standing on a chair together. They both fell off, and Connor landed on top of his friend. His friend began to howl, and Connor immediately began to hug him, saying, "I'm sorry. I'm sorry." I've never seen another child of two display such concern. I believe that he is this way because he's always been given empathy and love when he cries. His injuries, his pain, his fears are taken seriously. Because he has received such loving concern for his emotions, he is able to show that same concern toward others.

AP IS CONTEMPORARY

Nowadays there are computers in classrooms, in homes, and even in hands, and more and more toddlers are pointing and clicking their way into the high-tech age of instant access to entertainment and information. This is fast-tech life in the twenty-first century, and it's unlikely to slow down. Attachment parenting adds a high-touch balance to this high-tech pace. It's important for infants and toddlers to relate to people before machines. The AP child becomes programmed to the importance of interpersonal relationships before the high-tech toys take over.

THE PAYOFF FOR PARENTS

Not only does attachment parenting increase the chances of turning out sensitive, caring, and well-disciplined children, but this style of caregiving benefits parents, too. Listen to what these AP parents have to say:

AP has completely changed my life. I'm a totally different mother — more nurturing, more patient, more focused on what really matters in life, less hurried, with a better sense of humor — and I want to help others discover this marvelous way of parenting. It has made my husband and me closer as we share in providing something special for our children. AP has also led us to adopt healthier values, a more spiritual life, and even a better diet, and it has helped us correct some of the mistakes we made with our first two children.

◆ ◆ ◆

AP has made me a more discerning person. I am much more likely to research any parenting or medical decision that I make for myself and my children because I know it can have long-term effects. It has made me a much more giving person — to my children, my husband, my family, and my friends. I evaluate the decisions that I make much more thoroughly now and try to anticipate how my actions will affect those around me. I have learned how important it is to be in tune with those around me and to work cooperatively with my family.

◆ ◆ ◆

AP is teaching me more about life and myself than I ever would have learned without it.

◆ ◆ ◆

If we make life better for our baby, we make it better for ourselves.

AP softens every member of the family. You will find yourself gradually becoming more caring and considerate to everyone around you.

What Attachment Parenting Is Not

POPULAR PARENTING PHILOSOPHIES have always had their critics, and attachment parenting is no exception. Although the criticism is deserved when attachment parenting is taken to extremes, most of the criticism of attachment parenting stems from misunderstandings of what attachment parenting is and what makes it work.

Attachment parenting is what parents would do naturally without the influence of "experts." Attachment parenting is regarded as controversial only because it goes against certain social trends, such as those that suggest that it is more important for new parents to train their baby to fit into their lives than it is for parents to get in touch with their baby.

Once you both become securely attached to your baby, together you will become the experts most qualified to balance the needs of your baby with contending needs of the family. Decisions involving staying at home or returning to work (part-time or full-time), weaning, childcare, or alternative caregivers, are *your* decisions, and I know they can be tough ones. But one of the great things about the tools of attachment parenting is that they can be passed along. The instinctual biological wiring between mother and child is important in the early months, but luckily the maternal instinct is not limited to new mothers. Later in this book, we will return to these subjects at length.

Looking at attachment parenting from the point of view of its critics is a useful way to clarify the what and the why of this parenting style. That's why this chapter is devoted to explaining what attachment parenting is not. Constructive criticism can help restore balance to what an individual is doing. We hope that this chapter will help you make wise choices and put balance into your attachment parenting.

CLEARING UP MISUNDERSTANDINGS

AP is not a new style of parenting. There's nothing newfangled or even faddish about attachment parenting. Actually, attachment parenting is an old way of caring for babies. It's based on the ways that many traditional cultures care for babies and mothers. In this country, it wasn't until childcare advisers came on the scene that parents began to follow books instead of their babies. The more restrained style

SCHEDULING THE AP BABY

Schedule isn't necessarily a bad word, even in AP circles. What we mean by schedule, however, is merely having some regular routines. A sense of order can become an important part of attachment parenting if these routines are handled sensitively and with flexibility. Remember, you want to give your child the tools to succeed in life — not just skills and education, but also attitudes and ways of managing time and emotions.

There will be days when you need to be able to feed your baby at predictable times. If you have to leave home at 9:00 to catch a plane at 10:00, you can't stop to nurse at 8:55. Here's where your steady attention to baby's needs pays off: you can use what you know about your baby to trick him into nursing earlier. Just click into the routines he knows and trusts. If baby is used to being nursed in a certain chair, you can sit down with him in that place and offer the breast, even if he hasn't yet told you he's hungry. He'll go along with the routine, fill his tummy, and free you up to grab baby, baby sling, and your luggage and get to the airport on time. Or there will be nights when you know your baby needs to sleep, even if he doesn't think so, or nights when you

desperately need to sleep. If baby is accustomed to falling asleep during a walk in the baby sling, you can put him in the sling when you're ready for bed, walk for a while, lie down with him, and he will probably nod off — even if it's an hour earlier than his usual bedtime.

The cues to start a routine are called setting events. Use them regularly and predictably, and you'll be able to rely on them when you need them. You can use breastfeeding to settle baby at a time when you need him to be calm because you have other things to do. Babywearing is another comforting tool that helps you ease baby into a peaceful state that allows you to take care of other important matters. In fact, if you think about it, you may discover that you already rely on routines like this without even being aware of it.

Critics of attachment parenting often warn that an AP baby will run the family, and everyone will have to adapt to baby. On the contrary, because the attached baby is not tied to the clock and goes where Mom and Dad go, AP parents have a lot of freedom. Baby fits more easily into the unpredictable days and nights of modern family life.

of parenting — the kind that advocates letting baby cry lest you spoil her — became popular really only in the past century.

Picture your family on a deserted island. You've just delivered a baby. There are no books, advisers, or relatives around to shower you with advice. The Baby B's of attachment parenting come naturally to you. They are what you have to do to ensure that your baby sur-

vives. The Baby B's are based on baby's biological needs. When we cite new research in this book, we are describing studies that confirm what mothers have always known: good things happen when mothers and babies are allowed to be in tune with one another.

I'm happy that I was doing attachment parenting long before I even knew it had a name.

AP is not indulgent parenting. Few parents make it through their offspring's babyhood without being told that all their efforts to nurture and respond to their baby will surely spoil her. And if it's not spoiling that they're warned against, they're told not to let themselves be manipulated by baby. Attachment parenting is not the same as giving your child everything she asks for. We stress that parents should respond *appropriately* to their baby's needs, which means knowing when to say yes and when to say no. Sometimes in their zeal to give children everything they need, parents give their children everything they want, and this is indeed harmful. Parents must learn to distinguish between a child's needs and a child's wants.

During the first six months, being able to tell the difference between baby's needs and wants is not a problem that parents have to wrestle with. In the first several months of life, a baby's wants *are* a baby's needs. A consistent yes response teaches babies trust, which makes them more accepting of no later on, when they start wanting things they should not have. If you learn to know your baby by responding readily to his needs in the early months, you'll have a good sense of when it's appropriate to say no later on. (For a discussion of how attachment parenting makes discipline easier, see page 19.)

AP is not exclusively child centered. Healthy parenting styles respect the needs of all family members, not just the child's. Sure, it's true that in those early high-maintenance months of infant care, baby's needs must come first. Baby is, after all, a baby, who doesn't have the cognitive equipment needed to handle waiting. But a mother can't do a good job of taking care of her baby's needs if she is ignoring her own. In the early months, attachment parenting asks her to focus a lot of attention on her baby, so that she can grow more self-confident as a mother. AP also emphasizes that taking care of Mother is one way that other family members can take care of baby. As parents create a healthy attachment with their infant, they learn to be discerning about balancing baby's needs, Mother's needs, and the needs of the rest of the family. We often describe AP as being family centered. Learning to balance the needs of everyone in the family helps Mom and Dad mature as parents and the whole family operate at a higher level. If baby is thriving, but Mom is completely burned out because she is not getting the help she needs, something has to change.

AP parents are attentive to their children, but not to the point where they neglect their own needs. Mothers (and fathers) who are completely worn out and who don't take care of themselves are not balanced attachment parents.

When you do everything for your child, you are giving him the message that you don't believe he can take care of himself. Being possessive, or a "smother mother" (or father) is unfair to the child, as it fosters an inappropriate dependency on the parent. Remember, the key word in AP is *responsiveness*. When you smother your child, he doesn't get a chance to give you cues to initiate the interaction so you can then respond to these cues. As you and your baby grow together, you will develop the right balance between helping him and letting him help himself. For example, you don't usually need to respond to the cries of a seven-month-old baby as quickly as you would to those of a seven-day-old baby. And by the time your baby is seven months old, you'll know which cries need a quick response and which cries stem from problems that baby can probably handle on his own.

It's easier for me to say no to my attachment-parented child when she wants a lot of stuff, because I know I have given her so much of myself.

AP is not permissive parenting. Permissive parenting says anything goes. Whatever a child wants to do must be the right thing. AP is not permissive. Attached parents don't shrug their shoulders and let their children do "whatever." They shape their children's behavior. They encourage good behavior and make it easier for a child to behave well. They quickly intervene and gently correct problems. For example, if you realize your curious toddler is beginning to open all the kitchen drawers to explore their contents, give him his own toddler-toy drawer in the kitchen to shape his behavior, guiding him toward what he can touch rather than slapping his hands, as some controlling style of parenting would advise, when he approaches "no touches."

Shaping is different from controlling. The critics who charge that attachment parenting is permissive say that parents should be in control of the baby, and not the other way around. This may sound like it makes sense, and it is one of the selling points in books and classes that advocate baby training. One problem with this approach is that the fear of the baby being in control creates an adversarial relationship between parents and baby: baby is out to manipulate you, so you better control him first. This approach to parenting keeps parents and babies at a distance from each other, and they run the risk of never really connecting and trusting one another.

Attachment mothering is not martyr mothering. Don't think that AP means baby pulls Mommy's string and she jumps. Because of the trust that develops between attached parents and their attached children, parents' response

---

CLARIFYING THE CONTROL ISSUE

When a baby cries from hunger or is upset, she wants to be comforted, not to control. The confusion between communication and control is a carryover from a time when experts were advising parents to raise babies by the behavior-modification model, with rewards for being "good" and withholding for being "bad." This went along with rigid schedules for feeding, sleeping, even playing. The problem was, these experts didn't understand what babies are really like. Their version of scientific parenting wasn't based on any science.

What goes on between parents and babies is not a battle for control. The real issues are trust and communication. A baby in need communicates by signaling to the person whom he trusts to meet that need. The person responds, which is another way of communicating. By responding, parents are teaching their baby to trust them, which ultimately makes it easier for the parents to guide the child. Trust is a much better foundation for discipline than behavior modification. When your child trusts you, you can shape her behavior in gentle, subtle ways. For example, because AP parents know their child so intimately and their radar is always tuned toward their child's behavior, they can come up with on-the-spot prompts that redirect an about-to-be mischievous toddler into a more desirable pursuit.

time gradually lengthens as baby gains the ability to control himself. Then mother jumps only when it's an emergency.

Admittedly, a mother who has no help may come to feel tied down by constant baby tending. Mothers need baby breaks. It's especially important for fathers and other trusted caregivers to share infant care in AP families. But with attachment parenting, feeling tied down is an issue less than you might think. Instead of feeling tied down, attached mothers feel tied together with their babies.

Even though you enjoy being with your infant, you don't necessarily want to stay home all the time. Remember that attachment parenting, by mellowing your child's behavior, makes it easier to go places with your baby. AP will make you more discerning about when and with whom to leave your baby. You don't have to feel tied down to your house or apartment and a lifestyle that includes only babies.

The mutual sensitivity between mother and baby makes it possible for women to do lots of other things while caring for their babies. Because they are so naturally tuned in to baby, attached mothers can also pay attention to jobs, projects, or other children, knowing that they can trust their own sensitivity to bring their focus back to baby when he needs it, even when parents' needs and baby's needs collide. It's amazing how attached mothers can handle a multitude of tasks and still know exactly when to look down with a reassuring smile at baby in the sling.

AP is not hard. Attachment parenting may sound like one big give-a-thon, and initially, there is a lot of giving. This is a fact of new parent life: babies are takers, and parents are givers. Yet the more you give to your baby, the more baby gives back to you. You grow to enjoy your child and feel more competent as a parent. Remember, your baby is not just a passive player in the parenting game. Your infant takes an active part in shaping your attitudes by rewarding you for giving him good, sensitive care, and by helping you become an astute baby reader.

With attachment parenting, baby and parents shape each other. An example of this is how you and your baby learn to talk to each other. A baby's early language is made up of cries, facial expressions, and movement. To communicate with your baby, you must learn to use more than words. You become more intuitive. You learn to think like a baby. But even as you are mastering your baby's language, your baby is learning to speak the language of the family. Both of you have helped each other develop communication skills that you didn't have before. Each of you gives, and each of you gets back.

Attachment parenting is actually the easiest parenting style in the long run. What is hard about parenting is feeling like you don't know what your baby wants or can't seem to give her what she needs. If you feel you really know your baby and have a handle on the relationship, parenting is much less frustrating. True, getting to know your baby and responding to his cues takes a tremendous amount of patience and stamina, especially in the first three months, but it's worth it. The ability to read and respond to your baby carries over into the childhood and teenage years, when you'll have the ability to get behind the eyes of your growing child and see things from her point of view. This will make it easier to understand and shape her behavior. When you truly know your child, parenting is easier at all ages.

AP is not rigid. On the contrary, attachment parenting offers options and is very flexible. It's not about rules, and "never do this" and "always do that." Attachment mothers speak of a flow between themselves and their baby — a flow of thoughts and feelings that help the mother make the right choice at the right time when confronted with daily childcare decisions. You don't have to follow rules, you just have to read the situation and respond.

AP is not spoiling. New parents ask, "Won't holding our baby a lot, responding to her cries, nursing on cue, and even sleeping with our baby spoil her?" Or they ask if this kind of parenting will create an overly manipulative child. Our answer is an emphatic no! In fact, both experience and research have shown the opposite to be true. A child whose needs are met predictably and dependably does not have to whine and cry and worry about getting his parents to do what he needs. Spoiling does become an issue a few years down the road when overindulgence or permissiveness signals a parent's inability to set limits and provide boundaries.

The spoiling theory may seem scientific. It seemed logical to the childcare "experts" who popularized this idea in the early part of the twentieth century. They thought that if you responded to crying by picking your baby up, he would cry more so that he could get picked up more. It turns out that human behavior is a little more complicated than this. It is true that if you carry a newborn baby in your arms much

of the time, the baby will protest when you put her down in her crib. This baby has learned how to feel right, and she lets you know when she needs help getting that feeling back. However, in the long run, this rightness within her will make her less likely to cry for attention.

AP does not create dependent children. The possessive parent, or "hover mother," is constantly in a flurry around her child, doing everything for him because of her own fears and insecurity. Her child may become overly dependent, because he has been kept from doing what he needs to do. An attached mother recognizes when it is appropriate to let her child struggle a bit and experience some frustration, so that he can grow. This is why we continually emphasize putting balance in your chosen parenting style. Attachment enhances development; prolonged dependency hinders development. (See Attachment vs. Enmeshment, page 109.)

AP is not the same as doting on your infant. In certain situations, such as a long-awaited child, the first child of older parents, the first child of parents who have struggled with infertility, or a special-needs child, parents may become overprotective and doting. They have so much of themselves invested in this child that they have trouble separating the child's needs and happiness from their own. This can interfere with the child's emotional development. It's healthier to keep AP in balance. Yet, at the same time, you shouldn't be afraid of getting too close to your baby. (How can you give your baby too much love?)

AP is not weird. Don't believe that AP is a back-to-nature cult of earth mothers. In my medical practice, I have mothers of all kinds who practice AP quite successfully, including

---

ATTACHMENT TIP

Attachment parenting is about responding appropriately to your baby. Spoiling is the result of responding inappropriately.

single teen moms and executives. What is true is that AP carries over into other areas of your life, so that you want to become more informed and discerning about social issues and about your family's lifestyle choices.

AP is not all or nothing. You may be unable to do all seven Baby B's all the time, either because of medical reasons or the competing demands of your work life. That does not mean you're not an attached mother. Practice as many of the attachment tools as you can as much as you can. That's all your child will ever expect of you.

AP is not only for mothers. Attachment parenting works much better when dads are active and involved in baby's care. Dads bring another perspective to parenting. Many AP mothers give so much to their babies that they forget to care for themselves. One day Martha complained, "I don't have time to take a shower, my baby needs me so much." Clearly, it was time for me to step up and make sure my wife found some time for herself. That day I hung the following reminder on the bathroom mirror: "Each day remind yourself that what your baby needs most is a happy, rested mother."

MYTHS ABOUT ATTACHMENT PARENTING

Myth: Attachment parenting requires a stay-at-home mom.

Fact: Not at all. Attachment parenting is even more important for the mother who works outside the home.

As you will learn in chapter 11, it's even more important for a mother who works outside the home to practice attachment parenting.

The Baby B's will help Mom and infant stay attached even if they are apart during much of the day. When you and baby are separated, you must be more conscious of building that connection. The attachment-parenting tools of breastfeeding, believing in your infant's cries, babywearing, and bedding together will help you do that.

Myth: Attachment parenting might cause a baby to become clingy and dependent.

Fact: Attachment-parented infants become less clingy and more independent. Critics of attachment parenting maintain that babies who are held all the time, who are fed on demand, and who sleep with their parents will become excessively clingy and never want to leave their mothers. Yet it is our experience, and research supports us, that attachment-parented infants become less dependent children.

Independence is the American dream, and all parents want their children to grow up to be independent and self-sufficient. However, you can't push a child to be independent. Children will naturally become independent — in their own good time. To understand how this happens, you have to know something about infant emotional development and how children gain a sense of who they are as independent persons.

A newborn does not know that he is a separate individual. Baby has no real sense of who he is or of what it means to be in the world. Baby knows only that when he is with his mother he feels right. Other sensitive and familiar caregivers, such as Dad, Grandma, or a regular baby-sitter, may also feel right to baby. But an attached baby knows that he can't experience that same sense of rightness with just anybody. Some very sensitive babies make it quite clear that only Mother will do, at least in certain situations.

Add to this the fact that babies do not understand the concept of *person permanence* until sometime between nine and twelve months of age. They don't realize that objects and people continue to exist when they are out of sight. So when Mother goes away, baby feels that the one person who can make him feel right has completely disappeared, perhaps forever. Baby just can't hang on to a mental picture of Mother to reassure himself, and he can't understand the concept of time, so "Mom will be back in an hour" means nothing to him. If a caregiver is brought in when a mother returns to work, a baby must learn to transfer his attachment. This is harder for some babies than for others. Sometime between twelve and eighteen months, out of sight is no longer out of mind. A baby can re-create a mental picture of Mom, even though she may be across town.

Because babies have these developmental limitations, they experience separation anxiety when Mother is away. Nearly all babies, whether securely attached or not, experience varying degrees of separation anxiety. Babies of mothers who practice attachment parenting may protest more strongly when Mother is away, or they may happily accept another caregiver in her place. Active protest is actually a sign of how accustomed they are to feeling right. Because they are used to having their signals understood, these babies let their mothers know when all is not well with them. They need substitute caregivers who are sensitive to their cues and who will try to help them feel calm and comforted.

This period of dependency during the first year of a baby's life is important to a child's later ability to be independent. Critics of attachment parenting don't seem to comprehend this, but child-development specialists understand it well. During the first year, when baby needs familiar caregivers to help him fit, he learns what it's like to feel right most of the time. As his thinking ability matures during the second year of life, he is able to pull up a mental image of his mother or his caregiver that gives him this same sense of rightness even when they are apart. The better the quality of baby's early attachment to mother, the more secure he will feel as he is ready to move away from her. This secure base along with his growing understanding that "Mommy will come back" make the toddler better able to tolerate separation from his mother.

You can see the development of independence at work when you watch a toddler explore new surroundings. She bravely ventures forth, but checks in with Mom at regular intervals. This might be just a glance backward over her shoulder or a vocal request for information or reassurance. Mom smiles and says, "It's okay," and baby continues to explore. If baby is headed for danger, Mom says, "No," or "Stop," or maybe just frowns, and baby retreats. The space between the baby and mother is like a rubber band, stretching and retracting. An older toddler will venture farther, even out of her mother's sight. But you may still hear her telling herself, "No-no," speaking out loud the words of her mother that she hears in her mind.

In an unfamiliar situation, the mother gives a sort of "go ahead" message, providing the toddler with confidence and, perhaps, information. The next time the toddler encounters a similar situation, he can recall how his mother helped him the first time, and this time he handles things on his own, without enlisting his mother's help. The consistent emotional availability of the mother or another responsible caregiver helps the child learn to trust, first in his caregivers, later in himself. Trusting himself leads to the development of a very important quality of independence: the capacity to be alone.

Babies, toddlers, and preschoolers differ greatly in how quickly they move from complete dependence to greater independence. In addition to the quality of their attachments, their own personalities influence this process. Outgoing toddlers, for instance, are less anxious about moving away. They carry their feeling of rightness with their attachment network into their explorations.

A toddler who is less securely attached may have to adopt a strategy of clinging to his parents in order to be sure they are available when he needs them. Or he may spend a lot of energy managing his own anxiety. Being preoccupied with how to keep Mother close gets in the way of developing independence and of learning other important skills. Studies have shown that infants who develop a secure initial attachment to their mothers are better able to tolerate separation from them when they are older. Once again, a child must go through a stage of healthy dependence in order to later become securely independent.

Myth: Attachment parenting is just for a certain kind of mother.

Fact: Actually, there is no stereotype of the mother who practices attachment parenting. All kinds of parents choose this parenting style for all kinds of reasons. Here are some "types" we've seen.

Some women are what we dub *gut-feeling mothers.* They practice attachment parenting because the attachment style of parenting just feels right.

> **SCIENCE SAYS:**
> Early attachment fosters later independence.
>
> Researchers Dr. Sylvia Bell and Dr. Mary Ainsworth at Johns Hopkins University studied babies who had varying degrees of attachment. Those infants that were the most securely attached turned out to be the most independent in later follow-up. Researchers who have studied the effects of parenting styles on children's later outcome have concluded, to put it simply, that the spoiling theory is utter nonsense.

It would tear me up inside to let my baby cry.

Next, there are the *logical mothers.*

It just makes sense to me. Listen to them when they're young, and they'll listen to you when they're old.

Then there are the *researcher mothers,* part of the growing number of parents who are having their babies later in life.

Doctor, this is a well-researched baby. We have waited a long time. We have read a lot of theories about child raising, and attachment parenting is the one we've chosen.

Special-situation parents nearly always practice attachment parenting. These may be parents who have gone to a lot of effort to have a baby, including couples who have struggled with infertility or whose baby is born with special needs, such as a developmental delay or a physical handicap.

We worked hard to have this baby, and we're certainly going to go the extra mile to help our baby be all that she can be.

Adopting parents find attachment parenting attractive because the physical closeness gives their intuition the jumpstart to bonding that they missed out on by not being pregnant.

I believe attachment parenting will help me get to know our adopted baby better and, hopefully, make up for those hormones I missed out on by not being her biological mother.

Parents who are less likely to practice attachment parenting are those whom we tag *daily-planner parents,* couples who like order and predictability in their lives and want to train their babies to fit conveniently into their scheduled lives. These babies are likely to be fed on a schedule, be trained early to sleep through the night, and be regularly put in playpens and cribs. If breastfed, these babies are weaned early and seldom fed on cue. Some babies with easy, laid-back personalities seem to do okay with this more distant style of parenting, at least on the surface. Babies with persistent personalities continue to protest this low standard of care until they are upgraded, or they give up trying and seldom become all that they can be.

Myth: AP doesn't prepare the child for the realities of the real world.

Fact: The criticism that AP doesn't prepare the child to cope in the modern world reflects not on the parenting style but rather on the world. This high-touch parenting style complements rather than competes with a high-tech world. It's important for a child to develop some high-touch roots before entering our high-tech age. You are raising your children to improve the world they live in, not stay in their own little bubble. The "real world" is only as good as the sum of its parts, which are the parents and children who make it up.

Myth: You're a bad mother if you don't practice attachment parenting.

Fact: Nonsense. Attachment parenting is about getting connected to your baby, not about meeting a list of requirements for the "good mother" merit badge. There may be circumstances in your life that prevent you from practicing all of the Baby B's, or there may be some attachment-parenting tools you just plain don't want to use. For example, you are certainly not a bad mother if you don't sleep with your baby. There are plenty of thriving infants and parents who sleep in separate rooms and have wonderful relationships. Consider the Baby B's as starter styles of parenting. Take what works for you and your family, and discard what doesn't. As you and your infant get to know one another, you'll create your own list of attachment tools — things you do that help build your connection with your baby. The point is to get connected any way you can. Do the best you can. Your baby doesn't compare you with other mothers. To your baby, you are the best mother.

Bonding at Birth and Beyond

WE TAKE IT FOR GRANTED that parents love their children, but where does that love come from? What makes it so intense? When does it develop? These may seem to be questions that have no easy answers apart from "It's the way we're designed." But when it comes to mothers and babies (and fathers and babies), nothing about love is left to chance. As we have already seen, the process by which a mother learns to love her baby gets lots of support from biology. Mothers and babies are biologically programmed to produce good feelings in one another. This helps love grow.

We'll use two terms for the process of growing love between infant and parents: *bonding* and *attachment*. Bonding describes the way parents and baby get to know each other at the beginning, especially when they are together in the hours following birth. Attachment describes the whole caregiving relationship between mother or father and baby. Attachment begins in pregnancy, intensifies after the baby is born, and continues as the child grows.

BONDING AT BIRTH

Dr. Marshall H. Klaus and Dr. John H. Kennell explored the concept of bonding in their classic book *Bonding: The Beginnings of Parent-Infant Attachment,* published in 1976. These researchers suggested that for humans, just as for other animals, there is a "sensitive period" right after birth when mothers and newborns are uniquely programmed to benefit from being in contact with each other. Studies done by Klaus and Kennell and others have shown that a mother's early contact with her baby makes a difference to how she cares for her infant. Mothers who spend lots of time with their babies in the hours and days following birth breastfeed longer, are quicker to respond to their babies' cries, and feel more attached to their babies. Of course, these parenting behaviors in human beings are not solely the result of bonding at birth. They are influenced by many factors, including the mother's choices and beliefs. But this kind of parenting, in which parents feel very close to their child, gets a boost from biology if mother and father and baby are together immediately after birth. Here's how the miracle happens:

The physical and chemical changes occurring in the mother's body during pregnancy signal the presence of a new being, and the beginning of attachment. Mother's focus turns inward, and she pays attention to the nurturing of this new life and to the changes ahead in her own. Fathers plan for the new baby as well but in different ways. They may focus on providing financially for the child, on being a role model, and on supporting the mother. While they are not yet experiencing the reality of having a child, both mother and father are growing attached to the idea.

Then the drama of labor begins. After much hard work, both physical and emotional, the parents receive their new baby into their arms. This is the moment they've been waiting for, when the dream of a baby suddenly becomes a reality. The movements felt in the uterus and the heartbeat heard through instruments belong to a real human being.

The experience of seeing and touching your newborn at birth is precious. It's a time when your life-giving love for the infant in your womb is transformed into caregiving love for the baby in your arms. Inside, you give your body and your blood; outside, you give your milk, your eyes, your hands, your voice — your entire self. Your baby gazes intently at you, studying your face as if to say, "I know already that you are the most important person in my world." The attachment begun during pregnancy grows into the kind of love that ensures that this baby will get the care and protection he needs in order to survive and thrive.

While parents bring a lot of love and a great deal of anticipation to this first meeting, babies bring something, too. All babies are born with a group of special qualities called attachment-promoting behaviors, or APB's — features and behaviors designed to alert the caregiver to the baby's presence and draw the caregiver, magnet-like, toward the baby. These include the big, round eyes, the penetrating gaze, the softness of the skin, the incredible newborn scent, and, perhaps most important of all, baby's early language, the cries and precrying noises. When allowed to work their incredible appeal, newborn babies can make almost anyone fall in love with them. APB's are an infant's attachment toolbox to keep mother close by.

As you plan ahead for the birth of your baby or think back to those moments after the birth, it's important to understand that bonding is not an all-or-nothing event that happens only in the first hour after birth. You can't say, "Yes, we bonded," or, "No, we didn't bond," based on whether or not you got to hold your baby right after delivery. Bonding is not like using a super, quick-set glue, where the two surfaces must make contact at a critical moment if they are going to stick at all. The attachment between parents and infant develops over many days and months, and it happens differently for everyone. Medical complications sometimes take precedence over mother and baby being together, or sometimes mother is just too worn out from labor to enjoy holding her infant for long. When I was attending pediatrician at a prolonged and exhaustingly difficult labor, the mother said to me, "Let me take a shower and nap, then I'll bond."

EIGHT TIPS FOR BETTER BONDING

While there are situations in which mother and baby must be separated at birth because of

Birth bonding.

medical problems, there are also many good reasons why mothers, fathers, and babies should be encouraged to stay together and enjoy some privacy during their first hours as a family. During this time, mother and baby are unusually receptive to one another. They are programmed by nature to do good things for each other during this first meeting. Unnecessary medical routines or the mere convenience of health-care givers should not intrude on this special time. The way in which mother and baby get started with each other sets the tone for how they get to know each other. Spending time together as a family is not a frill — it's an important part of getting the new family off to a good start.

While you certainly don't need step-by-step instructions for how to bond with your baby (you'll know what to do), here are some tips to help you understand and enjoy your first meeting. Some of them you will need to discuss with

your doctor or the delivery-room staff ahead of time.

1. Hold your baby skin-to-skin immediately after birth. The needs of your newborn after birth are similar to your needs during labor: peace, quiet, warmth, and the arms of someone who cares. Request that your newborn be placed skin-to-skin on your abdomen, baby's head nestling on your breast, and baby's back and head covered by a warm towel. This is not just good psychology; it is also good medicine. Newborns get cold easily. Draping baby over the mother tummy to tummy and cheek to breast allows a natural heat transfer from mother to infant that is at least as effective as putting baby in an artificial warmer. Skin-to-skin contact also soothes the newborn. The gentle rise and fall of the mother's chest as she breathes and her rhythmic heartbeat, familiar to baby from the womb, relieve baby's distress.

2. Notice baby's state of quiet alertness. Don't be surprised if during this first meeting your newborn seems to be relatively still. Within minutes after birth, the newborn enters a state of quiet alertness, the state in which, researchers have discovered, a baby is most able to interact with her environment. It's almost as if she is so enthralled by what she sees, hears, and feels that she doesn't want to waste any energy squirming. During this alert stage, the baby looks directly at the mother's eyes and snuggles at the mother's breasts. Your baby drinks in the sound of your voice, the feel and smell of your

---

ATTACHMENT TIP

Don't let technology keep you out of touch with your newborn.

warm skin, and the taste of your breast. Within minutes after birth the infant begins to sense to whom she belongs.

The quiet, alert phase lasts for only an hour or so, and then the baby contentedly drifts into a deep sleep. You'll see this stage again in the days to come, but for shorter periods of time. That's one reason for making the most of this first hour after birth. Babies should spend this time with their parents, not in a plastic box in the nursery, bonding with a wall.

3. Touch your baby. Gently stroke your baby, touching her whole body. We have observed how mothers and fathers touch their newborn differently. A mother may stroke all over her baby's body with a gentle caress of her fingertips, while a father often places his entire hand on his baby's head as if symbolizing his commitment to protect the life he has fathered. A parent's touch is often tentative at first, but it grows more confident with each passing minute.

Besides feeling good, stroking has medical benefits. The skin is the largest organ of the human body, and it is very rich in nerve endings. At a crucial transition time in baby's entry into the world, when breathing patterns are often very irregular, stroking stimulates the newly born baby to breathe more rhythmically. Your touch has therapeutic value.

4. Gaze at your baby. Your newborn can see best at a distance of about ten inches, which, incidentally, is the approximate distance from a mother's nipple to her eyes. When mothers look at their babies, they usually tilt their head to match baby's, so that their eyes can meet in the same geometrical plane.

During the first hour after birth, a baby's eyes are wide open (if the lights aren't too bright!), as if wanting to relate to his new world. Adults find this steady gaze irresistible — even adults who aren't the baby's parents! Staring into your baby's eyes may make you feel as if you never want to part from this little person whom you have labored so hard and long to bring into the world.

Klaus and Kennell's book *Bonding* has a wonderful story about women medical students who assisted in a research project on newborns' gaze. None of them had plans for having children soon. By the time the study was over, they were all planning to have babies and were coming back to visit their research subjects every afternoon.

5. Talk to your newborn. Studies have shown that newborns can distinguish their mother's voice from that of everyone else very early in life. Baby can also recognize Dad's voice, as well as siblings'. During the first hours and days after birth, a natural communication will develop between mother and infant. Mother's voice comforts her baby and helps baby feel at home in the world. Mothers adjust the pitch and rhythm of their speech when they talk to babies, using a high, sing-song language sometimes called motherese. Babies — even newborn babies — move to the rhythm of their mother's speech, a phenomenon that suggests that human beings are uniquely programmed to use language.

6. Delay routine procedures. Oftentimes the attending nurse takes care of routines first, such as measuring the baby, cleaning him up, giving him vitamin K, and putting ointment in his eyes, and then presents baby to mother for bonding. This is backward. Ask the nurse ahead of time to delay these procedures for an hour or so, until you and your new baby have enjoyed the initial bonding period. Also, ask that they be done in your room to avoid any separation. This time with your baby is more important than these routine procedures. Think about the very important lesson your baby has learned during this first meeting: distress is followed by comfort. She is learning the single most valuable lesson in infant development, that she can trust her environment.

7. Breastfeed your baby in the first hour after delivery. Contact with the mother's nipple is part of the design for bringing out mothering behavior, to ensure that an infant will be protected and cared for. The baby's sucking and licking of the nipple releases the hormone oxytocin into the mother's bloodstream. Oxytocin causes the uterus to contract and lessens postpartum bleeding. It also produces feelings of affection. Most babies need time to find the nipple on their own, to nuzzle and lick before latching on. Researchers have filmed newborn infants who have had no separation and whose mothers were not medicated actually inching their way up their mother's abdomen on their own to explore and latch on to her breast within the first forty minutes after birth.

Your baby's first sucking experiences should take place at the breast. Sucking on an artificial nipple — whether it's a pacifier or attached to a bottle of water or formula — requires a different sucking action from the one that gets milk from the breast. Newborns need to breastfeed early and often in order to learn correct sucking based on the sucking instincts they are born with. Your baby's first breastfeedings are very important.

8. Ask for privacy. This first hour after birth should be a quiet one in which Mother and Father focus on their new baby. Ask that you be left alone as much as possible during this time, so that your attention is not diverted from your baby by the hustle and bustle of nurses and other hospital personnel. There will be time for phone calls and family and friends later.

ROOMING-IN: THE ATTACHMENT CONTINUES

Studies of the parent-newborn attachment process provided the impetus behind the more family-oriented hospital maternity policies of today. They brought babies out of nurseries to room-in with their mothers. This makes sense. Mother and baby are cared for as a unit, as they were during pregnancy. Birth has separated them, but only physically. Baby is born with a sense of oneness with Mother and, of course, depends on mother for milk and comfort. Since mother still feels that her baby is a part of her, she needs to keep her baby close to be sure that he is safe and happy.

Whenever possible, the mother, not the hospital staff, should be the newborn's primary caregiver. When mothers get to know their babies by caring for them right from the start, they feel more confident of their abilities. Most hospitals will allow babies born by cesarean to room-in once they are stable, as long as someone else will be in the room to assist the mother. The beauty of rooming-in in the hospital is that it allows nurses and doctors to care for the baby's mother and remain on standby should she need help with her baby.

Unless a medical complication prevents it, we encourage mothers and infants to remain together from the moment of birth until they are discharged from the hospital. Full-time rooming-in allows you to exercise your mothering instincts at a time when your hormones are making you uniquely receptive to your baby's

BONDING WITH A SICK OR PREMATURE NEWBORN

Newborns in the intensive-care unit — and their parents — need attachment parenting intensely, but all the medical equipment and parents' own fears can easily interfere. In the past few decades, medical science has made it possible for ever-smaller premature infants and others with health problems to survive and develop well, but in the midst of all this technology, it's easy for parents to feel displaced and detached from their baby. Parents, however, are valuable members of the team caring for a sick infant. Long before the baby is ready to come home from the hospital, parents' love and hands-on care can make a significant difference in their baby's health and development. The two big B's of attachment parenting — breastfeeding and babywearing — are especially important for these special infants.

The health benefits associated with breast milk are incredibly valuable to a tiny preemie. Infection rates are significantly lower in babies who receive their own mother's milk, and the immune protection babies receive from breast milk cannot be duplicated by special preemie formulas. Human milk is easier on immature digestive systems. Because it contains lipase, a hormone that helps with fat digestion, babies can use more of the calories available in the milk. Studies have shown that the milk of mothers who deliver a premature infant is higher in protein, fat, and other nutrients needed for catch-up growth. Pumping milk for a preemie requires a significant commitment from a mother, but she is giving her baby something that only she can give. Giving your baby your milk will help you feel attached and important even before baby is ready to nurse at the breast.

Babywearing has a different name in the neonatal nursery. It's called kangaroo care, an affectionate term that refers to the way the kangaroo mother carries her infants, who are born at a relatively early stage of development. With kangaroo care, the diaper-clad baby is placed skin-to-skin on the mother's chest, between her breasts, with a blanket over his back. Mother's body keeps baby warm, which is important since these tiny babies lack body-insulating fat. Studies of kangaroo care show that the mother's skin temperature automatically goes up when baby's drops, so responsive is her body to the needs of her infant. Babies in kangaroo care respond to this closeness by becoming beautifully calm. Their heart rate and breathing become regular, and they sleep more peacefully nestled close to their mother than in their high-tech beds. Babies also explore the breast during kangaroo care. They may lick the nipple or make attempts to latch on. Mothers find that kangaroo care helps them pump more milk. Their bodies respond to baby's touch by boosting milk production. Babies given kangaroo care cry less, so they conserve energy and oxygen. Kangaroo care is not just for mothers; fathers of these tiny babies enjoy it, too. Most parents find kangaroo care very rewarding, as it helps them get in touch with their hospitalized babies.

Research by Dr. Gene Cranston Anderson at Case Western Reserve University in Cleveland has shown that preemies receiving kangaroo care gain weight faster, have fewer stop-breathing episodes, and have a shorter hospital stay. And babywearing continues to be important to preemies when they leave the intensive-care nursery. After baby comes home, the baby sling helps mother and baby nurture their attachment, encourages frequent feeding, and helps baby grow and thrive.

When I learned that my baby was about to be born eleven weeks premature, I went into a state of depression and detachment. I held back from becoming attached to my baby because I was afraid I was never going to have a baby to bring home. While he was in the intensive-care unit, I was afraid to touch our baby, afraid with every gasp for air that he was going to get sick. My husband was wonderful. He held, nurtured, loved, and cried over our little boy.

After our baby came home from the hospital, my husband stayed home with us for two weeks, caring for both of us. I then heard about attachment parenting. I immediately purchased a baby sling and began wearing my baby, all day, everywhere. Slowly I began bonding and healing by wearing my tiny baby.

needs and cues. Mothers and newborns who room-in enjoy the following benefits:

- Rooming-in babies are more content because they can count on a prompt and predictable response to their fussing and about-to-cry behavior.

- Rooming-in newborns cry less because they are more likely to receive a quick and nurturing response to their cries. Mother (or Father) helps them calm down before they have a chance to get really wound up and cry uncontrollably. Babies in a large nursery are sometimes soothed by tape recordings of a human heartbeat or of music. Rather than being soothed electronically, the baby who is rooming-in with Mother is soothed by real and familiar sounds.

- Rooming-in babies learn sooner about day and night. They organize their sleep-wake cycle more quickly than nursery babies because they are near their mothers, who are trying (mostly) to sleep at night in a room that is darkened.

- Mothers who room-in usually have fewer problems with breastfeeding. Because baby is right there, he can nurse frequently through the day and night. Baby gets lots of practice breastfeeding, Mother's milk appears sooner, and baby seems more satisfied at the breast. This motivates mothers to continue breastfeeding.

- Rooming-in babies get less jaundiced, probably because they get more frequent feedings and more milk.

- While nurses or concerned relatives may suggest that a mother send her baby to the nursery at night ("so you can sleep"), a rooming-in mother usually gets more rest than one who is separated from her baby. The mother whose baby is by her side experiences less anxiety. She does not need to wonder what's going on with her newborn in the nursery, and if her baby wakes her in the middle of the night, she wakes up gently and has the calming effect of breastfeeding to help her fall back asleep. In the first few days, newborns sleep most of the time anyway, and rooming-in mothers can just watch and enjoy.

- Full-time rooming-in encourages hospital personnel to focus their attention and care on the mother, too, rather than just on the new-born. The mother benefits from the attention to her needs and from the psychological support. She feels important and better able to focus on her baby.

- Rooming-in mothers, in our experience, have a lower incidence of postpartum depression. They leave the hospital feeling more confident about caring for their baby and are better able to weather the ups and downs of the first weeks postpartum.

More and more, rooming-in is becoming the usual standard of newborn care. Yet there are still too many babies left in plastic boxes in their mothers' rooms. For true rooming-in, get your baby out of the box and into your arms as

---

ATTACHMENT SAFETY TIP

It is not safe for postpartum mothers who are deeply tired or under the influence of sedatives or pain relievers to hold their baby in their arms or sleep with their baby without help. In these situations, a mother is not as aware of her baby as she would be otherwise. Mothers who have received medications that affect their sleeping patterns or level of consciousness need supervision and assistance from a nurse or other helper. While Mother sleeps, Father (or another caregiver) can hold the baby and care for baby's needs.

---

much as possible. Your newborn's home is in your arms, not just by your bedside.

HOW ROOMING-IN BUILDS ATTACHMENT

You may be thinking that you'd rather rest while you're in the hospital after your baby's birth. "Let the nurses care for him. I'll wait till I've recovered from childbirth to take on this job full-time." Think again. Rooming-in is especially helpful for women who are hesitant to jump right into mothering.

One day while making rounds I visited Jan, a new mother, only to find her sad. "What's wrong?" I inquired.

She confided, "All those gushy feelings I'm supposed to have about my baby—well, I don't. I'm nervous, tense, and don't know what to do."

I encouraged Jan. "Love at first sight doesn't happen to every couple, in courting or in parenting. For some mother-infant pairs, learning to love is a slow and gradual process. Don't worry, your baby will help you. But you have to set the conditions that allow the mother–infant care system to click in. The most important condition is that you keep your baby close to you."

Mother-infant attachment depends on mother-infant communication, which is a two-way system. The opening sounds of the baby's cry activate a mother's emotions. This effect on the mother is physical as well as psychological. As the mother thinks, "What is wrong?," her body is preparing to comfort her baby. The blood flow to her breasts increases, and she may even feel her milk-ejection reflex cause her milk to "let down." She has a biological as well as an emotional urge to pick up her baby and comfort him — with her voice, with her touch, with her milk. She gently picks up her newborn and tries different ways to soothe him. She speaks, she sings, she pats, she nurses, she moves around the room. The first thing she does may not work, but she keeps trying until her baby calms down. She thinks, "Ah, that was it. He wanted to be up on my shoulder [or he wanted to nurse, or he needed to hear my voice]." Meanwhile, baby thinks, "I was upset and I cried. I got picked up. Now I feel better." Both of them have learned something that they will apply to their next attempts at communication. There is no other signal in the world that sets off such intense responses in a mother as her baby's cry.

When babies and mothers room-in together, they have many opportunities to practice their communication. Because Mother is right there, she can begin to notice what baby does before he cries. She picks him up as he awakens, squirms, or grimaces and settles him right down, before the crying even starts, certainly before it is out of control and hard to stop. She has learned to read her baby's precrying signals and to respond appropriately, and because these more subtle cues get a response, baby begins to use them more often. After rehearsing this dialogue many times during the hospital stay, the mother and baby are working as a team. Baby learns to cue better; mother learns to respond better. Even the mother's hormones begin to work better. Since she can respond to her baby calmly and confidently, her milk-ejection reflex functions smoothly, and baby gets the milk he needs when he needs it.

What goes wrong when mother and baby are apart? Contrast this rooming-in scene with what happens when mother stays in her room and her infant is cared for in the hospital nursery. Baby awakens in a plastic box. He is hungry and starts to cry, along with other hungry

babies in plastic boxes who have managed to awaken one another. A kind and caring nurse hears the cries and responds as soon as time permits. But if she has other babies to bring to their waiting mothers, some babies have to wait. Since the nurse has no biological attachment to any of these babies, she does not feel any particular urgency to quiet the babies' cries. Her hormones aren't responding, her milk isn't rushing down to her nipples. So the crying, hungry baby is taken to his mother as quickly as time permits.

The problem with this scenario is that a baby's cry has two phases. The early sounds of the cry have an attachment-promoting quality: they arouse sympathy and prompt a response. A cry that goes unattended escalates. It becomes more and more disturbing, more grating on a listener's nerves. At this point, it may no longer call forth a sympathetic response. Instead, it may actually promote avoidance. (See The Crying Curve, page 85.)

Nevertheless, the mother who has missed the opening scene in this biological drama is expected to give a nurturing response to this baby. However, baby is much more difficult to soothe once he has worked himself up into a full-blown cry. Mother becomes agitated and anxious. Nothing she does seems to help her baby. She is tense, so her milk-ejection reflex doesn't work, and her baby is too frantic to latch on and nurse anyway. Some babies simply give up after a prolonged period of crying, and by the time one of these babies is brought to his mother, he may have gone back to sleep as a way of withdrawing from pain or the discomfort of hunger. Then the mother has the frustrating experience of trying to wake and feed a baby who only wants to sleep.

If this happens a lot, Mother grows to doubt her ability to comfort her baby, and the infant

THE ATTACHMENT PARENTING BOOK   45

may wind up spending more time in the nursery, where, Mother feels, the nurses can do a better job of caring for him. Mother and baby go home from the hospital strangers in a way, not really knowing each other.

The cure for feeling as if you don't understand your baby or don't know what he wants is to spend time with your baby. That means rooming-in. When baby awakens in your room, you can respond to his precry signals, before his whimpers escalate into a disturbing cry that turns you into a fumbling wreck. Both parents, in fact, can begin to teach their baby to cry better, not harder. If you hold your baby in your arms much of the time, he may hardly need to cry at all, and you will feel like you really know how to do your job. The two of you (or the three of you) really do fit together. A better term for rooming-in may be *fitting-in.* By spending time together and rehearsing the cue-response dialogue, the baby and mother learn to fit together well. Already they are experiencing one of the payoffs of attachment parenting: knowing and enjoying each other. They are bringing out the best in each other.

BONDING BLUES

Bonding is both a useful term and a loaded one that could set you up for failed expectations. Bonding blues can occur in mothers who have cesarean births, mothers whose babies go directly from the delivery room to intensive-care nurseries, or mothers who are separated from their babies for other reasons after birth. A mother may naturally feel sad or worried when she does not get to hold her baby or keep him with her. Her body and mind are programmed to expect an infant in her arms after the work of giving birth. When this doesn't happen, some mothers are understandably upset. They may describe feelings of being empty or not whole. They miss their babies and worry about them, and that is very real. But they should not worry about missing out on bonding.

In some animal species, disrupting the sensitive period after birth can permanently damage the mother-infant relationship. The mother may reject or abandon her infant, or the infant may not recognize the mother. Unlike these animals, humans, who are able to think about people and things even when they are not present, have other ways to bond with their babies if they are apart in the hours after birth.

When bonding became the birthing buzzword of the 1980s, there were some unfortunate results that persist today. Bonding is sometimes seen as a now-or-never phenomenon: if you miss your chance in the first hour after birth, you've blown it, and your relationship with your baby will never be quite as good as if you'd had that early opportunity to bond. The overselling and distortion of the bonding concept have caused needless worry for mothers who, for one reason or another, were temporarily separated from their babies after birth — especially those mothers who expect perfection in everything they do. While being together during the biologically sensitive period that follows birth does give the parent-infant relationship a boost, there are ways to compensate for missing out on the opportunity to hold your baby at this time. Here are some suggestions:

Father bonding. If Mother cannot be with baby, Father can. He can hold and talk to the baby in the nursery or a quiet room if Mother is groggy from an anesthetic or too tired from the birth to focus on the baby. In this situation, baby gets the benefit of intense human contact in the time after birth, and Father has an op-

BONDING AFTER A CESAREAN BIRTH

A cesarean section may be a surgical procedure, but first and foremost, it is a birth — the time when Mother and Father first meet their child. When a cesarean is necessary, parents can still enjoy the opportunity to bond with their baby during the sensitive period after birth and in the days to come. Here are some ways to foster bonding following a cesarean delivery.

For the mother. Most cesareans are done using regional anesthesia, so that you feel nothing from your navel to your toes but can still greet your baby as he enters the world. Unless there is an emergency, requiring quick action and general anesthesia, ask that you be given medications that will allow you to be awake and aware during the procedure. When your baby is born, ask to see and touch him as soon as the doctors have checked him over. You may have only one arm free because of the IV, but with assistance you can still enjoy your baby's soft skin and gaze into his eyes. Your time with your baby may be somewhat limited, and you may feel physically overwhelmed, but make the most of the time you have together. The important thing is that you connect with your baby immediately after birth, and not just from across the room.

For the father. Plan on being with your wife during the operation. (You don't have to view the surgical area.) You can sit next to her and hold her hand. Once baby is out of the uterus and has been pronounced stable and healthy, you or a nurse can bring baby to Mother and help her to see and touch him. Then, while the surgeons are finishing the operation and your wife goes to the recovery room, you stay with the baby. Even if your baby needs special care, you can still be there next to the incubator. Ask for help from the nursery staff so you can touch your baby and let your baby hear your voice; he may recognize it because he's heard it for several months in utero. I have noticed that fathers who spend this special time with their babies after a cesarean birth find it easier to get attached to their babies later.

portunity to get to know his baby and absorb his new role. If baby must go to a special-care nursery, or even be transferred to another hospital, Dad can go along and be the one to talk to medical personnel about the baby's condition and then relay the news to Mother. He may be able to touch and stroke the baby, even in an incubator.

Catch-up bonding. So you miss the first hour of your baby's life because of medical complications or procedures. Make the most of the hours to come. As soon as you are feeling up to it, request that your baby be brought to you. (You may have to keep asking and be assertive.) Even if he is sleeping, pick him up and hold him. Gaze at his face, examine his tiny fingers and toes, watch him breathe and make faces and sucking motions while he dreams. Keep him close to you. If you don't feel as if you can be completely responsible for his care in your room, enlist the help of your husband, a grandma, or a special friend during your hospital stay. When he wakes, hold him skin-to-skin against your chest and let him nuzzle the nipple and latch on.

If your baby can't come to you, go to your baby. Ask to see your baby, to touch him, to hold him — whatever is possible. If your baby is receiving special care, it may be hard to see your little one with tubes or monitors attached, but not seeing your baby is even harder. Call the nursery nurses for a report on your baby several times a day and plan to be with him whenever possible. Leave something special with your baby, perhaps a receiving blanket that has the scent of your milk on it. Take a picture of your baby with you and keep it by the phone or by your breast pump to look at when you are thinking or talking about your baby.

Bonding at home. We have seen adopting parents who, upon first contact with their one-week-old newborn, release feelings as deep and as caring as those of biological parents in the birth room. If you can focus on the baby after you are both at home, the feelings of attachment will come. Keep your baby with you. Give him plenty of skin-to-skin contact as you breastfeed and hold him. Don't let chores or visitors or even your own worries get in the way of tuning in to your baby.

Relax. Many mothers do not feel love for their infants the first time they meet, whether it's in the birthing room or days later. What you feel matters much less than what you do. If you practice the parenting behaviors described in this book, the feelings of love will follow. The best cure for wondering if you love your baby is to spend time with her. Study her face, hold her even when she sleeps, comfort her when she cries, nourish her at your breast, honor her likes and dislikes. Responding to her cues, holding her, and comforting her will help her feel loved, even if your own emotions are not quite what you expected. Don't worry. You will fall in love with your baby. It's inevitable.

HOMECOMING: TEN TIPS FOR STAYING ATTACHED THE FIRST MONTH

We call the first four weeks at home a period of nesting-in, a time when parents and baby (and older children) learn to fit together as a family. It's a time for parents to focus on their baby and themselves. During these weeks of nesting-in, your main job is to build a strong mutual attachment between yourselves and your baby. Growing attached means that you come to feel as if you and your baby really fit together. Just as you asked for privacy in the first hour after birth in order to bond with your baby, guard your privacy now, too. Don't let outside demands or worries intrude on this special time for building the attachment between baby and parents.

Here are some tips to help you make the most of this time and keep your attention centered on your baby and your family.

1. Take maternity leave. Maternity leave means just that: taking leave of everything else so that you can concentrate on being a mother. Whether you're taking leave from a full-time job or from the preschool car pool, give yourself the gift of time to spend with your new baby.

Mothering a new baby takes more time and energy than most parents ever believe is possible. Building your attachment to your newborn requires that you be there, with your newborn, focusing on her needs and responding to her signals. You can't do this if you're also trying to run a busy household, play host to visitors, or keep up with the details of a paying job. It's not that you're frantically busy all the time when you're getting to know your newborn. You'll spend lots of time doing "nothing," just holding and nursing your baby. But time spent re-

THE SCIENCE BEHIND "MATERNITY LEAVE"

Since ancient times, traditional cultures throughout the world have treated "those first forty days" after birth as a special time in the lives of mothers and babies. A mother receives household help during this time, and her activities may be restricted so that her attention stays on her baby. This traditional maternity leave has a strong basis in biology.

During the first six weeks postpartum, prolactin levels are high in a mother's blood. Frequent nursing during the first six weeks helps a mother to establish a good milk supply. Six weeks is about how long it takes for a woman's body to recover from childbirth and for her to establish a good milk supply for her baby. Lactation scientists have recently established that frequent nursing during the early weeks of breastfeeding is important to a mother's milk supply over the months to come. Frequent breastfeeding leads to the establishment of more prolactin receptors in the milk-making cells of the breast. Prolactin is the hormone that causes the breasts to make milk. Blood levels of prolactin are high in the first weeks, but they decrease as the baby grows older. Having more prolactin receptors in the breast ensures that even lower levels of the hormone will be able to keep the milk-production process going. Taking the time to nurse your baby often during the first six weeks will help you have plentiful amounts of milk when your baby is three and four months old.

Six weeks is the minimum maternity leave you should consider. Aim for three months, which is now what the law allows. As we said, it takes six weeks to recover from childbirth, establish your milk supply, and settle into a routine and parenting style that work for you and baby. During the next six weeks you'll begin to cash in on your investment and enjoy your baby more.

Mother burnout occurs frequently in our culture, not so much because of the incessant needs of the tiny baby, but because new mothers try to do too much, too soon. Take those valuable weeks of maternity leave and make it clear to the rest of the family just what your plans are.

laxing with your baby isn't really doing nothing. You're observing and learning, resting together, and settling in together. Taking leave of your other responsibilities frees you to relax and enjoy this leisurely time with your baby, without fretting about what isn't getting done. What you are getting done is actually more important than anything else you could do — mothering your baby.

Parents often describe the first couple of weeks as wonderful but exhausting. Mothers need lots of rest as their bodies recover from the effort of giving birth and adjust to the process of making milk. Your life changes on the most basic levels: sleep patterns, eating schedules, when you get up in the morning, what you do all day, when you go to sleep at night. The women who cope with these changes most successfully are the ones who are able to relax and go with the flow. Four weeks, the first month of your baby's life, is a very short time. Almost anything can wait for that long.

FATHER-NEWBORN BONDING

Research has focused mainly on mother-infant bonding, with the father given only honorable mention. But when fathers have been the subjects of bonding studies, researchers have noted that they are as responsive to their newborns as mothers are. A father's reactions to his infant have been given a special name, *engrossment.* This term describes father involvement to a high degree, a feeling of absorption, even preoccupation with the infant. A new father will be quick to tell you that his newborn is perfect and that he himself feels incredibly happy and very proud of his new offspring. Spending time with baby right after birth and in the first few days helps to bring out these feelings. Dads who have the opportunity to care for their newborns, to talk to them, and to enjoy eye-to-eye contact can quickly become as sensitive as any mother to their baby's cues.

Unfortunately, fathers are often portrayed as well meaning but bumbling when caring for newborns. Sometimes they're relegated to the position of secondhand nurturers — nurturing the mother as she nurtures the baby — but that's only half the story. Fathers have their own unique way of relating to babies, and babies can recognize and respond to this difference. Men can be just as nurturing as women, especially if they're given a chance to enjoy their baby in the hours and days right after birth.

2. Take paternity leave. Dads, if possible take a week or two away from the job to help your new family get the best start. You have important responsibilities during the nesting-in period that involve your wife, your new child, and any siblings baby may have.

First, do everything you can to make your nest a place where mother and baby can concentrate on each other. Take over whatever housekeeping needs to be done (and keep this to a minimum — this is not the time to scrub carpets or retile the bathroom). See that your wife has good food to eat, whether it's prepared by you, brought in by friends and relatives, or delivered from her favorite restaurant. Hire some help if you can afford it, or enlist the aid of supportive friends and relatives. An organized environment helps a mother direct her attention to feeding and caring for her baby. Look around — take a walk through the house every day, and then take care of any potential problems that may upset your peaceful nest and your vulnerable partner.

Second, take some time to get to know your newborn. Babies don't always have to be in Mom's arms. Dad's willing arms and chest can provide a welcome respite for Mother. While she takes a shower or a nap, you can be the one to care for the baby. Help out as Mom is getting ready to feed the baby. Hold and talk to him while your wife settles into the rocking chair. Hand her the baby, get her a drink of water, and then sit down, watch, and marvel at this miraculous new life the two of you have created together. If baby is still awake when he's done nursing, take another turn at walking and enjoying your baby until you soothe him off to sleep.

Third, take over the care of any siblings. Let them know what they can do to help Mom at this time, such as pick up after themselves, keep quiet while Mother naps, or bring snacks and diapers. Let them know that they must be givers during this time, not takers. This is the time for the whole family to give to Mom. (As future mothers and fathers, this is good training for them.) If your baby's sibling is a toddler or preschooler having fits of jealously over the amount of attention paid to the baby, step in and give this child a good dose of fun with Dad. It won't quite make up for having to share Mother's attention, but it will come close.

3. Ban the baby trainers. The early months postpartum are a time to let yourself go and follow your heart and your baby's cues. This is not the time to worry about getting your baby on a schedule, reducing the number of daily feedings, getting baby to sleep through the night, or teaching baby "who's in charge." A tiny baby's wants are the same as a tiny baby's needs. Your job is to get to know your baby, not to get your baby to follow someone else's advice.

When you're a new mother, love for your baby and your desire to be the very best mother you can be may make you vulnerable. When someone tells you that the way you are mothering might not be the best way, you may get anxious — and confused. Even the most confident of mothers finds it hard to follow her heart and her mothering instincts when books, relatives, and advice in the media are telling her to do something else. This is Dad's opportunity to shine. Get between your wife and the advisers who upset her. Let her know that you think she is doing a wonderful job of giving your baby exactly what he needs.

4. Ask for help. After you and your baby return home from the hospital, it is wise to limit visitors and phone calls. Entertaining and so-

cializing take energy that should be directed primarily toward taking care of yourself and your baby. Keep visits and phone calls short and pleasant, but do ask friends and family for help. When people ask if there's anything they can do for you, say yes! Ask them to bring a meal or to stop by the grocery store. Friends can start a load of laundry, clean up the kitchen, or take baby's big brother or sister to the park. Most people are glad to help; they just need some direction. You can return the favor later by helping out other postpartum families in the years to come.

When helpers (such as your mother, mother-in-law, or best friend) come to visit, be sure that they actually help you. Don't be the one to wait on them while they hold and play with your baby. They should be mothering you by helping your household run smoothly. You should be the only person acting like the baby's mother. It's a good idea to make this clear before Grandma comes to spend a week or two. Be clear about your needs: "I need you to straighten up the kitchen and put dinner in the oven so that I can sit and nurse the baby." If it's hard for you to ask for help directly, post a list of jobs to be done on the refrigerator or near the phone. Then let your helpers do the job their way.

Relax and let yourself be on the taking end of this relationship. Thank your helpers profusely for freeing you up to do the one job only you can do: mothering your baby. And yes, you can let them hold the baby — if you go and take a shower or do something nice for yourself while they do.

A couple of phrases that worked for Martha when our children were demanding more than she could give were "Go ask Daddy" and (during sibling squabbles) "That's disturbing my peace." Also, she dressed for the occasion. She took the advice she gave in her childbirth classes: "Don't take your nightgown off for two weeks. Sit in your rocking chair and let yourself be pampered." She realized that if she didn't get dressed, the kids would get the message that Mom was off-call for any of their needs that could be met by someone else.

5. Hire help. If it's financially possible, consider hiring household help while your baby is small. The investment is well worth it. Pay someone to do the cleaning or the laundry. Hire a teenager to play with an older child for an hour or two. You can even pay someone to come into your house and prepare meals for you.

Many communities have doula services. *Doula* is a Greek word meaning "servant." A doula specializes in mothering the mother (not the baby, as a baby nurse would), freeing her to focus on and learn to care for the baby. Just as you can hire a doula to support you during labor, doulas also provide postpartum support, including help with breastfeeding and assistance with the household. If you can't hire a doula, ask your husband, relatives, and friends to be doulas for you. Introduce them to the word and the concept as a way of explaining what you need them to do for you. To learn more about doulas, consult Doulas of North America (DONA) at www.dona.com.

You can even be your own household help if you plan ahead during pregnancy. Cook double amounts for dinner during the month before the birth and freeze half. Stockpile groceries. Keep your home clean and neat as your due date approaches so that you won't have to look at a mess when you get home from the hospital. And start collecting menus from take-out restaurants so that you'll have lots of options

besides pizza when you choose to make a phone call instead of making dinner during those first weeks at home.

6. Avoid isolation. Too many visitors can be a problem, but coping with a newborn baby all by yourself is not a good idea either. Stay in contact with friends and family members who support your parenting choices and make you feel good about yourself. If you are far away from family and friends, make an effort to find some kind of support system for yourself in your community. Experienced parents can be a good source of support, especially ones who understand the wisdom of standing back and letting you discover what works best in your family. Get together with other couples from your childbirth class or from your church. Investigate activities in your community for mothers and babies. Going from full-time employment with lots of people around to being home by yourself with a baby all day long is a big adjustment. You need social outlets that you and baby can enjoy together, ones that leave you feeling good about yourself. (See the list of resources on page 177.)

7. Eat well and often. When you're experiencing stress, good nutrition is more important than ever. This means lots of fresh fruits and vegetables, along with whole grains, low-fat dairy products (if you or baby are not sensitive or allergic), and fish, lean meat, and chicken. Have plenty of healthy food on hand for snacks and quick meals so that you won't be tempted to load up on sweets and junk food.

Babies are notorious for needing to breastfeed just as Mom and Dad are sitting down to dinner. There will be times when you have to grab a meal when you can, but be sure that what you grab is good for you. Smaller, more frequent meals keep your blood sugar steady and your energy level high and help you be more responsive to your baby. It's amazing, but true: eating well will help keep your emotions on an even keel.

The first six weeks postpartum are not the time to worry about losing pregnancy pounds. They will come off in their own good time, especially if you are nursing. If you stick to healthy food, exercise and time will take care of the weight loss. You're a new mother now — you're designed to carry a little extra padding for the first few months.

8. Get some exercise. Taking care of yourself doesn't mean sitting around doing nothing. Physical exercise is a tremendous way to combat stress and boost your mood. Exercise releases endorphins, brain chemicals that make you feel happier and more relaxed. Take advantage of this natural antidepressant.

Walking is excellent exercise for postpartum women. You don't have to worry about who will mind the baby — just bring your baby along. Carry her in the babysling. She'll be cuddled close to you, and your movement will probably put her to sleep. Take a brisk forty-five-minute walk daily or at least several times a week. You'll be outside, you'll feel better, you'll sleep better, and some of those extra postpartum pounds will disappear as well.

9. Rest, rest, rest. You can't be very responsive to your new baby if you are tired and cranky. Newborn sleeping patterns are unpredictable, and you will often find yourself awake in the middle of the night and worn out in the middle of the afternoon. Naps are great for postpartum mothers (dads, too). Take the phone off the hook and hang a sign on the front door that says "Do not disturb. Mom and baby resting." Go to bed early if your baby does, or sleep late. Teach your baby to nurse lying down so that the two of you can drift off to sleep together. Getting enough rest will lift your mood, help you care for your baby better, and give your body a chance to recover from childbirth.

10. Delegate to Dad. Husbands and wives cannot read each other's minds. Having a new baby brings major change to your lives, but mothers and fathers meet these challenges in different ways. It's important to talk to one another, and important to listen.

Wives, be specific in telling your husband what kind of help you need, both practical and emotional. You may think that it's obvious that you need help with housework, or that you need a hug and holding rather than advice. But many men are unable to sense what their wives are thinking and feeling. Be nice but direct. Your husband will probably be grateful for the information.

Husbands, let your wives know what you're thinking and feeling. If you're feeling left out, as if there's no place for you in the family because of your wife's intense focus on the new baby, talk with her about this. Then take over the baby care for a while so that your wife has a chance to take a nap, go for a short walk, or do something else for herself. If you can give her opportunities to care for her own needs, she will be more likely to have some energy for you as well as for the baby.

Breastfeeding

O NE OF THE BABY B's that greatly influences the physiology of mother-infant attachment is breastfeeding. This should not be a surprise, since breastfeeding is an attachment tool that is "built in," or part of mother and baby's biology. It is also the prime example of the mutual giving at the heart of attachment parenting, since both babies and mothers benefit from breastfeeding.

BREASTFEEDING MAKES ATTACHMENT PARENTING EASIER

Even though bottle-feeding mothers can feel as close to their babies as breastfeeding mothers do, breastfeeding does make attachment parenting easier. Here's how:

It gives you a hormonal head start. Every time a mother gives her baby her milk, baby gives something back to mother by stimulating the production of her lactation hormones. The hormones associated with breastfeeding, namely prolactin and oxytocin, do more than cause the mother's body to produce and release milk.

They also help the mother get connected to her baby. Think of these hormonal helpers as attachment hormones.

Levels of these attachment hormones are highest in the first ten days of breastfeeding, just when mothers need all the hormonal help they can get in learning to care for their babies. Besides signaling the body to make milk, prolactin acts as an antistress hormone, helping mothers stay calm while dealing with the challenges of a new baby. Oxytocin causes the milk-making cells to release milk, and it also makes a woman feel content and peaceful. Both of these hormones are released in response to the baby's sucking, making breastfeeding a natural tranquilizer.

These hormonal perks are a mother's reward for nursing her baby, and the sense of relaxation that mothers come to associate with breastfeeding makes them want to be with their babies even more. Because of this biochemical boost, breastfeeding is particularly helpful for the mother who is slow to feel connected to her baby after birth. Repeated nursing sessions not only give her lots of hands-on time with her baby, they also generate good feelings within

TEN HEALTH BENEFITS OF BREASTFEEDING

Thousands of research studies over the years have shown that breastfeeding is best. Here are just a few of the health benefits enjoyed by breastfeeding babies and mothers:

1. Breastfed babies see better. Studies show that visual acuity is better in breastfed babies because of the "smart fats" it contains. Breast milk contains the type of fats needed to build better nerve tissue in the eyes and the brain.

2. Breastfed babies hear better. There are more middle-ear infections among formula-fed infants, and these can contribute to hearing problems. Even temporary hearing impairment can affect a child's language development.

3. Breastfed infants have better smiles. Because breastfeeding improves jaw alignment and the development of facial muscles, children who were breastfed experience fewer orthodontic problems.

4. Breastfed babies breathe better. Breastfed babies have fewer and less severe upper-respiratory infections, asthma, and nasal allergies.

5. Breast milk is easier for babies to digest. Because human breast milk is designed specifically for human infants, it is easier to digest than formula. Human milk empties more quickly from the stomach, which makes it less likely that breastfed babies will have problems with gastroesophageal reflux (GER), the regurgitation of stomach acids into the lower esophagus. GER is a common, though hidden, cause of colic and painful night waking.

6. Breast milk protects immature intestines. Breast milk contains immune substances that act like a protective paint, coating the digestive tract to keep germs from entering the bloodstream. This friendlier environment means that breastfed babies have less trouble with intestinal infections and diarrhea. Breastfed babies are also less likely to develop food allergies, because they are protected from exposure to foreign proteins that inflame the intestinal lining.

7. Breastfed babies have healthier skin. They are less likely to experience the allergic, rough, dry, sandpaperlike rashes found in some formula-fed babies. Breastfeeding is especially important if there is a family history of eczema or skin allergies.

8. Breastfed babies are less likely to become obese adults. Breastfeeding teaches healthy eating habits right from the start. Infants learn to match their intake to their appetite, without anyone prodding them to finish the last $\frac{1}{2}$ ounce. Breastfed babies tend to be leaner (just the right amount of fat for their body weight) than their formula-fed friends, and leanness is an important contributor to overall health.

9. Breastfed babies are protected from many diseases. Breastfeeding is associated with a lower incidence of virtually every kind of infectious disease, including bacterial meningitis, urinary tract infection, and infant botulism. Children who were breastfed are less likely to develop juvenile-onset diabetes, Crohn's disease, and childhood cancer. Rates of Sudden Infant Death Syndrome (SIDS) are also lower among breastfed babies.

10. Breastfeeding makes Mommy healthier. At least one study has shown that breastfeeding mothers have a lower incidence of postpartum depression. Other studies have shown that breastfeeding reduces the risk of breast, uterine, and ovarian cancers. It is also associated with a lower incidence of osteoporosis. Many women also find that breastfeeding helps them to lose weight postpartum.

the mother when she is with her baby. Breast-feeding thus jump-starts the mother-infant attachment.

Studies comparing mothers who breastfeed with those who don't have shown that breastfeeding mothers have lower levels of stress hormones. Research has also shown that breastfeeding mothers tend to be more tolerant of life's stresses. In other words, what breastfeeding does for the mother tends to balance the otherwise tiring effects of high-maintenance baby care. This may explain why mothers who are breastfeeding and practicing attachment parenting often say that their lives are made easier — not more difficult — by their parenting choices. While attachment parenting may

look like a lot of work, mothers often describe this parenting style as more relaxed.

I'm a busy person, and I tend to get overly committed and have a hard time setting priorities. Breastfeeding forces me to take time out, relax, enjoy my baby, and put less important obligations on hold. Breastfeeding makes me realize that other

---

ATTACHMENT TIP
Working and Breastfeeding

The hormonal perks of breastfeeding are particularly helpful for mothers who work outside the home. Breastfeeding helps you unwind from a busy day's work and reconnect with your baby, especially after a tense day.

SCIENCE SAYS:
Enjoy your hormonal helpers.

How do you keep your hormone levels high? Studies show that the more a mother and baby nurse, the higher the mother's prolactin levels. Prolactin has a short biological half-life of approximately half an hour. This means that prolactin levels drop by 50 percent only half an hour after a feeding. Oxytocin has a half-life of only a few minutes. These biochemical facts suggest to scientists that mothers and babies are designed to breastfeed frequently. The more frequently a baby feeds, the better the mother's milk supply and the greater the hormonal benefits.

things can wait. Those frequent nursings are special times that will pass all too soon. My baby has this special need only once in her life, and only once in my life do I have the privilege of meeting it.

It helps you become an expert on your baby. Breastfeeding is an exercise in baby reading. Successful breastfeeding depends on learning to read your baby's cues, which means you have to spend a lot of time paying attention to your baby, not to the clock. Baby gives a cue, and it's up to you to figure out what is an appropriate response. If his mouth is opening and closing and he's searching for the nipple, you offer your breast. If he's whimpering and you're not sure what's wrong, you try walking with him or patting his back. If that doesn't calm him, you try a new position, or perhaps you try nursing. With each new cue-response session, you become a more intuitive cue reader, and baby becomes a more accurate cue giver. You seem to "just know" what baby wants, and baby's cues become more organized because he's learning to understand his own needs as well.

Breastfeeding gives you lots of practice at reading your baby's cues because breastfed babies nurse eight to twelve times a day, and those feedings are not evenly spaced throughout the day and night. Baby may sleep for three or four hours in the middle of the day, have a feeding, play for a while, and then want to nurse every twenty minutes during the dinner hour. You learn to be flexible, to recognize and respond to your baby's body language. You learn that sometimes she needs to nurse vigorously and fill her tummy, and other times she needs some leisurely sucking and a few sips of milk to calm her. A veteran breastfeeding mother once told us, "I can tell my baby's moods by the way she behaves at the breast."

Breastfeeding as a tool for helping mothers get to know their babies is especially useful for mothers who may not feel they have any intuition. Learning to read your baby's cues is a mental exercise that will build your confidence in your own intuition. At first you may feel as if you have no way of knowing whether your baby is hungry, upset, or something else, but the more you respond, the better you get at responding. You feel good about yourself as a mother, and you also become convinced that your baby can be trusted to tell you what he needs.

Sometimes I have to give my baby a bottle. While she bottlefeeds she can look anywhere. When she breastfeeds, she looks at me.

It helps you develop empathy. As a parent, you need to develop the ability to get behind the eyes of your child and see things from his viewpoint. Learning to tell when your baby wants to breastfeed is a good first step toward developing empathy. Following your baby's cues for feeding gets you in the habit of looking at life through your child's eyes.

As a psychotherapist, I have noticed that breastfeeding mothers are better able to empathize with their children.

It builds healthier babies and healthier mothers. Everything about mothering is easier when both baby and mother are healthy, and research shows that breastfed babies have significantly fewer health problems than formula-fed babies. Every organ and every system in a baby's body works better when that baby is fed human milk. Consider breastfeeding like immunizing your baby with periodic booster shots throughout the day. Your milk, like your blood, is a living substance full of infection fighters. In the

Koran, mothers' milk is called white blood. A drop of breast milk contains around one million infection-fighting white blood cells. Your baby's own immune system is weakest during the first six months, a time when the antibody-rich mother's milk fills in this gap, until baby's immune system matures toward the end of the first year. Problems with allergies are also less likely when babies are breastfed. The incidence of nearly every kind of disease is less in breast-fed babies.

The mutual sensitivity that we described above in connection with baby's and mother's cues and responses exists on a physical level as well. Mother's body responds to the baby's need for protection from germs in the environment. Mother's body also adjusts the nutritional content of the milk to suit baby's growing and changing needs.

ATTACHMENT TIPS FOR SUCCESSFUL BREASTFEEDING

At this point, you may be agreeing with us about the importance of breastfeeding but wondering if breastfeeding will work for you. Friends and relatives may have shared their stories of sore nipples or insufficient milk, or maybe you already have experienced problems with breastfeeding. We know from our thirty years in counseling breastfeeding mothers in our pediatrics practice and from Martha's eighteen years of breastfeeding our eight children that breastfeeding has its challenges as well as its rewards. The key to successful breastfeeding is believing that you can do it. We have found that the mothers who truly enjoy the breastfeeding relationship are the ones who take the time to learn about breastfeeding and who look

> ## NATURAL CHILD SPACING: THE RULES OF THE GAME
>
> The same hormone that makes milk, prolactin, also suppresses ovulation. Most mothers who breastfeed exclusively find that their periods do not return until sometime around or after baby's first birthday. Although the system is not foolproof, this prolonged period of infertility means that they can naturally space their children two or more years apart. For prolonged infertility to work, you must breastfeed according to these rules: You must practice frequent, unrestricted breastfeeding throughout the day and night (prolactin has the highest response to breastfeeding between 1 A.M. and 6 A.M.). You must also avoid the use of supplemental bottles and pacifiers and delay introducing solid foods until the second half of the baby's first year.

for support. Here are some tips and resources for getting your breastfeeding relationship with your baby off to a good start:

- **Read all about it.** Read our *Breastfeeding Book* from cover to cover. Then reread the parts about getting started at breastfeeding. This book contains lots of helpful information on getting the right start in breastfeeding and on overcoming breastfeeding problems. Because we believe that confidence is an important part of breastfeeding successfully, *The Breastfeeding Book* also talks about feelings. It will help you build a positive attitude about breastfeeding.

BOTTLE-FEEDING FOR ATTACHMENT

Can a bottle-feeding mother experience the same closeness with her baby as a breastfeeding mother does? We believe she can, though it will require more conscious effort, since the bottle-feeding mother doesn't get the biochemical boost that comes with breastfeeding. Remember, nursing means *caring for* and *nourishing*, whether by breast or bottle. The breast is the original model for infant feeding, but it is possible to bottle-feed in a way that follows the breastfeeding blueprint.

Feed according to baby's cues. Feeding is more than delivering nutrition. It is a time for social learning, and babies need lots of daily lessons in the cue-response pattern, in which the baby gives a signal and his mother figures out that he's hungry and offers food. Bottle-feeding mothers may be tempted to put their baby on a three-to-four-hour feeding schedule. Because formula takes longer to digest than human milk, it is easier to get a formula-fed baby on a schedule and to feed that baby less frequently. This is not how breastfed babies are fed. Feed your baby as frequently as you would if you were breastfeeding: eight to twelve times a day for newborns and younger babies. Small, frequent feedings are not only good for mother-infant attachment, they're also easier on baby's immature digestive system.

Forget the fear of spoiling. Becoming sensitive to her baby's cries is a bit easier for a breastfeeding mother. Since the baby's cry will often stimulate her milk-ejection reflex, she has a strong biological motivation for picking up her baby and offering the breast. The baby can then decide whether he needs to fill his tummy, suck for comfort, or take just a few sips of milk to ease into sleep. When a baby is bottle-fed, Mom has to think more about her responses: "Is baby hungry? Should I go to the kitchen for a bottle? Or does he just need to suck — where's the pacifier? Maybe his tummy is too full and he needs to burp." Faced with many possible solutions to baby's cry, a formula-feeding mother may take longer to come up with the right response. If baby keeps crying, she may have to tune him out while she prepares a bottle or deals with the intestinal discomforts formula may cause or the extra burping bottle-feeding babies may need. Tuning him out keeps her from getting to know her baby better, and it can make the baby trainers' advice to let baby cry it out more acceptable. We find that a bottle-feeding mother has to work harder to respond consistently and sensitively to her baby's cries and to overcome worries about spoiling the baby.

Hold your baby during bottle-feedings like you would at the breast. Besides giving your infant the bottle, give her your eyes, your voice, and your touch. Give your baby the warmth of skin-to-skin contact, like she would experience were she breastfeeding. Wear short sleeves and open your shirt during feedings. Hold the bottle alongside your breast, as though it were coming from your body. Don't distract your baby from sucking, but do watch for pauses in your baby's feeding rhythm; these are opportunities to smile or talk. Give lots of eye-to-eye contact. You want your baby to feel that the bottle is part of you.

Avoid bottle propping. Like breastfeeding, bottle-feeding should be a social interaction — with a human being at both ends of the bottle. You want your baby to know that a person, not a thing, is feeding him. Propping a bottle is not safe, since baby could choke on the formula. Also, falling asleep with a bottle allows sugary formula to pool against the teeth, causing tooth decay.

Practice the other Baby B's of attachment parenting, especially babywearing. Your relationship with your baby is about much more than just the way he is fed. The best way to get connected to your baby is to spend lots of time with him — bonding in the first days after birth, bedding close to him, being responsive to his cries. Babywearing is a very practical way to get to know your baby and build the attachment. With baby cuddled close to your body, you'll nurture the feeling of harmony that helps attached parents relax and enjoy their child.

Don't beat up on yourself. Above all, don't worry that you will somehow be less of a mother or less attached to your baby because you have chosen to bottle-feed or because breastfeeding did not work out for you. Breastfeeding is just a part of the whole attachment-parenting package, and the ways in which breastfeeding builds the mother-infant attachment have more to do with behavior — which you can duplicate — than with physiology. Don't let anyone make you feel guilty about not breastfeeding. It's your choice to make, whatever your reasons. Your commitment to mothering your baby will shine through in many other ways.

- **Join La Leche League International (LLLI).** More than anything, breastfeeding mothers need support from other mothers. La Leche League publications are full of mother-to-mother stories about breastfeeding that will help you see yourself as a nursing mother. Local La Leche League group meetings are a wonderful source of support, a place where you can share both your joys and complaints about life with a new baby. La Leche League leaders can answer questions over the phone and tell you about lactation resources in your community. (See Breastfeeding Resources on page 63 for information on how to contact your local La Leche League group.)

- **Consult a lactation specialist.** A session with a professional lactation consultant on the first day or two after birth is a good investment. She can show you proper positioning and latch-on techniques that will keep sore nipples to a minimum and maximize your baby's milk intake. Most breastfeeding "failures" are due to mothers not getting the right advice soon enough. Breastfeeding problems are easiest to fix in the first days of life, before babies develop poor latch-on and poor sucking habits. (See Breastfeeding Resources on page 63 for information on how to contact a professional lactation consultant.)

  A veteran AP mom hung this little note on her baby's bassinet in her hospital room: "Because I don't want my baby to develop bad sucking habits, please do not give him any bottles or pacifiers. Thank you." She wasn't taking any chances!

• **Teach baby how to latch on efficiently.** The most common cause of early problems with breastfeeding is baby not learning to latch on and suck efficiently. While some babies are natural suckers, others don't position their tongue or their lips properly to get enough milk. As a result, nipples get sore, babies don't get enough milk, and mother feels like a failure. Breastfeeding should not hurt if baby is latching on correctly. Careful attention to latch-on and sucking right from the start will prevent problems.

I thought breastfeeding would just come naturally, but I soon learned that there is a definite technique to successful breastfeeding. In the first couple of weeks, Cheyenne had trouble latching on and sucking properly. My nipples were sore and bloody, which only made me dread every feeding. We were both frustrated, and my confidence as a new mother was completely shot. Only after we hired a lactation consultant to train Cheyenne how to suck and latch on properly did breastfeeding become an enjoyable experience.

• **Nurse frequently according to baby's cues.** Newborn babies nurse a lot, eight to twelve times in twenty-four hours. Their tummies are tiny and empty quickly, and they get hungry at night as well as during the day. Newborns also rely on breastfeeding to calm them down and to help them fall asleep.

All this nursing is good for your milk supply. Studies have shown that frequent nursing in the first days and weeks after birth helps you have a good milk supply when baby is older. Milk production works on the principal of demand and supply: the more your baby demands, the more milk you can supply. Don't worry about waiting for your breasts to fill up between feedings; your breasts actually make milk for your baby while he sucks. And re-

member that babies like snacks and dessert at the breast as well as full meals. If baby wants to nurse soon after the end of a feeding, it may be that he needs just a little more milk or a little more sucking to feel content or to fall asleep.

• **Ban the naysayers.** If you lived in a time and place where everyone breastfed their babies, there wouldn't be anyone around to put negative ideas into your head. You can create this kind of environment by surrounding yourself with breastfeeding-supportive friends.

SCIENCE SAYS:
Cache or Carry? A Biological Clue to AP

The nutritional content of the milk made by each species of mammal contains clues to the way the young of that species are cared for. Some animal parents leave their young for long periods while they are away hunting. These mammals are called intermittent-contact species. The milk of these mammals is high in fat and calories so that the babies need to feed only a couple of times a day. Human milk, on the other hand, is relatively low in fat and calories, which indicates that nature intended human infants to be fed frequently. Human infants are therefore called a constant-contact species. Humans' closest genetic relatives in the animal world are the primates, and these mothers carry their babies constantly and feed them throughout the day. Anthropologists dub these two parenting styles "cache" (meaning infants are left alone for long periods) and "carry" (infants are kept in arms and nursed frequently).

You don't need to hear remarks such as, "Maybe you don't have enough milk." Stay away from people who tell you this, or change the subject quickly. A statement like that can get you wondering about your milk supply, and pretty soon you're interpreting every bit of your baby's behavior as a sign that he's just not getting enough milk from you. Soon you're offering supplements, baby is nursing less at the breast, and your milk production declines. If you think you don't have enough milk, you'll start acting like you don't have enough milk, and eventually you won't.

- **Choose supportive health-care providers who are knowledgeable about breastfeeding.** While most health-care providers will agree that breast is best, look for evidence that they practice what they preach. Make it known to your health-care provider that breastfeeding is important to you and that you want help finding solutions to breastfeeding problems, not just the advice to "offer a bottle." Is there a lactation consultant in the health-care provider's practice or one that's affiliated with the practice? What percentage of mothers in the practice breastfeed and for how long? What is the doctor's own experience with breastfeeding?

- **Be confident.** Sometimes during a prenatal interview an expectant mother will say, "I'm going to try to breastfeed." The word *try* reveals doubt in her mind. Be confident that your body will work for you. La Leche League often advises that breastfeeding is a confidence game. Believe you can breastfeed successfully, and you will.

- **Make a commitment.** Many first-time mothers are not prepared for the fact that breastfeeding does not always come easily.

Some babies have to be taught to latch on and suck properly, and some mothers require help and support to produce enough milk. Those friends of yours who are veteran breastfeeders may have had a difficult period at the beginning, when they had to work through two or three weeks of challenging problems. Breastfeeding really does work, but for reasons that are not always clear some mothers and babies get off to a more difficult start. This may be a result of difficulties during labor and birth, anatomical variations in mouths and nipples, or other reasons that are not clear. Make a commitment to a "thirty-day free trial." Many mothers who have been tempted to give up during the first two weeks find that with professional help problems work themselves out by the third or fourth week, and mother and baby go on to enjoy a long and happy breastfeeding relationship.

The first two weeks of motherhood were anything but perfect. My daughter and I were having so much trouble breastfeeding. I didn't know how to latch her on properly, and she didn't know how to suck properly. My nipples were cracked and bleeding, and breastfeeding was not enjoyable. The best money we ever spent was on having a lactation specialist come to our home. She found that my daughter was sucking my nipple in the front of her mouth rather than drawing it to the back of her mouth. She trained her how to suck in the back of her mouth using her index finger. She advised me that I might have to occasionally retrain her with my index finger. That was the beginning of a beautiful breastfeeding relationship. I had never realized what an art breastfeeding is. I can honestly say that if I hadn't had training from an experienced lactation specialist who reassured me I could breastfeed and then helped me to be successful at it, both my daughter and I would have been robbed of something very special.

♦ ♦ ♦

Despite an unmedicated birth, lots of early bonding time, and many attempts to get my first-born son to breastfeed, he had a great deal of difficulty latching on to the breast. He lost a lot of weight, and we ended up giving him bottles of formula. In fact, for a day or two he was exclusively formula-fed because I was so exhausted and so discouraged. But still I wanted to breastfeed, so I began the job of teaching him to nurse at the breast, using an SNS (a supplemental nutrition system that delivers milk through a tube while baby learns to suck on the mother's nipple correctly). This was an uphill struggle, and I'm sure many people wondered why I was putting myself through this. I often wondered myself.

Then one afternoon my sister came to visit, bringing her four-and-a-half-month-old chubby breastfed son. We sat and talked, and she started to nurse her baby. He sucked for a while, then pulled off the breast, reached for her face, and gave her a big smile. I thought to myself, "I want that. That's why I'm working so hard at breastfeeding now." I realized that the struggle to get breastfeeding to work for us wasn't about how my baby was being fed today, or how he would be fed tomorrow. It was about this whole first year (and, as it turned out, well beyond the first year). If I gave up now, I wouldn't have that later. So I persevered, and before long, I had my own real breastfeeding baby — with the smiles, the cuddliness, the simplicity of breastfeeding. It was well worth the effort.

- **Look at the big picture.** We urge parents to think of breastfeeding in terms of years, not just months. While breastfeeding for only a few months is the cultural norm for Western society, what we know about breastfeeding in

primitive cultures and weaning times for other mammals suggests that human infants were designed to breastfeed for several years. If you are the parent of a new baby, you may not be ready yet to think about nursing your child through toddlerhood. But you will soon recognize that breastfeeding means much more than delivering nutrition to your baby, and that will be your first step toward an appreciation of breastfeeding as a parenting tool.

THE BENEFITS OF LONG-TERM BREASTFEEDING

I have heard many an expectant mother say, "I'm not going to be one of those women with a two-year-old who pulls at her blouse and asks to nurse." I'm happy to report that many of these same mothers later go on to nurse toddlers. As the saying goes, "Don't knock it till you've tried it." Long-term nursing is the one feature about attachment parenting that really stands out as different from the way most women in Western culture mother their children. Yet ideas about weaning are beginning to change. Here's why:

What the experts say. In 1990 then–surgeon general Dr. Antonia Novello wrote, "It's the lucky baby, I feel, who continues to nurse until he's two." If you look at the recommendations of the American Academy of Pediatrics' Committee on Nutrition over the years, you'll find growing support for extended nursing. In this committee's 1997 statement on breastfeeding, they recommended that breastfeeding continue "for at least twelve months, and thereafter for as long as mutually desired." The World Health Organization recommends breastfeeding for at least two years. So if uninformed friends raise

---

BREASTFEEDING RESOURCES

- *The Breastfeeding Book: Everything You Need to Know About Nursing Your Child — From Birth Through Weaning*, by Martha Sears and William Sears (Little, Brown, 2000).
- *www.breastfeedinginfo.com.* Operated by lactation consultants (Martha among them), this Web site is a valuable at-home resource for the breastfeeding mother. It contains answers to common questions and concerns about breastfeeding, video clips demonstrating positioning and latch-on techniques, as well as support for overcoming breastfeeding problems.
- La Leche League International. LLLI offers support and information for breastfeeding mothers. Contact the organization by phone (800-LALECHE or 847-519-7730) or through their Web site (www.lalecheleague.org) to find a leader or group in your community. You can also receive a catalog of books, breast pumps, and other merchandise for nursing mothers. Their Web site contains answers to many frequently asked questions about breastfeeding.
- International Lactation Consultants Association (ILCA): 919-787-5181 or 919-787-4196 (fax) or www.ilca.org.

SCIENCE SAYS:
Health Benefits of Long-Term Breastfeeding

In recent years a flurry of studies have all come to the same conclusion: the longer mothers breastfeed, the greater the health benefits to their babies and themselves. Studies correlating the duration of breastfeeding with intellectual development conclude that the longer infants are breastfed, the greater their intellectual advantage. And in a recent study from China, mothers who breastfed for two years had at least a 50 percent lower risk of developing breast cancer.

---

their eyebrows and say, "What! You're still nursing!" just tell them that you are following the advice of experts.

What mothers say. The real experts on nursing into toddlerhood are the mothers who do it. Their reasons for continuing to nurse these walking, talking little persons are often very practical: "Nursing heals boo-boos"; "It's the only time I ever get to sit down"; or "I don't know how I'd get her to sleep at night if it weren't for nursing." Mothers also find that nursing helps to soothe a child who is beginning to stretch his boundaries but who is often frustrated by the things he can't do. Breastfeeding helps a mother and toddler reconnect on days when they find themselves in constant conflict. For many mothers, the reason they continue to nurse is that they simply can't imagine weaning: "Nursing means so much to my daughter. How could I refuse to give her something that is so important to her emotional well-being?"

It's fun. How charming it is to hear toddlers talk about their nursing relationship. Your toddler will have his own way and his own vocabulary for letting you know that he needs to nurse. Choose your family's term for breastfeeding carefully — be sure it's something that's okay to say out loud at the mall or during

SCIENCE SAYS:
Breastfed babies have higher IQs.

Breastfeeding is smart! Because breast milk contains brain-building nutrients, namely the omega-3 fats DHA (docosahexanoeic acid) and AA (arachidonic acid), that are not in formula, breastfed infants tend to be smarter. Recent scientific studies comparing breastfed and formula-fed infants have shown that breastfed babies enjoy as much as a 10-point higher IQ. And the more frequently and longer babies are breastfed, the greater this intellectual advantage.

church. Most mothers prefer, for example, *nana* over *booby.* Terms of endearment we hear include *nummies, milkies, nee,* and *nur.* Few things can make a mother feel more special than having her toddler snuggle up to her expecting to nurse.

Long-term breastfeeding builds beautiful memories. Many children who nurse past the age of two can remember when they get older being at their mother's breast. These are moments to treasure — for both of you.

BEWARE OF THE BREASTFEEDING SCHEDULERS

Feed on schedule is a dangerous dictum passed along by the baby trainers, parenting advisers who advocate crying it out and other ways of letting babies know that parents, not infants, are in control. But babies pay a high price for this ill-conceived approach to feeding. Only a baby knows when he needs to eat. (You don't let other people tell you when you're hungry, do you?) The body is programmed to satisfy hunger with feeding. When parents ignore their baby's hunger signals and watch the clock instead, their baby learns that her hunger signals are unreliable. This is not a healthy feeding habit for a child to learn. Baby even may stop asking to be fed, and her growth and weight gain will suffer along with the baby's relationship with her parents. (For a story of a scheduled baby who failed to thrive, see page 122.)

Besides affecting infant growth, feeding schedules can keep breastfeeding mothers from making enough milk for their babies. Milk production works on the principle of demand and supply. The more milk baby takes from the breast, the more milk the breasts make. When you space feedings farther apart, milk production slows down. Another interesting fact about human milk production is that the fat level in milk is higher when the time in between feedings is shorter. Frequent feedings allow babies to receive more high-fat milk — the kind with lots of calories for growth.

Studies of infant growth and maternal milk production have shown that babies who are allowed to breastfeed on cue have a remarkable ability to decide for themselves how much milk they need to grow. Mothers' bodies respond by producing the milk their baby needs. Schedules get in the way of this finely tuned system. They also get in the way of parents and babies learning to trust one another.

ATTACHMENT TIP
Avoid Scheduling Feedings

Watch your baby, not the clock.

Babywearing

WHERE DOES A BABY BELONG? We believe that most of the time, young babies should be in the arms of their parents, wherever their parents may be. That's why we've become great advocates of the baby sling, a simple cloth baby carrier that holds an infant close to Mother or Father's body. You use the sling when you go out, and you use it around the house as well. It's like wearing your baby — which is why we call this parenting style babywearing.

The beauty of babywearing is that you are, literally, attached. Baby is held in the baby sling and goes around the house with you as you sort through the junk mail, make beds, or start supper. When Mom or Dad goes out for a walk, baby does, too, but he is carried in the sling, not wheeled in a stroller. Baby becomes a part of your regular activities. The payoff is that the two of you are learning about and enjoying each other all the time.

We enjoy collecting stories about babywearing in other cultures. After returning from the island of Bali, one of our patients told us about witnessing a ground-touching ceremony. Balinese babies are worn in a sling for the first six months of life. Mother or some other member of the extended family wears the baby all day long. Baby is out of someone's arms only when sleeping, and even then, baby sleeps next to the mother. The baby literally does not touch the ground for the first six months. Then a ground-touching ceremony is held, and for the first time baby touches the ground, in a ritual that acknowledges that baby will soon be learning to crawl and eventually won't have to be carried by mother.

THE BACKGROUND TO BABYWEARING

Babywearing, like other parts of attachment parenting, is not a new idea. For centuries women in various cultures around the world have carried their babies in different kinds of slings and shawls. Experience taught these women that babies are happiest in the arms of their mother or another person who cares about them. Buggies and strollers are relatively new inventions, in use only in modern times, when "experts" have advised women not to "spoil" their infants by paying too much attention to them.

Over the past two decades, we have learned a lot about babywearing. Our education started with the birth of our fourth child, Hayden,

BABYWEARING BASICS

There are a number of different kinds of baby carriers on the market. In our experience, a sling-type carrier is the easiest to use, the most comfortable, and the most versatile. The baby sling has a simple design patterned after the slings used in many traditional cultures, which are used to tying an infant to Mother's back or hip or to holding a tiny baby near Mother's breast. A sling can be used for older babies and toddlers as well as for newborns, and it slips on and off easily. Baby can ride in many different positions, and in most positions baby enjoys eye contact with Mom or Dad.

Baby slings come with directions for using them at different ages and stages of your baby's development. Use these suggested positions as a starting point, then fine-tune your sling-wearing style to suit yourself and your baby.

Newborns are most comfortable in the cradle hold or the snuggle hold. In the *cradle hold,* baby rides sideways across your body, aligned with the lengthwise direction of the sling. Baby can ride in a horizontal position or semi-upright, with his head peeking over the top railing. If you put the sling on backward, the sling's shoulder pad can help to steady your newborn's head.

In the *snuggle hold,* you carry baby vertically, his head between your breasts and his tummy against your abdomen. Hold baby up on your chest and pull the top edge of the sling out and up over baby as you ease his bottom into the pocket. Then cinch in the tail of the sling to snuggle baby securely against your body. Tiny babies may like to keep their feet tucked inside the sling. Older babies can sit in the sling with their feet hanging down.

Here are some points to keep in mind as you learn to use your baby sling:

- Babywearing takes some practice. You may feel a bit awkward at first and may wonder if your baby is really comfortable, especially if he fusses. Stick with it. The sling offers such great convenience to mothers that it's worth some trouble to learn how to use it and to teach your baby to enjoy it.
- In the beginning think of your sling as part of your clothing. If you put it on when you get dressed in the morning, you will remember to use it. It will become the place you put your baby instead of putting him down. This is a great way for you and baby to get used to the sling.
- When you put your baby in the sling, start walking immediately, as soon as you're sure he's safe and secure. The movement will help to calm him and accustom him to this new nest. If you just stand still, he may start to fuss. While you walk around, pat him reassuringly on his bottom.
- Be sure to adjust the sling to fit your personal dimensions. A newborn should nestle into your body just below breast level, his weight supported by your hips as well as your shoulders. If you wear the sling too low, you may not feel as confident of baby's position, and your shoulders and lower back will take more of the weight.
- The sling should fit snugly around your baby. Pull the tail further through the rings

to take up the slack, or in the snuggle hold, hold the tail snug against baby's back by tucking the slack of the tail under your arm. You can make adjustments while baby is in the sling. Support baby's weight with one arm while you adjust the cloth with the other.

- There's no need to set a crying baby down in a safe place before "slinging" him. You can put the sling on while holding your baby. Slip it over your head with one hand and ease baby into position. Then start walking.
- Experiment with different positions as your baby grows. Between three and six months, many babies like to sit in the sling facing forward (the *kangaroo carry*), so that they can see everything. As baby develops the strength to sit by himself, he becomes ready for the *hip straddle* — the classic baby-holding posture made much easier with a baby sling.
- If you need to pick something up from the floor while wearing your baby, steady the baby with one hand and bend at the knees, not at the waist. (This is better for your back as well as safer for baby.)
- Learn to breastfeed while wearing baby in the sling. Someday when you're in line at the grocery store, you'll be glad you practiced this ahead of time at home.
- Shop around to find a sling in a color and pattern you like. You'll be happier using it if you know you look great. Keep Dad's preferences in mind as well.
- Keep your sling in a handy place — on a hook by the back door, draped over a kitchen chair, on the bedroom doorknob. Then you can just grab it — and your baby — and go! Keeping a spare one in your car can be a lifesaver if you're the forgetful type.

See the list of resources (page 177) for information on where to buy a baby sling and how to wear it.

who simply was not happy unless she was held. Through the years, we have experimented with different types of carriers and have taught many new parents to use soft front baby carriers, beginning in the newborn period and continuing well into toddlerhood. We've observed a long parade of babywearing families over the years and have come to believe that babywearing is an old idea whose time has come. The option of bringing baby along in his familiar place on Mom's or Dad's hip or cuddled near Mom's breast makes it possible for parents to stay in touch with baby in the midst of their busy lives. We've found that the baby sling, in particular, is easy to use and very versatile.

In 1989 I (Bill) spoke at a conference attended by parents from all over the world. One day, as I was wearing baby Stephen in a sling, I stood next to two women from Zambia who were also carrying their babies in slings. I asked them why parents in their culture carried their babies on their bodies most of the time. One woman replied, "It makes life easier for the mother." The other woman responded, "It's good for the baby." These women went on to describe the feeling of completeness that babywearing gave them and added that keeping their babies with them reminded them of their importance as mothers. These mothers have taken to heart their cultural tradition, which

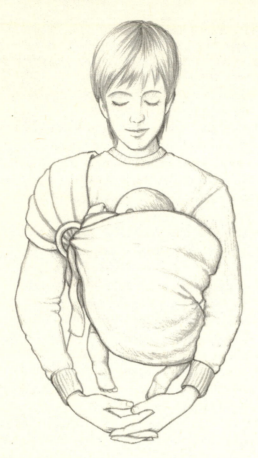

Babywearing.

has taught them that something good happens to women and their offspring when they wear their babies.

THE BENEFITS OF BABYWEARING

Over the years we have continued to study the beneficial effects of babywearing. We've talked with hundreds of parents about why they have embraced this style of parenting. They always come back to those two simple, yet profound, benefits cited by the two mothers from Zambia:

Babywearing does good things for babies, and it makes life easier for mothers. But they also describe many specific ways that babywearing benefits their families. Here are some ways that modern parents use babywearing to simplify their lives and enjoy their babies more.

Babywearing Calms Babies

Parents in my practice often report, "As long as I wear her, she's content!" Even parents of fussy babies find that their complainers seem to forget to fuss when they're held in the sling. This is more than just my own impression. In 1986, a team of pediatricians in Montreal studied ninety-nine mother-infant pairs. Half the parents were asked to hold their babies for at least three extra hours a day, even if the babies weren't crying or fussing, and they were provided with baby carriers to help them do this. The other parents were the control group, and they were not given any specific instructions about carrying. After six weeks, researchers found that the infants who received the extra carrying time cried and fussed 43 percent less than the noncarried group.

Further evidence comes from anthropological studies of infant care in other cultures. In cultures where babies are worn or are in adult arms much of the time, prolonged periods of infant crying are unheard of. Studies of babies in Western culture have measured infant crying in hours per day, but in cultures where babies are held most of the time and they sleep next to their mothers, total daily crying can be measured in minutes. We tend to think that it is normal for babies to cry a lot, but in other cultures this is not the norm. Babywearing gives parents in "more advanced" cultures an opportunity to discover what these other cultures have known for a long time: Holding or wear-

SLING TIME FOR STRESS TIME

Once our sling babies were past the "fussy toddler hanging onto mom's leg" stage, we stopped carrying them around in slings before naptime and bedtime. But we kept one sling handy even after our toddlers had turned two. We found that there were times when misbehavior called for "time in" the sling rather than "time out." A few minutes in the sling calmed a child who could no longer control herself in the face of life's challenges. When one of our toddlers was, well, just being a toddler, we would announce, "You need sling time." Reconnecting with Mom or Dad in this old, familiar way would melt away stress and boost the child's confidence. A few moments of babying the baby inside that assertive two-year-old made her easier to live with.

ing your baby saves you from having to put up with a lot of crying.

Babywearing is especially helpful in those early months for colicky babies who, it seems, save up all their energy for a long blast of crying in the evening. These "P.M. fussers" can fray the nerves and shake the confidence of any parent. But if you plan ahead for this "happy hour" and take baby for a walk in the sling, you may be able to forestall the crying. The fresh air and the motion calm baby and help him sleep. And you get some exercise, which puts you in a better mood for whatever happens later.

I find the sling is an apartment dweller's savior. Crying pierces walls. The sling keeps my baby quiet for my student neighbors.

Babywearing Teaches Babies How to Be Content

When describing the benefits of babywearing, you could say that familiarity breeds content. For a baby to be content, he must be organized. This means he can pay attention to some stimuli and block out others. He can stay in a quiet, alert state for an extended period of time. He can focus on nursing when he's hungry and can fall asleep when he's sleepy. The womb takes care of these things automatically for babies. Food comes into their bodies continuously through the umbilical cord. They are never too cold or too hot, and their legs and arms seem to be under control, because there's no room to fling them out. They hear Mother's heartbeat, feel her breathing, and are rocked by the gentle motion of her body. Mother's rhythms are baby's own. Birth temporarily disrupts baby's sense of organization in the womb. Without the support of the womb, baby can't remain calm. This is why babies like to be swaddled. But with babywearing, the newborn has an external regulating system. Father's rhythmic walk recalls the womb experience and calms baby. Cuddled next to his mother's body, baby hears her heartbeat, beautifully regular and familiar, and senses her breathing. These parental rhythms become baby's own, and the sling itself controls baby's arms and legs, so that baby's own movement doesn't upset him. As babies get older they still need to return to the familiar feeling of being close to a parent's body, especially when they are in new places or meet strangers. With a secure seat on Mom's hip or chest, baby is less fearful of new experiences.

Babies are not used to being alone and still. What may happen if the baby spends most of his time lying horizontally in a crib, with parents coming into the room only for feeding and comforting and then leaving again? The new-

LIFE IN MOTION: THE VESTIBULAR CONNECTION

Babywearing benefits the infant's vestibular system. This is what controls a baby's sense of balance. Three tiny structures, like carpenter's levels, are located behind the middle ear. One tracks side-to-side motion, another up-and-down motion, and a third back-and-forth motion. Every time baby moves or is moved, the fluid in these "levels" moves against tiny hairlike filaments that vibrate and send messages to the brain. The data collected in this way are used to keep the body in balance.

The gentle motion a baby experiences during babywearing stimulates the vestibular system, and scientists are finding that this stimulation helps babies breathe and grow better, regulates their physiology, and improves motor development. This is especially true for premature infants. Some

babies recognize on their own that they need vestibular stimulation. When deprived of it, they often attempt to put themselves into motion and develop self-rocking behaviors.

Infants who are carried a lot, especially those who ride along with Mom in a baby sling during her daily activities, get lots of vestibular stimulation. They move with Mom in all directions. Compare this to spending hours in a horizontal position in a crib or playing on the floor. Critics of babywearing sometimes suggest that it doesn't give infants sufficient opportunities to move about on their own. They forget that a baby in a sling is making constant adjustments to his mother's motion, especially as he gets older and sits upright in the sling.

born will eventually find ways to become organized, to fit into his or her new environment; but without the regulating presence of the mother, babies develop behaviors that take a lot of energy that could better be used to grow, such as fussy crying, purposeless, jerky movements, or self-rocking behaviors that are behaviors of disorganization. Even sleep disturbances can be an indication that baby's physiology is disturbed by an unnatural distance from mother.

As a psychologist, I see a lot of older children and adults with sensory-motor integration problems. I wonder if babies who were worn in a sling, because they feel so included in the sensory world of the parents, grow up with a greater capacity for making appropriate sensory-motor adaptations.

Babywearing Teaches Babies About the World

If infants in slings spend less time crying and fussing, what do they do instead? Sleep? No, they learn! Contented babies spend more time in the state called quiet alertness, the behavioral state in which they are best able to interact with other people. And, of course, when babies are worn, adults are right there to interact with them. Baby is intimately involved in Mom and Dad's world. Baby can study her mother's face and watch how it changes. She can see what her mother sees, hear what she hears, even share her emotions. This is how babies learn the subtleties of human expression and body language. Babies also learn more about their environment while carried in the sling. The view is constantly changing, and because they're near adult eye level, the view is also more interesting than it would be from a buggy or stroller.

Baby watches the dishes go in and out of the water in the sink. He peeks in the mirror when Mother combs her hair. He moves with Dad as he bobs up and down doing laundry and swoops back and forth with the vacuum. He views the bedroom from every angle as Mother puts clothes away or arranges books or pillows. These are all learning experiences for baby.

It's no surprise that researchers have reported that babies who are carried more are more responsive to visual and auditory stimulation. A stimulating environment is important to brain growth in babies. Interesting experiences cause neurons in the brain to grow, branch out, and connect with other neurons. Babywearing helps the infant's developing brain make the right connections as Mother helps baby filter out unimportant information. Baby stores her experience of the world in the developing brain as patterns of behavior. Think of these patterns as thousands of short movies that are rerun in baby's brain when a similar situation reminds her of the original film clip. For example, mothers often tell me, "As soon as I sit down in the rocking chair with my baby, he squirms into a horizontal position, turns his head to the breast and gets excited about nursing. I can't get my bra open fast enough!" Or, "She likes to be in the sling and 'loads' herself by adjusting to different positions." So, don't rush to enroll your baby in lots of classes. She'll learn a lot by just literally hanging around with you all day.

Here's an excerpt from our journal about one of our babywearing observations:

Like breastfeeding, babywearing allows baby to practice his innate desire to mold his body to the contours of his mother's body. He keeps moving and adjusting himself until he feels comfortable. In doing so, he learns that practice makes perfect. The more he tries, the more comfortable it becomes, until he settles in a position that feels right to him. A baby lying flat on his back in a bassinette, playpen, or crib much of the day is deprived of that comfort level and the joy of earning it. In those early weeks of squirming to mold to the just-right contours of his mother's body, the newborn begins to develop the capability to satisfy himself and create a comforting world around himself, especially when it is so predictable. The detached baby, on the other hand, does not get that "Ah, life is good" feeling. The AP baby begins life with a high standard, has a goal to shoot for, and conceivably could spend the rest of his life trying to keep that standard up. The unattached baby has no standard to shoot for or motivation to keep his standard up. His norm is less.

Babywearing Enhances Speech Development

Sling babies talk better. We've noticed that they seem more attentive, clicking into the conversations as if they were part of it. Because baby is

---

SCIENCE SAYS:
Carried babies cry less.

Researchers at Stanford University found that babies settle best when held by caregivers who move in all planes of motion (up and down, side to side, and back and forth), and they cry less than babies who are only rocked side to side. Babywearing enables a caregiver to provide vestibular stimulation, moving in all three planes while carrying baby rather than standing and rocking from side to side.

up at voice and eye level, he is more involved in conversations. He learns a valuable speech lesson — the ability to listen.

Normal ambient sounds, such as the noises of daily activities, may either have learning value for the infant or disturb him. If baby is alone, sounds may frighten him. If baby is worn, these sounds have learning value. The mother filters out what she perceives as unsuitable for the baby and gives the infant an "it's okay" feeling when he is exposed to unfamiliar sounds and experiences.

A mother who is a speech pathologist once described for us all the ways in which she thought babywearing contributed to infant language development. Here's what she said:

As a speech pathologist, I feel that using the attachment style, especially the use of the sling, has greatly contributed to our children's abilities to communicate. My husband and I used the sling from about one month to one year with both of our children. They were always exposed to adult conversations, listening from birth to their parents' voices and those of others. When they were able to sit upright in the sling, they began watching speakers use turn-taking and eye contact to communicate. Children's emotions develop when they listen to intonation patterns connected to happiness, sadness, frustration, and so on. By viewing the speaker's mouth up close, children learn to imitate correct speech movements for accurate articulation patterns. When they've been attachment-parented, they start practicing words and sounds at an early age. When language develops early, children have the ability to "store" many more memories at an earlier age. All these patterns contribute greatly to early communication skills. Our six-year-old is bilingual and would like to add a third language. He recently told me he wanted to learn French so he could "talk to even more people." No one can

be sure that the sling and other attachment-parenting components are the reasons our children have turned out so well and speak so well thus far, but if we have another child, I sure wouldn't want to take a chance and not use these helpful techniques.

Babywearing Makes You a More Attentive Parent

Talk about keeping a close eye on your baby! With baby sitting right under a parent's nose, a babywearing parent spends more time relating. Since parents are baby's first and most important teachers, all this interaction makes your baby smarter. Baby learns much in the arms of a busy person.

We carried her in the sling wherever we went, and we talked to her, sort of like a running commentary, as we washed dishes, walked along the beach, visited the bookstore, prepared food, talked to the neighbors and pets, went shopping, visited the zoo, and so on. Oftentimes people looked at me like I was crazy, talking to a baby as I did, but I just smiled and continued to comment on the lovely red apples or the loud airplane. We spent much time reading books together. She began talking very early. My goal was never to create a superbaby or to drill ABC's or 123's into her early, as some education-anxious parents are apt to do. I simply wanted to show her the fascinating world on a daily basis, and she has responded in turn by being fascinated by colors, sounds, textures, numbers, music, new people, and new places.

Babywearing Makes Breastfeeding Easier

The two Baby B's of breastfeeding and babywearing naturally go together. Babies need to travel with their food supply, and babywearing makes it easier. In fact, there are many situa-

BEST BABYWEARING POSITIONS FOR BREASTFEEDING

As you experiment with babywearing positions, test out different ways to breastfeed in the sling. Try them out while you're alone with your baby at home and you won't feel so awkward the first time you try breastfeeding in the sling while surrounded by friends or extended family.

In our experience, the *clutch hold* is the easiest way to breastfeed a fairly young baby in the sling. Shift baby into a sideways position on the side of your body away from the sling's rings. Baby's head is in front of the breast, supported by the padded edge of the sling, and baby's legs are curled up beneath your arm on that side. Use that hand to hold baby's back and head close to your breast, and use your opposite hand inside the sling to support your breast as baby latches on. You can usually let go of your breast once baby is nursing, but continue to support his back and neck with your other hand to keep him in close to you. If your baby needs extra help learning to latch on, use the clutch hold to give yourself a good view of what baby is doing at the breast. The sling can help you keep baby's body bent so that he can suck better. Baby can't arch away from the breast in this position, and his chin stays down, which relaxes his jaw for better sucking.

As your baby gets older and more skilled at breastfeeding, you can switch to using the *cradle hold* in the sling. Baby's head will be in the pocket of the sling, away from the shoulder rings. Turn baby onto his side so that he can latch on without turning his head. Use the arm on that side to support baby, since the sling alone probably won't hold baby close enough to the breast to maintain a good latch-on. Slip your other hand inside the sling to support the breast while baby latches on. In the early weeks, you may need to continue to hold your breast with this hand, or prop it up with a cloth diaper or hand towel to keep it at the right level for baby to maintain the latch-on.

To burp baby while babywearing, shift baby into the *snuggle hold* (upright against your chest). The upright position, plus the gentle patting on his back, should help baby burp. You may have to lift baby up and drape him over your shoulder to put pressure against his tummy.

The most common mistake beginning babywearers make is wearing their baby too low. Baby should ride at around breast level, with the rings just below your collarbone. Start with a higher position, and lower it until it feels right for you. The various holds may feel better higher or lower, depending on each wearer's proportions.

---

tions in which a baby sling helps feedings go better.

Babywearing makes discreet nursing easier. Babywearing enables you to nurse discreetly when you are away from home. Many breast-

feeding mothers worry about how they will feed their baby when they are in public places. Of course, there's nothing wrong with breastfeeding on a bench at the mall or even in a pew at church. You don't have to hide the fact that you are breastfeeding your baby. But many mothers feel more comfortable nursing in public when both breast and baby are out of sight. The baby sling makes this easy. Simply pull the sling up over baby's head, and your baby has her own private nook. The sling helps support baby's weight, so that you can nurse comfortably even while standing in the checkout line in the grocery store. Waiting — whether it's in a store or at the doctor's office — is much easier if you can calm and feed baby.

Babywearing satisfies the frequent nurser.
There are times when babies like to nurse frequently — for example, when they are going through a growth spurt, when they aren't feeling well, or during the late-afternoon fussy period. Breastfeeding while babywearing makes life easier for Mom when baby wants to nurse constantly. Tuck baby into the sling, and you

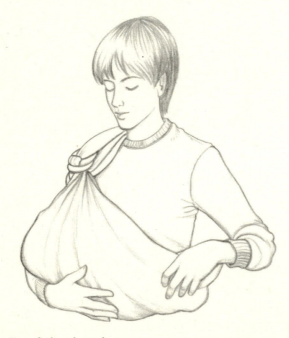

Breastfeeding discreetly.

can still walk around the house while nursing. You can get simple chores done or play with your preschooler.

Babywearing organizes problem suckers.
Some babies breastfeed better on the move than when they are still. Tense babies (such as those with a tight latch) and archers (those who dive backward and arch their back while pulling off the breast) often breastfeed much better in the sling. It coaxes their bodies into a curved position, chin down toward their chest, which makes latch-on easier. The walking motion blocks out other stimuli. As baby's body relaxes, so do the sucking muscles. With the sling and a bit of walking, a baby who is fighting sleep or for some other reason refusing the breast can be "tricked" into latching on, sucking, and relaxing.

Babywearing helps the slow-to-gain-weight baby. Babies who are close to their mothers nurse more often and gain more weight. When we encounter a breastfeeding baby who is gaining weight slowly, we encourage the mother to wear the baby in a sling for at least several hours a day and breastfeed frequently. Mothers report that babywearing entices their babies to feed more frequently and in a more relaxed way, and we have seen weight gain increase dramatically. This breastfeeding-while-babywearing technique is especially valuable with babies who were born early and those who need more stimulation to get them to eat more.

Anthropologists have observed that in cultures where mothers wear their babies or hold them most of the time infants may nurse three or four times in an hour. The fat content of the milk is higher when the time between feedings is shorter, so it makes sense that feeding more often produces better weight gains. You may not nurse your baby every fifteen minutes while he's in the baby sling, but if you are wearing your baby, it will be easier to read and respond to his feeding cues. As another perk, when baby is near the source of milk and comfort, he does not have to use much energy to get Mother's attention; he can use this energy to grow instead.

Babywearing Makes Going Out Easier

Remember, for an AP baby, home is where Mother is, but there's no reason Mother has to be stuck at home. After a few weeks of nesting-in at home, you'll probably be ready to go out

and meet the world once more. You don't have to become a recluse in order to stay close to your baby.

Shortly after the birth of Stephen, I was experiencing the "when will I get my wife back?" feelings common to postpartum dads. One night I said to Martha, "Honey, how about a date? Let's go out to dinner." Martha was just about to object when we both looked at the baby sling draped over the couch and had the same idea at the same time: "Let's wear Stephen to the restaurant."

Babies in slings are usually quiet and content. This makes them much more acceptable in adult surroundings, such as nice restaurants. You can keep your baby quiet and content while you're out by breastfeeding him in the

Breastfeeding while babywearing.

sling. Patrons in a restaurant much prefer a discreetly breastfeeding baby to one who is crying and fussing because he is not attached to the breast. The sling is the key to taking your baby places where being a baby and acting like a baby are not socially acceptable.

Our most memorable breastfeeding-in-public experience was the morning that Martha wore Stephen (almost two) on national television on Phil Donahue's talk show. Stephen watched contently for fifteen minutes, then breastfed and slept in the sling for forty-five minutes as we discussed the benefits of attachment parenting. We are sure that what the audience saw made more of an impression than what we said. This experience made us brave, so we decided to see a Broadway show while we were in New York. We went to the *Cats* box office to purchase tickets and saw a sign that read "No Infants Allowed." Undaunted, we asked for the manager, and while Martha was wearing Stephen, I very politely said, "Please, we would love to see your show. I guarantee Stephen will be quiet, and if he does fuss, we'll exit within a millisecond of the first peep." The manager let us in, and Martha and I enjoyed *Cats* while Stephen didn't make a peep. Later when we went to thank the manager, he confided, "There was something about the look of your baby that made me want to take a chance."

When Stephen was two months old, we were invited to a black-tie affair. Rather than decline the invitation, as new parents usually do, Martha wore Stephen in a fashionable sling, and we all had a great time. During the three-and-a-half-hour affair, Stephen nestled peacefully in the sling and nursed on need. Obviously, the other guests were puzzled and watched us, no doubt wondering, "What's that she's wearing?" Eventually, we could see them conclude, "Why, it's a baby. How cute!" By the end of the evening, as the other guests noticed how content we were with our babywearing arrangement, there was an air of acceptance throughout the room. Our formal babywearing had achieved not only social approval, but social admiration.

I think one of my favorite tools of attachment parenting is wearing my baby. The first year I wore him in the sling all day. I could take him with me anywhere. My husband and I went on a ski trip with thirteen other people when our son was six months old. We were the only ones with a baby, and a few people were concerned about the fact that we were bringing him. We were able to go out at night with everyone. He hung out in the sling, and I was able to nurse him without anyone knowing what I was doing. They just thought he was sleeping! No one was awakened in the middle of the night by a crying baby since he slept with us and all I had to do was roll over and take care of his needs. After the trip was over, they all said what a "good" baby he was — even after we were stuck in an airport for eight hours and then had a five-hour flight!

◆ ◆ ◆

Having a "pouch baby" has caused some conflict with certain family members. On our first trip back home, my family just couldn't understand why we chose to carry Kristof in a sling and nurse him wherever. God forbid sharing our bed with him! Everyone kept trying to get me to put him down and "get him out of that thing." They also couldn't understand why we just didn't let him cry. On our next trip home, they all saw that I was still carrying him and how happy he was, and they stopped bugging us.

◆ ◆ ◆

My son is now thirteen months old, and I still use my sling every day. Yesterday we had an extremely challenging day, and I was able to put him in the sling and calm him. He slept for two hours. I was able to pamper myself with a little shopping. When he awoke, we were both renewed and able to conquer the challenges of toddlerhood together.

◆ ◆ ◆

I am often told that this is the hard way of parenting. But, really, in the long run, I think it is so much easier!

Babywearing Makes Traveling Easier

Babywearing also makes traveling easier. When baby is worn close to Mom or Dad, the sights and sounds of airports, hotels, big cities, or wilderness retreats are not frightening. Babywearing makes it easier for babies to transition from one place to another. While you are standing in line at the airport or walking through a crowd, a baby worn is secure, happy, and, above all, safe. If you're traveling with a toddler, babywearing not only keeps your little one from wandering away, it boosts her up into the adult world, where there are interesting things to look at. Think how the world must look from a baby's seat in a stroller. She has a good view of the floor and adults up to their knees. People seem much bigger than she is. Worn on your hip in the baby sling, she enjoys your attention and also gets to see all the ads, signs, and merchandise displayed at adult eye level.

Babywearing also keeps a toddler close to your side in any situation where a free-roaming toddler may not be safe, such as when babies begin to walk and dart out from your protective arms to explore their environment. Busy shoppers or travelers often don't watch out for little

people. (Have you ever noticed that a walking or wheeling toddler's face is at the exact level that people let their cigarettes dangle?) Wear your baby or toddler up in your arms at a safe level and relax. He won't go anywhere without you.

Babywearing Makes Life Easy at Home

Babywearing is as useful at home as it is in stores and airports. If you keep the baby sling on a hook by the door, you'll remember to use it when you go out, but even better is to put it on when you get dressed in the morning. When baby wakes, you change his diaper and put him in the sling. Then you can make breakfast together, do a load of laundry, take a morning walk, or vacuum the living room. Later in the day, babywearing allows you to make dinner, even if baby is fussing and needs to be held. At night, you can put baby in the sling and take a relaxing walk through the house to ease baby off to sleep while you tidy the nest for the next day.

Babywearing makes it easier to enjoy dinner with your spouse at home. Over the years, Martha and I made a point of scheduling a once-a-week dinner at home for just the two of us. We'd put the younger children to bed and have a late supper together. However, in the days when there was a new baby in the house, this often turned out to be dinner for three. One of us would wear the baby in the sling, and we could usually eat and talk while baby stayed quietly attentive to our conversation, or stayed lulled to sleep so we could finish.

Babywearing at home helps parents survive all the times when babies just can't be happy anywhere but in the arms of an adult. If your baby seems to be asking for your attention all the time, put him in the sling and go on with your usual activities. You may not get as much done as you did before you had a baby, but you'll be more productive than you would be if baby continued to fuss.

I feel like having the sling bronzed.

SIBLINGS AND BABYWEARING

With baby cuddled near you in the sling, you can give your toddler or preschooler focused attention while meeting your baby's need for closeness. It's easier for an older sibling to share you with the new baby if your hands and eyes are free to focus on her and her activities. While feeding and holding baby in the sling, you can read a book to a sibling, supervise art activities, or cheer from the sidelines at a soccer game. Baby needs the physical sensation of being close to you; siblings need your mind. The baby sling allows you to give your body to your baby while talking and playing with baby's older brother or sister. This will make it much easier for the sibling to accept the presence of the new baby.

Breastfeeding our new baby in the sling gives me an extra pair of hands to play with and enjoy our toddler. This has done wonders to lessen sibling rivalry, and it allows me to mother both children well.

◆ ◆ ◆

A sibling says: I wish I could be in the sling. My little brother loves being carried in the sling. He seems so relaxed. The stroller seems so noisy.

BABYWEARING AND WEARING BABY DOWN

Oftentimes, babies are not ready to sleep when parents want them to sleep. This sleep-inducing technique is a lifesaver for weary parents; it's peaceful, struggle-free, and it works.

As bedtime approaches, put your baby into the sling in the cradle hold, the snuggle hold, or if your baby is older, the hip straddle (see Babywearing Basics, page 66). For most babies, the forward-facing kangaroo carry is too stimulating to induce sleep; for others it's the only one they'll accept. Then wear your baby around the house. You can do some simple jobs, talk quietly to your spouse, or just stroll through your home until baby is lulled to sleep. If baby is fighting sleep, go for a walk outside. Ten minutes outside in a sling is usually worth forty-five minutes of rocking indoors.

Keep baby in the sling even after his eyes have closed and he has drifted off, until you can tell by his limp arms and regular breathing that he is in a deep sleep. Then walk slowly to the bed, bend over, and ease yourself out of the sling while you put baby down on the mattress. If baby starts to stir, he may need to be in physical contact with you a while longer. Put baby back in the sling and lie down with him, letting him drape across your chest with his head nestled into your neck (see the illustration on page 149). The rhythm of your breathing will soon ease baby into a deep sleep. Then roll over carefully, deposit baby on the bed, and slip the sling over your head and quietly slip away.

This practice of wearing down is like having a secret formula that you can use to wind baby down to sleep even when he is hyperstimulated. Putting baby in the sling contains his energy. The gentle motion of your walk, the familiar position, and your hand on his back are all familiar cues to relax. Wearing down will help you relax, too, since you can be pretty certain that this technique will get baby off to sleep shortly.

WORK AND WEAR

In many cultures, mothers carry their babies with them while they work. "Work and wear" is not the usual practice for mothers in American culture, but it could be. Mothers in our pediatrics practice who work outside the home have tried babywearing on the job and report that it works very well until about six months of age, when babies grow more mobile. We've also had our office staff take this approach to baby care while on the job. Mom can get her work done while baby listens in and observes. Babies find the adult world of work very interesting.

Babywearing works better with some jobs than others. We've known mothers who sold real estate, demonstrated various products, or worked in baby stores with baby riding in the sling. These mothers felt that being attached to their babies was important, so they found a way to make babywearing work for them on the job. We've even known teachers who have worn their babies to classes for the first few months after returning to work. (These teachers are teaching wonderful lessons about parenting along with their usual subject matter!) If your employer is not too keen on this arrangement, ask if you can give it a two-week trial period, and promise that you'll reevaluate this choice regularly as baby grows. Most people are amazed at how productive mothers can be when they know that baby is safe and secure in the baby sling.

ATTACHMENT TIP

Babies learn a lot in the arms of a busy caregiver.

BABYWEARING IS ATTACHMENT INSURANCE

Leaving baby with a substitute caregiver is hard for an AP mom. You don't want to be away from your baby, and you know how important it is for baby to feel secure in the arms of someone who cares about him. Insisting that your baby be worn in a sling for two or three hours a day ensures that he gets a daily dose of high-touch, responsive care while you're away.

BABYWEARING FOR SUBS

When babies are accustomed to having their mother around, accepting a substitute caregiver may be difficult. Yet even attached mothers need the occasional break, especially if they are blessed with a demanding, high-need baby. Babywearing can give your baby many of the familiar comforts of Mom, even if he's being worn by someone else.

Jason is so happy when he is in the sling that I feel comfortable leaving him briefly with a sitter. Sometimes if I'm in a hurry, I greet the sitter at the door, transfer Jason to her while in the sling — sort of like the transfer of a baton in a relay race — and she takes over the wearing. He forgets to fuss, and I feel better knowing his routine is not disrupted.

AP babies adapt better to substitute care if the sub uses the tools of attachment parenting. Grandma or the sitter can't breastfeed, but she can respond promptly to cries, lie down with baby at naptime, and wear him in a sling as much as possible. Sling babies are used to first-class care and don't take kindly to being down-

BABYWEARING FOR THE NEXT GENERATION

When adults wear babies, we let our children know that babies are important and that they belong with their parents. We teach our children — and other children, too — that big people care for little people and that babies are fun to be around. When you wear your baby, you are modeling a parenting practice that others will imitate. When you bring your baby with you in the baby sling, other parents will feel more comfortable keeping their babies with them. Your own children will practice babywearing with their dolls and teddy bears.

My family commented on how Zoe was always moving when she was in the sling, doing a "sling dance." Now, twenty-two-month-old Zoe has her own sling. She puts it on by herself and puts animals, dolls, and whatever is around in the sling. Then she begins to sway like I did with her for so many months. She often decides that her sling friends need to be nursed and will offer them her breast. My favorite part is when she says, "More, please," speaking for the animals, as if they were asking to be switched to the other side.

graded. Techniques such as wearing baby down to sleep will help substitute caregivers duplicate what Mom does.

Our toddler calls his sling his "little house."

Babywear for day care. One of my patients had a high-need baby who was content as long as she was in the sling. When the mother had to return to work when her baby was six weeks old, I wrote a "prescription" for her day-care provider, stating that this baby needed to be worn in the baby sling three hours or more daily. This mother felt much better about leaving her baby, knowing that the substitute caregiver understood the baby's need for close physical contact with an adult.

Belief in the Signal Value
of a Baby's Cry

THE BABY B that flows most instinctively from an AP mother is her belief that her baby is trying to tell her something when he cries. At first she may not know what the cry means, and trying to respond in the right way may be frustrating. As she gets to know her baby better and the attachment between them grows, she will also believe in her ability to decode her baby's crying language and to offer the right kind of comfort. Baby's cries really are a language, but early in the mother-child relationship they may seem more like a foreign language. The more you listen and respond, the better you will get at understanding what your baby is saying.

CRYING IS AN ATTACHMENT TOOL

A baby's cry is a baby's language. It's baby's way of saying, "Something is not right, please make it right!" The infant's cry is designed to help the baby survive by calling attention to her needs. (And we want our babies to not just survive, but thrive.) Researchers who have studied the sound of crying regard the infant's cry as the perfect signal: disturbing enough to command attention but not so disturbing that parents want to get away rather than respond. Crying is how a baby keeps her parents close and attached. Respond to your baby's cry with your ear and your heart.

Babies generally stop crying when their parents respond. This is another feature of crying that builds attachment. When, by your presence, your arms, and your nurturing, you can calm baby's fears, you feel good about your baby and about yourself. The more you respond, the better you get at understanding your baby's cues and the more attached you feel. Babies everywhere cry, but the sensitivity of parents' listening varies greatly, as does the intensity of cries from one baby to another.

Responding to baby's cries isn't always easy. It can be quite frustrating, especially in the early weeks, when you are still struggling to learn baby's language and baby's signaling skills are disorganized. But hang in there and keep responding. How you handle your baby's cries can teach baby to cry less and to cry less disturbingly. As parents and baby practice their cues and responses hundreds of times in the early months, baby learns to cue better. Her cries become less disturbing and more commu-

ATTACHMENT-STYLE CRYING

How often have you heard someone say, "I just needed a good cry"? A good cry can relieve tension, a phenomenon that has some basis in physiology. Dr. William Frey, in his book *Crying: The Mystery of Tears,* cites studies that show that stress hormones are present in human tears and that tears stimulated by emotions are chemically and hormonally different from those caused by irritants to the eye. Studies have also found endorphinlike hormones in tears (endorphins are hormones that bring good feelings to the brain).

There may be situations in which baby actually needs to cry in order to relieve tension and relax. This observation is not a license to let a baby cry it out, but rather a reminder to parents that you can't always do something to stop your baby's cries. In fact, stopping your baby's cries is not your job. Your job is to respond and to be there for your baby while he is upset. Don't feel guilty or inadequate if you can't fix what's bothering baby. He may just need to cry for a while. Pain cries, though, are different from tension cries. Keep working at finding the cause. As an AP mother you will know the difference.

Here's a story that a sensitive AP mother shared with us about a friend:

I went to visit my friend, who had just had a baby. While we were talking, her three-week-old started crying in another room. The baby kept crying, louder and louder. It really bothered me. My breasts were ready to leak milk! Yet my friend seemed oblivious to her baby's signals. Finally, I couldn't stand it anymore, and I said, "It's okay, go attend to your baby. We can talk later." Matter-of-factly she replied, "No, it's not time for his feeding. I want my baby to learn I'm in control, not him." Incredulous, I asked, "Where on earth did you get that idea?" "From a parenting class," she proudly replied.

Clearly, this mother and infant pair were becoming disconnected, and it was very hard for this sensitive AP mother to see it happen.

I believe that if you listen to them when they're young, they'll listen to you when they're older.

nicative. It's as if baby has learned to talk better. You learn to respond more appropriately; eventually you know when and how quickly to say yes or no. In time, baby becomes so good at cueing and you become so good at understanding her signals that the two of you can communicate with only minimal amounts of crying. This is what we mean when we say that attachment parenting teaches babies to cry *nicer.* Here's how you can make it happen.

Create conditions that lessen your baby's need to cry. "My baby seldom fusses; she doesn't need to." The mother who said this shaped her baby's environment so that her baby would be calm and content most of the time. All the Baby B's lessen a baby's need to cry. Breastfeeding babies cry less because they are held and fed more often. Sling babies cry less because they are carried more. Bed-sharing infants cry less because they don't have to summon food and comfort from another room. Early newborn bonding, breastfeeding, babywearing, and bed sharing all create such a feeling of rightness within the baby that there is less need to cry and there are fewer occasions when baby completely falls apart. Babies don't need to cry as intensely when a caregiver is only inches away. Why turn the volume up when the listener is close by? Parents who practice the Baby B's can become so adept at anticipating a tiny newborn's needs that they can respond at the first hint of a problem, before baby even needs to cry.

Regard your baby's cry as communication rather than manipulation. Tiny babies cry to communicate. Feeling manipulated is in the mind of the parents. Think of your baby's cry as a signal to be listened to and responded to rather than immediately clicking into the "What does that baby want from me now?" mind-set. If you are worried about spoiling your baby or her controlling you, you will always be second-guessing your responses to baby's cry. Think of your baby's cry as a communication tool rather than a control technique. Babies don't cry to control, they cry to communicate.

Learn to read your baby's precry signals. Crying is what happens when a baby's anxiety builds to a peak. Before baby cries, there are other signs that baby needs comfort from an adult. These may be anxious facial expressions, flailing arms, excited breathing, quivering lips, a furrowed brow, squirming into a nursing position, or other body language that tells you something is not right. Being with your baby and observing your baby closely will help you learn to recognize these. Responding to these precry signals teaches baby that she doesn't always have to cry to get attended to. This is especially helpful with those babies whose cries escalate immediately into "red alert" and are difficult to calm once they start crying.

Respond early. Delaying your response to baby's cries won't teach her to cry any less, and it may lead her to cry harder and more disturbingly. Studies have actually shown that babies whose cries are promptly attended to learn to cry less as older infants. Think what you are teaching your baby. When you delay your response, baby learns that he has to cry full blast to get your attention. The next time he is upset, he'll go immediately to that level of crying. Some babies — those with mellow, laid-back temperaments — may quit crying when a parent fails to respond. But most are far more persistent. It's much kinder to comfort baby right away.

Try the "Caribbean approach." Taking a relaxed approach to baby's fussing will often keep a cry from escalating. Your close attachment to your baby means that not only can you read baby's mood, he can read yours. If your baby senses that you are not anxious, then he is likely to calm down. We call this the Caribbean approach. You shrug your shoulders, smile a little bit, and say, "No problem, baby."

Susan, a sensitive and nurturing AP mother, brought her eight-month-old, Thomas, into my office for fussy-baby counseling. As I talked with

---

SCIENCE SAYS:
Early Response Means Less Crying

In 1974 a group of researchers met to review studies on what makes competent children. In analyzing attachment research, they concluded that the more a mother ignores crying in the first half of the first year, the more likely her baby will cry more frequently in the second half.

her, I noticed that she always picked Thomas up within a millisecond of his first peep with an anxious look on her face. Watching them, it was clear to me that baby's anxiety triggered mother's anxiety, which in turn made baby feel more anxious and made them one anxious pair. In this case, mother's strong desire to do the best for her baby was working against her. Susan's responding quickly was not the problem; her responding anxiously was. I advised her to try the Caribbean approach. As soon as Thomas began to fuss, she was to relax her facial expression (even if she felt anxious inside), and instead of swooping him up into her arms, she was to simply turn toward her baby and utter some words of reassurance. What her baby needed from her was the message, "No problem, baby, you can handle this. Mama's here." Soon baby Thomas began to fuss less and play more.

As I sit here with Andrea by my side, I am amazed at how quickly she resettles just from a reassuring, "It's okay." Her fussing immediately stops, and she goes back to her nap almost instantly. She knows that I'm close by if she needs anything, and I know that makes her feel safe and secure. She never has to go into an all-out cry because the sound of my voice settles her when she begins to fuss. This also works when she begins to fuss in our bed at night. A reassuring "It's okay," a cuddle, and we all get a lot more sleep than if she had completely woken up, cried, and gotten angry.

SHOULD BABY CRY IT OUT?

Sometime during your parenting career, someone is going to suggest that the solution to your baby's crying is to let your baby cry it out. Don't do it, especially not in the early months!

Let your baby cry it out is a piece of advice that can do far more damage than good. Let's take this insensitive admonition apart so that you can see how unwise and unhelpful it is.

"Let *your* baby." It's very presumptuous for a person who has no biological connection to *your* baby to lecture you on how to respond to *your* baby's cries. Even if the advice comes from Grandma or another loving relative, realize that this person does not know your baby the way you do. She's also not the one who's listening to what those cries sound like at 3 A.M. To people who give this kind of advice, probably out of concern for you, a cry is an annoyance. You know it reflects a need.

"cry." What exactly is a baby's cry? To the cry-it-out crowd, a cry has no meaning. But in fact, baby is crying to communicate. He is desperate to communicate his needs. How you respond to the cry is also a way of communicating.

Not only is the cry a wonderful tool for babies, it is a useful signal for parents, especially the mother. Cries are designed to motivate parents to respond. And when a mother picks her crying baby up and nurses him, she enjoys the relaxing effects of the hormones released by breastfeeding, which help her become more nurturing and less tense about her baby's cry. Why would anyone want to miss out on that!

"it." What is the *it* in cry it out? Is it an annoying habit that must be broken? That's unlikely, since a need cannot be called a habit. And babies don't enjoy crying. Also, the belief that crying is good for a baby's lungs is just plain wrong. Excessive crying lowers baby's blood oxygen levels and raises levels of stress hor-

THE CRYING CURVE

A baby's cry is not the same from beginning to end. If you were graphing it, it would look like a rising curve. The opening sound of a baby's cry draws the listener magnetlike toward the baby. It promotes attachment by triggering an empathic response in the caregiver that leads to the desire to comfort the baby. However, if the infant's cry continues because no one has listened and responded, it becomes increasingly disturbing, until the infant is over the top and past the point where the cry has a positive effect on caregivers. The over-the-top cries provoke an avoidance response, and the caregiver has to fight the urge to get away from this screeching creature. When baby still isn't getting what he needs, the cry moves into the anger phase. The parent is angry about how difficult it is for baby to settle down, and baby is angry that his cries are not getting the response he's looking for. One reason for responding quickly to baby's cries is to keep them in the attachment phase of the crying curve, the phase in which babies cry nicer.

One day a child psychologist who was visiting us commented on the cry of our baby Hayden: "She has an expectant cry, not an angry cry."

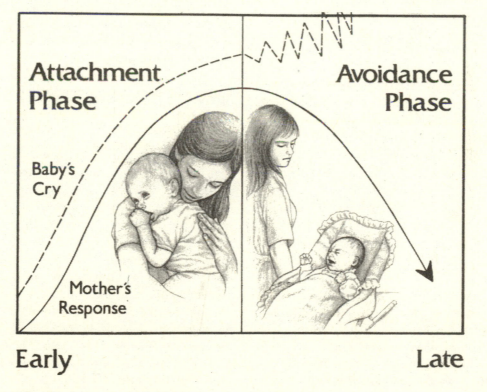

Effect of mother's response on baby's cries.

SCIENCE SAYS:
Crying it out is not scientifically correct.

Studies have shown that most babies who are left to cry it out don't cry less, but rather they cry in a more disturbing way and cling to parents more and take longer to become independent.

---

mones. To an attached parent, a cry stands for a need. The *it* in cry it out won't go away until the need is filled.

"out." What actually does a baby cry out when you let him cry, and where does it go? Does the infant cry out the ability to cry? Can he just get all that crying over with and be done with it? No! An infant can cry for hours and still retain the ability to cry. What the baby loses is the motivation to cry, and some other valuable things along with it. When no one responds to baby's cry, the baby has two choices: He can cry louder, harder, and produce a more disturbing signal, hoping desperately that someone will listen; or he can give up, become a "good baby" (that is, a quiet baby) and not bother anyone. Think how you would feel if you had a need and tried your best to communicate that need, but no one listened. You would be angry. You would feel powerless and unimportant, and you would believe that no one cares about you, since your needs matter little to anyone. What goes out of a baby left to cry is trust: trust in his ability to communicate and trust in the responsiveness of his caregivers.

Something goes out of parents as well when baby is left to cry it out. Parents lose sensitivity. Advisers may tell you that you must harden your heart against your baby's cries and even may suggest that you should do this for the sake of your baby. This is wrong. You go against your own biology when you consciously desensitize yourself to your baby's signals and shut down your instinctive responses. Yes, it's true that eventually crying won't bother you, but this has serious implications for your parenting. You will lose trust in your baby's signals, and you'll lose your ability to understand baby's primitive language. This is what happens when parents view crying as a control issue rather than as a way of communicating.

We tried the cry-it-out approach. I was so tired, and my friends all recommended this approach, so I thought I'd try it. Big mistake! It tore me up inside to hear her cry. The next morning my baby was hoarse and I had a hurting heart. She clung to me like a koala for the next couple of days. I will never do that again.

ADVICE FOR PARENTS WHOSE BABIES CRY A LOT

One day Leslie, a mother in my practice, and I were having a conversation about her baby's crying. Leslie was a nurturing, attached mom, blessed with a challenging high-need baby who was waking up frequently during the night. She responded sensitively to her baby's needs, but she was nearing burnout. Her marriage was suffering. She and her husband were at odds over parenting styles, and she confided that she was not enjoying motherhood. She loved her baby, but there were times when she felt angry about his frequent, lengthy crying spells. There were times when she needed to get away, and at times like this, she let her baby cry. She asked, "Am I a bad mother because I let my baby cry?" "You're not a bad mother, you're a tired mother," I replied.

IT'S NOT YOUR FAULT THAT YOUR BABY CRIES

Don't feel that it's your fault if you have a baby who cries a lot. If you are doing your best to respond sensitively to your baby's cries, don't feel that something is wrong with your mothering (or fathering) if you can't always soothe your baby. You don't have to stop your baby's cries. Just do the best you can to be sure there's no physical cause (this can become a long-term search, by the way) and then experiment with various ways of calming your baby. There will be times when you've tried everything you can think of and you still don't know why your baby is crying. Sometimes your baby doesn't know either. If you've done all you can to figure out why your baby is crying, then offer a caring set of arms, your breast, and a shoulder to lean on so your baby is not left to cry alone. The rest is up to your baby.

Babies who cry incessantly are no fun to have around the house. Their cries have a more disturbing sound, and they do not adjust easily to changes. Even with sensitive parenting, they continue to fuss, causing Mom and Dad to be tense and irritable. It may seem as if attachment parenting is not working for this baby, and in this family situation, the cry-it-out, get-your-baby-on-a-schedule advice may look like the parents' only salvation. But in fact, this is the baby who most needs attachment parenting. Otherwise, with all these negatives, parents are likely to distance themselves from their child. For attachment parenting to work well in this family, some adjustments are needed. A mother can't maintain a close connection to her baby if her baby's needs are so all-consuming that she is tense and exhausted.

If you find yourself in a situation similar to Leslie's, you need to take action. Don't shut your baby up in the nursery to cry every evening. Look for other solutions. Consider these:

Look for a medical cause for crying. In consultation with your baby's doctor, explore the physical causes for your baby to be a "hurting baby," one who is colicky (or fussy) because of an underlying medical condition. Consider the possibility of gastroesophageal reflux (GER), a formula allergy, or, in a breastfed baby, an allergy or sensitivity to a food in your diet. A baby who is in pain much of the time will be irritable. In this case, you must treat the cause to stop the crying.

Teach baby to cry better. The Caribbean approach (see page 83), where you use your own relaxed facial expression and body language to let your baby know that he does not need to cry, is especially helpful with fussy babies. When your older baby fusses or cries, instead of quickly scooping him up into your arms, simply make voice contact: "Mama's here." Make a funny face, or talk to baby about something. You're trying to distract baby from fussing and get him involved in something else. This approach might be difficult at first because you have to relax yourself in order to model this reaction to baby. Take a slow, deep breath, or just pause for a few seconds and let go of tension. As you learn to do this, baby will, too.

Change listeners. Persistent crying usually bothers moms more than dads. Sometimes mothers just need to get away for a while to save their sanity. Be sure baby is well fed and then hand him over to Dad while you take a walk or go somewhere on your own for an hour or so. Baby and Daddy benefit from time together, and fathers are often more tolerant of babies who continue to fuss despite their parents' attempts to comfort them. Crying in the arms of someone who loves you is not the same as crying it out alone with no one to at least offer comfort. Crying in Daddy's arms helps baby know he's not crying alone.

Teach baby that he can handle some problems on his own. Newborns and young babies need almost constant help from Mom or Dad to stay organized and calm. But by one year of age, babies can begin learning to do this for themselves. Use your own sensitivity to gauge whether baby needs an immediate response or if she needs a minute or two to try and settle herself. Listen to the intensity of the fussing. If it's increasing rapidly, you probably need to respond. If it peaks and then begins to taper off, hold back. Don't mistake this advice for the baby trainers' formula of scheduled crying. Be guided by your own knowledge of your baby. There is no magic formula for teaching a baby to handle his own emotions. Each session is a cry-by-cry sensitivity call that only you can make. Remember, your ultimate goal is to show your baby as he grows older and into toddlerhood that sometimes there are other ways to cope besides crying. At the same time, you don't want to teach baby that his cries have no value.

Bedding Close to Baby

NOT A WEEK GOES BY that I don't get a call from a writer wanting to interview me for an article on "the controversy about sleeping with your baby." I laugh and think to myself, what is so newsworthy about parents sleeping with their babies? Parents have slept with their babies for thousands of years, and even today the practice is not unusual. Most parents do sleep with their babies, at least some of the time — they just don't tell their doctors or their relatives about it. Why is this practice kept so hush-hush? The reasons go back to parents' and advisers' focus on making children independent, while failing to understand how children really become independent. Of all the Baby B's, bedding close to baby seems to be the most controversial.

Co-sleeping.

CONTINUING YOUR ATTACHMENT AT NIGHT

Attachment parenting at night is about more than where your baby sleeps. It is an attitude toward baby's nighttime needs, an acceptance of your baby as a little person with big needs — twenty-four hours a day, seven days a week. Your infant trusts that you, his parents, will be continually available during the night, as you are during the day. So you adapt your nighttime habits to fit baby's needs. Your nighttime parenting strategy may change, depending on baby's stage of development and your own adult needs. If you are willing to be flexible and let go of the expectation common in American culture that babies should be taught to sleep by themselves from the very beginning, you will recognize that you are not spoiling your baby or letting him manipulate you when you welcome him into your bed.

What to call it. Sleeping with a baby has various labels. The earthy term "family bed," while appealing to many, can be rather daunting to new parents who imagine the whole family sleeping together all the time — big kids, babies, parents, and even the family dog. "Co-sleeping" sounds more like what adults do, something like cohabiting. This is the term fa-

---

SLEEP — NOT A CONTROL ISSUE

Sleeping, like eating, is not a behavior you can force upon a child. The best you can do is create the conditions that allow sleep to overtake the child. After three decades of counseling parents on sleep problems, I have concluded that most night wakers are born, not made. It is not your fault your baby wakes up, nor are your baby's sleep habits any reflection on your parenting. If your friends brag about their babies sleeping through the night, trust us: they're probably exaggerating — a lot.

All the conflicting advice you hear can keep you awake more than your baby does. You worry that you're spoiling your baby if you take your baby into your bed or tend sensitively to your infant's night waking. You worry if you try a bit of baby training out of desperation and exhaustion and let your baby cry it out for a few nights. Sometimes it helps to realize that some babies are easy sleepers who are born knowing how to soothe themselves, while other babies wake easily at night and are hard to settle back to sleep. Every baby is different, and sleep behavior has more to do with inborn temperament (or with a medical cause in the case of night waking), than with any "bad habits" caused by Mom and Dad. There does come a time when even the persistent night waker's parents are rewarded with an uninterrupted night's sleep.

The night waking and night nursing don't really bother me. What does exhaust me are all those people who are constantly asking, "Is she sleeping through the night yet?"

The age at which families are rewarded with this nighttime bliss varies from child to child. In the meantime, keep experimenting with whatever nighttime parenting style works for you. The only sleep experts you need to consult are your baby and yourselves.

vored by anthropologists; it's clear and free of value judgments. "Bed sharing" appears in medical writings. We like the term "sleep sharing" because, as you will learn, mother and baby share more than just bed space. We also like the Baby B term "bedding close to baby," a reminder that nighttime sleeping arrangements continue the closeness parents and baby share during the daytime.

Let us add that there is no right or wrong place for baby to sleep. Your goal is not to make your baby's sleep habits follow someone else's advice — whether it's advice that comes from a baby trainer or from an advocate of attachment parenting. Your goal is to come up with a nighttime parenting strategy that enables everyone in the family to get a good night's sleep. We, along with many other parents, have found that sleeping close to baby is the best way to continue to be responsive to baby's needs while getting a good night's sleep.

OUR CO-SLEEPING EXPERIENCES

Martha and I did not sleep with our first three babies. The fact is, they were easygoing babies who slept well in cribs. We had no reason to challenge the medical profession's party line on letting your baby into your bed (it was weird, it might be dangerous, and it was not something modern parents did). Then along came our fourth child, Hayden, born in 1978. Her birth changed our attitude about a lot of things, including sleep. (Were it not for Hayden, many of our books might never have been written.) Once she outgrew her cradle right next to our bed, we moved her into a crib — and she hated it. It was very difficult to get her to stay asleep there. Martha was exhausted. Hayden was in Martha's arms constantly during the day, and

Martha was giving out. Finally one night, rather than dutifully returning Hayden to her crib, knowing that if she did, Hayden would be awake again within the hour, Martha nestled Hayden next to her in our bed. Hayden slept, and Martha slept, and from that night on, we all slept better together — so well, in fact, that Hayden slept with Martha and me for four years, until our next baby was born!

Still, I was trained as a pediatrician and felt I should get some advice on this daring sleep arrangement. The books all said, "Don't take your baby into your bed. You'll be sorry later." Martha said, "I don't care what the books say, I'm tired, and I need some sleep!" I couldn't argue with that, and slowly I overcame my worries about whether we were being "manipulated" and my uncertainty about exactly how and when we would get her out of our bed. We addressed our earlier doubts by writing books of our own in which we explained the many benefits of bedding close to baby.

When a mother and baby sleep together, they share a special connection. Whenever I watched Martha sleep with Hayden, I was intrigued by the harmony in their breathing. When Martha took a deep breath, Hayden took a deep breath. There was also harmony in their movements. I would see Martha move at the same time or just a few seconds before or after Hayden did. They would gravitate toward one another, and Martha would turn toward Hayden and nurse or touch her, and then both would drift back to sleep, often without even awakening. At other times, Hayden would stir and reach out to touch Martha, then take a deep breath, sigh, and go back to sleep, reassured by her mother's closeness. I also noticed that Martha, from time to time, would awaken partially, check on Hayden, rearrange the covers, and then drift easily back to sleep.

We slept with four more babies (one at a time!) after Hayden. For years, I observed Martha and our babies sleeping together. Martha and baby naturally slept on their sides, facing each other. Even if they started out at a distance, baby, like a heat-seeking missile, would naturally gravitate toward Martha, just a breath away. I wondered about this face-to-face, almost nose-to-nose position. Is it possible that a mother's breath stimulates her baby to breathe? Perhaps in the face-to-face position, mother's breath stimulates baby's skin, and this also leads to better breathing. I noticed that when I directed my breathing onto our babies' faces — as if it were a sort of magic breath — they would take a deep breath.

Martha and I now have our bed to ourselves, but we look back fondly on our years of sharing sleep with our children, and we do not doubt that these nighttime connections were an important part of how we built close and trusting relationships with them.

WHY BEDDING CLOSE TO BABY WORKS

Parents sleep close to their babies for two main reasons. First, sharing sleep continues the attachment that parents are working to build during the day. It makes sense that a baby who is not left to cry during the day should not be left to cry in another room at night either. Bedding close to baby is the nighttime equivalent of babywearing. Second, babies who share sleep sleep better, and this helps mothers sleep better. In other words, it works.

I regard sleeping with my baby as a "lazy mom" option. I like my sleep. Since she sleeps right next to me, I don't worry, and I don't have to get out of bed and wander down the hall when she wakes up to nurse. Besides, she likes nestling next to me. That makes me happy.

Babies sleep better. To understand how bedding close to baby helps baby sleep, you must first learn the basics about how infants sleep.

Infant sleep is different from adult sleep. You're probably aware that there are different stages of sleep, the main ones being light sleep, or REM (for rapid eye movement) sleep, and deep sleep. We dream during REM sleep, and baby's body is most active during this light stage. You'll notice his eyes moving under his eyelids, and he squirms, sucks, and makes noises. During deep sleep baby is still and quiet. Babies move back and forth through these sleep stages many times each night, more often than adults do. As baby passes from deep sleep into light sleep, he enters a vulnerable period for night waking. During this transition time, he may wake up and have difficulty settling back into sleep.

Scientists don't know why babies spend so much time in light sleep, though it's assumed that REM sleep has developmental benefits. It may help the brain grow and make connections. It may be that babies are not yet mature enough to be safe while sleeping deeply. If you accept that babies sleep the way they do for a good reason, it also begins to make sense that babies should sleep next to someone they love.

Snuggling down to sleep at the breast of Mother or in the arms of Father creates a healthy go-to-sleep attitude. Baby learns that sleep is a pleasant state to enter. Not only do sleep-sharing babies go to sleep more happily, they stay asleep longer.

If baby is alone, waking up can be scary. Without Mother — or another caregiver — there in the room, he concludes that he is alone and abandoned. Waking up is not so frighten-

THE ATTACHMENT PARENTING BOOK   93

ing if baby wakes up close to Mother. Baby understands that he's okay if he's with her. He can nurse if he is hungry, and the sucking will lull him back to sleep. And Mother may be able to just reach over, pat baby's back, murmur a few comforting words, and ease baby through this transition from light to deeper sleep without ever completely waking up herself.

Imagine you are a baby sleeping next to Mommy. As you enter a vulnerable period for night waking while passing from deep sleep into light sleep, you are near a familiar attachment person whom you can hear, smell, and touch. Her familiar presence conveys a reassuring "it's okay to go back to sleep" message, enabling you to peacefully drift through this vulnerable period of night waking and reenter deep sleep. Based on our experience with sharing sleep, our own research, and the research of others, we believe that co-sleeping mothers do far more for their babies than just settle them back to sleep, though. As you will later learn, bedding close to baby also has physiological benefits.

When my husband entered the bedroom and saw our newborn lying alone in the bassinet next to our bed, he said, "Our son is sleeping in THAT? He will get cold, and how will we know that he's breathing?" My husband took our son out of the bassinet and brought him into our bed. After nine months in my womb, my precious child continued to be part of me, breathing with me and sleeping to the sound of my heartbeat in our bed.

Mothers sleep better. Many mothers and infants who sleep together achieve what we call nighttime harmony: they get their sleep cycles in sync with one another. The mothers are aware of their baby's presence, yet they are able to sleep comfortably. They awaken when baby does and breastfeed, but they seldom have trou-

ble going back to sleep. Because they are so tuned in to their baby, they don't worry about rolling over onto baby. They feel sure that they will wake up if there is any reason that baby needs them.

How much nicer it is to be able to satisfy baby's needs at night without leaving your warm bed. This is how mothers of frequent night nursers not only survive, but thrive. Ask them in the morning, and they can't tell you when or how many times baby nursed during the night. (Since they are not anxious about it, they don't look at the clock.) They just know that they feel rested. Because babies and mothers who share sleep have similar sleep cycles, mother's sleep rhythms are not disturbed by baby's awakening.

Martha notes: I would awaken seconds before my baby. When the baby started to squirm, I would lay on a comforting hand, and she would drift back to sleep. Sometimes I did this automatically and didn't even wake up.

Contrast this with the mother of the baby who sleeps in another room. When the solo-sleeping baby wakes up — crying, alone, behind bars — and startles Mother out of a sound sleep, Mother must rouse herself out of bed and hurry to baby. Then she has to settle baby down so that he can breastfeed (or she has to go to the kitchen and warm a bottle). When baby is finally back to sleep, Mother eases him down into his crib and then has to get herself back to sleep. If she spends the next hour staring at the ceiling, she'll feel the effects in the morning.

Breastfeeding is easier. Breastfeeding mothers are sleep sharing's biggest fans. Breastfed babies need to nurse often even at night, and bedding close to baby makes this easy. Babies who sleep close to mother do tend to wake up more often to nurse than breastfed infants who sleep separately. Baby trainers take a dim view of this frequent night waking. If you're trying to train baby to need Mom less, they argue, Mom shouldn't stay close by all night long, tempting baby to nurse. In the baby-training philosophy, night waking is a habit to be broken, not a sign of baby's need to be attached to parents. Frequent night waking doesn't seem to bother most sleep-sharing mothers, though. The extra feedings, extra milk, and extra touching help a baby grow better. Frequent feeding also helps the mother's milk supply and keeps her from waking up in the morning with engorged breasts, which can lead to plugged ducts and mastitis. AP parents also realize that the frequent night waking helps baby reconnect with mother, especially if the two have been separated during the day. Breastfeeding mothers also find it easier than bottle-feeding mothers to get their sleep cycles in sync with their babies. They often wake up just before baby. They help baby latch on to the breast and go right back to sleep while baby nurses. The hormones released as baby sucks have a relaxing effect, which at 2 A.M. makes sleep almost inevitable.

It helps babies thrive. Sleep-sharing babies thrive, which means they not only get bigger but also grow to their full potential physically, emotionally, and intellectually. Why this developmental perk? It's probably the extra touch combined with the extra feedings that stimulate development. The added contact between mother and baby during sleep sharing also encourages frequent leisurely nursing sessions. Baby senses that mother is more relaxed and takes his time at the breast. The added sucking gets more high-fat hindmilk into baby and stimulates milk production. Mother's prolactin

goes up when she sleeps, so coupling breastfeeding with an afternoon nap is a good way to build the milk supply.

Sleep sharing as therapy for failure-to-thrive infants was known over a century ago, as evidence from this quote from a childcare book written in 1840: "There can scarcely be a doubt that at least during the first four weeks and during winter and early spring, a child will thrive better if allowed to sleep beside its mother and cherished by her warmth than if placed in a separate bed."

It helps babies and mothers make up for daytime separations. Sleep sharing takes on added importance given today's parents' busy lifestyles. When Mother and Father are away from their baby during the day, sleeping together at night helps make up for lost touch time. Babies know this as well as anyone. Breastfed babies often increase their night nursing when mother is gone during the day. Babies of working parents may take longer naps while at the babysitter's, so that they can stay up late and go to bed with Mom and Dad. Babies have a way of figuring out how to get what they need from their parents in order to thrive. If you go

---

ATTACHMENT TIP
Hindmilk is "mind" milk.

In our pediatrics practice, we often advise night nursings for the baby who isn't gaining sufficient weight. Night-nursing mothers produce higher-fat "grow milk." As an added perk, this higher-fat hindmilk, which is produced later in the feeding than the lower-calorie foremilk, is also good for baby's brain development.

along and enjoy your baby's presence at night, you'll feel happier and more attached to your baby.

Our two-year-old tells us when she's ready for bed ("Night-night, Mama"). She and I have a wonderful pattern: We go upstairs to bed together and read a few books. Then she climbs down from the bed and turns off the light before we go to sleep. We then quickly fall asleep engaged in a wonderful nighttime hug. This way of sleeping gives her a positive association with sleep, and we avoid evening battles.

It promotes trust between parents and infant. Sleeping with your baby enables you to give "I care" messages all through the night, without saying a word. Being close by when your baby wakes up in distress means you can respond quickly and appropriately. This tells your infant that you can be trusted to meet her needs and be there when she needs you. When you ignore the critics and the baby trainers and put your baby down to sleep next to you, you are sending her the message that you trust her cues.

Either you get up with your children when they're babies, or you'll have to get up with them when they're older.

SHARING SLEEP: HOW TO MAKE IT WORK

Who sleeps where? What about sex? These are some of the practical problems associated with sharing sleep. Here are some tips to help the whole family deal with sleep-sharing issues.

Make sure both parents are in agreement. The Baby B's of attachment parenting, especially bed sharing, should bring spouses closer together, not divide them. Sleep sharing seldom works unless both parents support the arrangement. Most fathers, even those who are reluctant at first, discover that bedding close to baby helps them feel closer to their baby. We usually advise Dad to go along with Mom's wishes on this issue, since she's the one whose sleep is most affected by baby's night waking.

My husband initiated sleeping with our baby because he was tired of getting up to get our baby out of the crib to bring him to me for breast-feeding.

Use a king-size bed. Take the money you would ordinarily spend on a crib and all that useless plastic baby stuff and splurge on a big bed. Bed sharing is more comfortable when there's lots of bed to share.

Extend your bed. Some mothers and babies find that they need a little distance in order for both to be comfortable and not wake up too often. If this sounds like you, you might want to try a new invention called a co-sleeper, a crib-like bed that attaches safely and snugly to the side of your bed. Baby's mattress is on the same level as yours, and you can easily move baby from the co-sleeper into your bed when she wakes up to nurse, then put her back again if you want. For more information visit www.armsreach.com.

Try different sleeping arrangements. While some dads like to have baby in the middle, between Mommy and Daddy, others find they don't sleep well with baby that close. Toddlers can be especially challenging to sleep with, since with their nighttime gymnastics, they often end up with their head toward Mommy and their cold feet against Daddy. Dad wakes up grumpy, demanding, "It's time for him to move

SAFE CO-SLEEPING

If you use common sense and take these precautions, sleep sharing is actually the safest nighttime arrangement for most babies and parents:

- Don't sleep with your baby if you are under the influence of any drug (prescription or otherwise) that affects your sleep or consciousness or that makes you less aware of baby's presence. This includes alcohol and sleep medications.
- Avoid sleeping with your baby if you are extremely obese. Obesity can affect a mother's sleep patterns, making her less aware of baby. Mother's large body and breasts can also present a danger of smothering.
- Be cautious about letting a baby-sitter sleep with baby, since a substitute caregiver is unlikely to be as aware as a mother is.

- Don't allow older siblings to sleep with a baby under nine months old.
- Don't fall asleep with a baby on a couch, beanbag chair, water bed, or any "sinky" surface. Baby's face may become buried or wedged into cushiony crevices, so that he can't breathe.
- Don't wear dangling jewelry or lingerie with string ties longer than eight inches. These can strangle.
- Avoid pungent hair sprays, deodorants, and perfumes that may irritate or clog baby's tiny nasal passages. Save these for when you and your spouse have your bed all to yourselves again.
- Put baby down to sleep on his back.
- Dress baby appropriately when sleep sharing. Adult bodies generate plenty of warmth. Heavy blankets or sleepers are for babies who sleep alone.
- Never smoke where baby sleeps.

out!" A better arrangement for many families is for baby to sleep between Mom and a guardrail or between Mom and the wall, if the mattress can be pushed snugly into a corner, leaving no gaps. Some parents feel safer removing the frame and headboard from the bed while they are sharing it with a little one.

Share sleep part of the night. Like all the Baby B's of attachment parenting, sleep sharing is not an all-or-nothing arrangement. Many parents find some privacy at night by putting their baby down to sleep in her crib at first. Parents can use this time when baby sleeps alone to enjoy some special time together. When baby

wakes up, Dad or Mom retrieves her, and she finishes the night sleeping with her parents. In situations where Dad doesn't sleep well with baby in the bed, mothers often elect to bring baby into bed only when baby awakens early in the morning. Then Mom and baby nestle off to sleep for a few more hours after Dad goes to work. In other families, parents sleep apart for part of the night, so that Mom and baby can sleep together and Dad can sleep soundly, too.

Don't have more than one child in the bed with you. In our experience, it rarely works, nor is it safe, to have a tiny baby and a toddler sleeping next to each other. A wiser arrange-

Bedding close to baby.

ment is for the baby to be in your bed and the toddler nearby in his "special bed" — a futon or toddler mattress at the side or foot of your bed. If you want everyone in one big bed, place a twin bed or mattress at the side of your bed. Then no one will feel left out, and there will be plenty of space for everyone.

What about sex? The master bedroom need not be the only place for couple time. Every room in the house is a potential love chamber. You can also move the sleeping child into another room or put her to sleep in her own room, enjoy some private time together, then bring baby into your bed for the rest of the night. Very young babies are not too aware of their surroundings and will not understand what is happening, so lovemaking in the family bed is not a problem when your baby is only a few months old.

MOVING OUT: WEANING FROM NIGHTTIME ATTACHMENT

"So when will my baby leave my bed?" New parents often ask this question, worried that their child will get so used to sleeping with them that he may never want to sleep alone. It's true that a baby who is used to sleeping first class is reluctant to accept a downgrade, but children do eventually wean themselves from your bed when they are ready — or when you are ready to help them. In many families, this process begins sometime around age two. Here are some ways to help it along:

- Increase the distance between Mom and baby at night. Ease your baby from your bed into a bedside co-sleeper or a crib next to your bed with the side rail down, mattress at the same

level, and the frames securely latched together. This is called the sidecar arrangement.

- Put a futon or toddler mattress on the floor at
the foot of your bed and lie down with him in
this "special bed" to help him fall asleep. (You
can get a lot of mileage out of the term *special*
in the todder and preschool years.) If baby
sleeps here through the night, baby-proof
your bedroom and keep the door closed.

- Encourage Dad to put baby down to sleep by
the "wearing down" technique (see page 78) or
with some other predictable bedtime routine.
This will teach baby other ways besides nursing
to fall asleep. With a toddler, the routine can
expand to include a stack of books to be read,
then the light off and a bedtime prayer and/or
story you can tell in a lulling tone, followed by
a back rub, and then a lullaby tape to listen to.
You can either fall asleep together or you can
get up after he falls asleep. You can also tell him
you'll be back to check on him, and leave the
light on until later if he needs it. As he gets
older, he'll enjoy looking at (or reading) books
by himself to fall off to sleep.

- When your child is ready, or when you feel
he could be and you are ready, start helping
him go off to sleep in his own bed in his own
room. Have an "open door" policy and night-
lights in the hall as needed, so if he needs to
join you during the night, he knows he's welcome. You decide if you want him to crawl in
with you or quietly slip into his "special bed"
next to yours.

- Expect your preschooler, or even school-age
child, to periodically return to the nighttime
security of your room, and maybe even your
bed, during stressful situations.

*When our attachment-parented co-sleeping
child was four years old, she proudly announced to
us she wanted to move into her own bedroom. For*
*a few days this worked out well, but one day she
came to me with such a troubled look on her face,
I thought she was about to cry. What had happened? She had just learned that the parents of her
two playmates down the street didn't love each
other anymore and were getting a divorce. After
this, Crista couldn't sleep in her own room; she
deeply needed the security of sleeping with her
family for a little while.*

Even parents who are eager to get a restless
toddler out of their bed may experience some
ambivalence about moving their child into
more grown-up sleeping arrangements. One
voice inside of you may say you're ready; another voice may say you're going to miss that
closeness. These feelings are normal, and you'll
experience them also when your child weans
from the breast, goes to kindergarten, to junior
high, and to college. If your child is truly ready
for this step, he'll move on to his new bed fairly
easily. If weaning from your bed is becoming a
huge struggle, back off for a while or take
smaller steps, like lying with him on a separate
mattress. Trust your instincts. You'll know
whether you're experiencing normal parental
nostalgia about babies that grow up too fast or
if you're pushing your child to do something he
is not ready to do.

NIGHT WEANING FROM THE BREAST: ELEVEN ALTERNATIVES FOR THE ALL-NIGHT NURSER

Babies love to night nurse. And who can blame
the all-night gourmet? The ambiance of their
favorite restaurant is peaceful, the server is familiar, the cuisine is superb, and they love the
management — ahhhh, life is good! Yet there
often reaches a point when nightlife is not so
restful for Mom.

WHEN SLEEP SHARING ISN'T WORKING

Some mothers are disturbed by frequent night waking and are unable to get their sleep cycles in harmony with their baby. In this case, keep experimenting with other sleep arrangements, such as a crib or co-sleeper at the side of your bed, until you find the one that gets all family members the best night's sleep.

Sharing sleep does not always work, and some parents simply do not want to sleep with their baby. Remember, sleep sharing is an optional attachment tool, and you are not less of a mother if you don't sleep with your baby. Try it. If it's working and you enjoy it, continue. If not, try other sleeping arrangements. There are babies who don't sleep well next to Mom and Dad, and there are parents who have tried sleeping with their babies and find it doesn't work as well for them as other ways of responding to baby's needs at night. Only you can decide what works best for you and your baby. As an attached parent, remain open to your baby's needs at night and be aware that baby's (and parents') needs change. Most families find that their sleeping arrangements change as baby changes.

If you're feeling tired from frequent night nursing, first ask yourself how much of a problem it is. Are you sleep deprived to the extent that you are barely functioning the following day? Or is this just a passing stage, and the frequent night nursing will eventually subside? A parenting principle we learned many kids ago is: IF YOU RESENT IT, CHANGE IT!

Try these alternatives to all-night nursing:

NIGHTTIME ATTACHMENT TIP

If you resent going to bed because it is work rather than rest, take this as a clue that you need to make some changes in your nighttime parenting.

1. Tank up baby during the day. During the day, toddlers are often so busy they forget to nurse, or Mom is so busy that she forgets to nurse. But at night, you're only an inch away, and naturally baby wants to make up for those missed daytime nursings. Nap nursing a couple of times a day will help you catch up on your rest and help baby catch up on feedings.

2. Increase daytime "nursings." As toddlers grow into independence, they take two steps forward and one step backward. Toddlers often increase their night nursing as they're going through a new developmental stage, such as from crawling to walking, or adjusting to a new caregiver or a change in the family routine, such as a move. Wear your baby around the house in a sling, take naps together, offer a daily infant massage, or whatever special touches your toddler seems to enjoy.

3. Tank up baby at bedtime. Waking baby for a full feeding just before you go to bed may encourage him to sleep for a longer stretch. Make sure baby gets a good feeding before he falls asleep for the night, even if you have to rouse him a couple of times to be sure he nurses long enough. When you feed in the middle of the night, wake up enough to pay attention to what baby is doing at the breast. Encourage him to suck well and get lots of milk so that he's not hungry again in an hour or two.

4. Get baby used to other "nursings." Try wearing baby down to sleep in a baby sling. After baby is fed but not yet asleep, wear him in a baby sling around the house or around the block. When he's in a deep sleep, ease him onto your bed and extricate yourself from the sling. This is a good way for Dad to take over part of the bedtime routine. Eventually, baby will associate Dad's arms with falling asleep, and baby will accept comfort from Dad in the middle of the night as an alternative to nursing. Other ways to ease your baby into sleep without nursing include patting or rubbing his back, singing and rocking, and even dancing in the dark to some tunes you like or lullabies you croon.

5. Make the breast less available. Once your baby has nursed to sleep, use your finger to detach him from the breast. Then pull your nightgown over your breast and sleep covered up. A baby who can't find the nipple quickly may just fall back to sleep. For toddlers who love to snuggle skin-to-skin — which naturally triggers the desire to nurse — place a pillow or teddy bear next to you to increase the breast-to-baby distance.

6. Just say no! It's very hard for attached mothers to say no to their babies, but sometimes saying no is necessary because your own emotional or physical tank is empty. Night nursing usually doesn't become truly overwhelming for moms unless there is a physical cause for night waking. Once baby is older he can accept delays and alternatives. One night, I woke up to Martha and Matthew, then eighteen months old, having this dialogue:

Matthew: "Nee!"
Martha: "No!"
Matthew: "Nee!"
Martha: "No!"

Martha was not feeling well and was so tired she couldn't begin to think about a more creative way to say no. It was clear that this "nee"-"no" conversation wasn't going anywhere, so I stepped in and got Matthew to accept a bit of "nee" from me. It was difficult for Martha to say no, but she also knew she had had enough nursing for one night. Matthew cried a bit in my arms but eventually settled back to sleep. Crying in the arms of a person baby knows loves and cares for him is not the same as being left alone to cry in another room.

Our next baby, Stephen, was typically content with waking twice at night to nurse, unless he was sick. This was working well for Martha. But at twenty-two months, after getting over an illness, he was waking up four times a night. This was too much for Martha, so we decided to switch to father "nursing" when Stephen awoke for the second time each night. There was some crying, and it took an hour to resettle him, but after three or four nights Stephen realized that Dad was a "milk dud" and began sleeping longer stretches again, waking only once or twice.

7. "Nummies go night-night." Now the marketing begins. Around eighteen months, your child has the capacity to understand simple sentences. Program your toddler not to expect to be nursed when she awakens, by saying something like, "We'll nurse again when Mr. Sun comes up." When you nurse her to sleep (or have the first or second night nursing), the last thing she should hear is, "Mommy go night-night, Daddy go night-night, baby go night-night, and nummies go night-night" (or whatever she dubs her favorite pacifiers). When she wakes during the night, the first thing she should hear is the gentle reminder "Nummies are night-night. Baby go night-night, too." This program may require a week or two of repetition. Soon she will get the message that daytime is for feeding, and nighttime is for sleeping. If "nummies" stay night-night, baby will, too — at least till dawn.

8. Offer a substitute. Nursing does not always mean breastfeeding. Honor your husband with his share of night "nursing," so your toddler does not always expect to be comforted by nummies. This gives Dad a chance to develop creative nighttime fathering skills and your child a chance to expand her acceptance of nighttime comforters.

One of the ways we survived a toddler wanting to nurse frequently during the night was for Martha to temporarily go off "night call." I would wear Stephen down in a baby sling, so he got used to my way of putting him to sleep. When Stephen woke up, I would again provide the comfort he needed by rocking and holding him in a neck nestle position, using the warm fuzzy, and singing a lullaby. Babies may initially protest when offered Father instead of Mother, but remember, crying and fussing in the arms of a loving parent is not the same as "crying it out." Dads, realize that you have to remain calm and patient during these nighttime fathering challenges. You owe it to both Mother and baby not to become rattled or angry when your baby resists the comfort you offer.

9. Increase the sleeping distance between you and baby. If the above suggestions do not entice your persistent night nurser to cut back, yet you still feel you must encourage him to do so, try other sleeping arrangements. When babies sleep inches away from their favorite cuisine, of course they're more likely to wake up to dine frequently. Let baby sleep next to Dad instead of next to you. For a younger baby (under six months), try a bedside co-sleeper (see page 95) or put baby in a crib in a sidecar arrangement next to your bed (see page 97) or across the room. You may discover that at a certain distance both you and baby sleep better.

10. Move out! This is the technique we advise when mother is exhausted and the whole family is detaching because of sleep deprivation — and it usually works. After you've tried all of the above night-weaning tricks to no avail, go sleep in another room for a couple of nights and let baby sleep next to Dad. In this compromise situation, baby still has a nighttime attachment figure, but he learns that he really can get through the night without breastfeeding. Also, you'll be surprised what father-nursing tricks dads can come up with when babies and daddies are left alone to work things out. Try this weaning-to-father arrangement on a weekend, or at another time when your husband can look forward to two or three nights when he doesn't have to go to work the next day. You will probably have to sell him on this technique, but keep in mind that we have personally tried it and it does work.

11. Don't persist with a bad experiment. Be sure to use these night-weaning tactics only when baby is old enough and your gut feeling tells you that your baby is nursing at night out of habit, not out of need. Here's where your previous training in baby reading will really pay off. If after several nights of working on night weaning you notice your baby is becoming more clingy, whiny, or distant during the day, slow down your rate of night weaning.

Like all the other Baby B's, bedding close to baby does come to an end — even if the few

---

ATTACHMENT TIP

If it's not working, baby is not ready.

months that you had planned to sleep with your baby become a few years. Keep in mind that the time in your arms, at your breast, and in your bed is a very short time in the total life of your child, but the memories of love and availability will last a lifetime.

CURRENT RESEARCH INTO SLEEP SHARING AND SIDS

When Martha and I first brought babies into our bed (and we were certainly not the first parents in late-twentieth-century America to try this), there was no research on bed sharing between babies and parents. Now, however, scientists in sleep laboratories are looking closely at what happens when mothers and babies share sleep and comparing it with what happens when babies sleep alone. Much of the research focuses on SIDS (Sudden Infant Death Syndrome), since advocates of co-sleeping, ourselves included, believe that this practice can lower a baby's risk.

Back in 1985, when I wrote *Nighttime Parenting,* I suggested that co-sleeping might have a protective effect against SIDS and proposed the following hypothesis: In those infants at risk of SIDS, natural mothering (breastfeeding and sharing sleep with baby) will lower the risk of SIDS. In 1995, in my book *SIDS: A Parent's Guide to Understanding and Preventing Sudden Infant Death Syndrome,* I updated this hypothesis (see the box on this page).

Normally, humans automatically take the next breath when their bodies tell them to. But this mechanism is immature in young infants and may not work well during deep sleep. Many experts believe that SIDS is caused by a baby's failure to arouse from deep sleep when his breathing stops.

Our newborn slept in a cradle next to our bed. One night I heard her gasping. I know baby noises, and these weren't normal. As soon as I picked her up and put her in bed with me, she breathed regularly. My pediatrician told me I was just a nervous mother. If her breathing didn't wake her up, it wasn't a problem. He told me it was my problem, and if I moved her out of my room, I wouldn't hear her. I kept badgering him to study her, and when he did, he found that she had apnea [breathing interruptions during sleep] 18 percent of the time. When she slept with me, I noticed a difference. She breathed with me.

While there is, as yet, no research that finds a direct correlation between the reduced incidence of SIDS and co-sleeping, there is a growing body of research, mainly by Dr. James McKenna, director of the Center for Behavioral Studies of Mother-Infant Sleep at Notre Dame University, on the sleeping behavior of mothers and babies who sleep together. Studies suggest that the mother's presence has a direct effect on her infant's physiology in the following ways that help protect against SIDS:

DR. SEARS'S SIDS HYPOTHESIS

I believe that in most cases SIDS is a sleep disorder, primarily a disorder of arousal and breathing control during sleep. All the elements of attachment mothering, especially breastfeeding and sharing sleep, benefit the infant's breathing control and increase the mutual awareness between mother and infant, so that their arousability is increased and the risk of SIDS decreased.

SCARY PSEUDOSCIENCE SABOTAGES SLEEP SHARING

On September 29, 1999, news reports about a U.S. Consumer Products Safety Commission study entitled "Review of Hazards Associated with Children Placed in Adult Beds," appeared in nearly every major newspaper in the United States as well as on television. This study and the way it was publicized put fear into many parents' hearts. After the reports appeared, I was interviewed by the *New York Times,* the *Washington Post,* CNN, and *20/20.*

This study appeared in the October 1999 issue of *The Archives of Pediatrics and Adolescent Medicine.* Researchers at the U.S. Consumer Products Safety Commission had reviewed death certificates in the United States from 1990 through 1997 and found 515 deaths of children under two who were placed to sleep in adult beds. Of these deaths, 121 were reported to be due to overlying by the parent, other adult, or sibling sleeping in the bed with the child, and 394 were due to entrapment in the bed structure, such as wedging of the child between the mattress and side rail or wall, suffocation in a water bed, or head entrapment in bed railings. Most of these deaths occurred in infants under three months.

As with so much research that is reported in the popular press, this study had both good and bad effects. On the positive side, the research alerted parents who choose to sleep with their babies — and many do — to do it safely. However, this study also caused unnecessary anxiety in the millions of parents who safely and responsibly sleep with their babies. It went too far and issued a blanket recommendation that parents should not sleep with babies under two years of age.

When science and common sense don't match, suspect faulty science — and that's exactly the case here. Co-sleeping is not inherently dangerous. The CPSC sleep study estimated that 64 deaths per year occurred in infants sleeping with their parents, but it failed to put these deaths in context. The fact is that many more infants die when sleeping alone in a crib than when sleeping in their parents' bed. Around 5,000 babies die of SIDS annually in the United States. That's a lot more than the 515 deaths of infants not sleeping in cribs over a seven-year period. If these researchers had examined the records of all infants dying alone in cribs during the same study period, the headlines might well have read: "Review of Hazards Associated with Infants Sleeping Alone in Cribs." Instead of making parents afraid to sleep with their babies, a more valid approach would be to teach parents who choose to co-sleep to do it safely.

A commentary on the CPSC study by Mark Vonnegut in the October 24, 1999, *Boston Globe,* entitled "Beware of Bad Science," put this fiasco into perspective: "Not many generations ago, the practice of breastfeeding was just about killed off by bad science that 'proved' that the practice was unsanitary. Now science can't say enough nice things about breastfeeding; just this week brought the news that breastfed babies are less likely to develop leukemia. Maybe in a few generations, we'll see studies that indicate that babies who sleep with their parents have fewer ear infections, do better in school, and don't engage in pseudo-science when they grow up."

OUR NIGHTTIME ATTACHMENT EXPERIMENTS

In 1992 we set up equipment in our bedroom to study our eight-week-old Lauren's breathing while she slept in two different arrangements: One night Lauren and Martha slept together in our bed, as they were used to doing. The next night, Lauren slept alone in our bed, while Martha slept in an adjacent room. Lauren was wired to a computer that recorded her electrocardiogram, her breathing movements, the air flow from her nose, and her blood oxygen. (The equipment was designed to detect only Lauren's physiological changes during sleep and did not pick up Martha's signals.) The instrumentation was nonintrusive and didn't appear to disturb Lauren's sleep. Martha nursed Lauren down to sleep in both arrangements and sensitively responded to her during the nighttime as needed. A technician and I observed and recorded the information. The data were analyzed by computer and interpreted by a pediatric pulmonologist who was blind to the situation; that is, he didn't know whether the data he was analyzing came from the shared-sleeping or the solo-sleeping arrangement.

Our study revealed that Lauren breathed better when sleeping next to Martha than when sleeping alone. Her breathing and her heart rate were more regular during shared sleep, and there were fewer "dips," that is, low points in respiration and blood oxygen from stop-breathing episodes. On the night Lauren slept with Martha, there were no dips in her blood oxygen, but on the night when she slept alone, there were 132 dips. The results were similar in a second infant whose parents generously allowed me and the technician into their bedroom. We studied Lauren and the other infant again at five months. As expected, the physiological differences between shared and solo sleep were less pronounced at age five months than at age two months.

In 1993 I was invited to present our sleep-sharing research to the 11th International Apnea of Infancy Conference, since this was the first study of sleep sharing in the natural home environment. Certainly our studies would not stand up to scientific scrutiny, mainly because of the small sample. We didn't intend them to; it would be presumptuous to draw sweeping conclusions from studies of only two babies. We meant this only to be a pilot study. But what we did learn was that with the use of new microtechnology and in-home, nonintrusive monitoring, my hypothesis about the protective effects of sharing sleep was testable. I wanted our preliminary study to stimulate SIDS researchers to study scientifically the physiological effects of sharing sleep in a natural home environment.

- Mother-baby pairs showed more synchronous arousals when sleeping together than when sleeping separately. This means that when one member of the pair stirred, coughed, or changed sleeping position, the other member also changed, often without awakening.

These arousals may be one way in which mother's presence keeps baby from sleeping too deeply.

- Mother and baby were more likely to be in the same stage of sleep (REM or non-REM) for longer periods if they slept together.

- Sleep-sharing babies spent less time in each cycle of deep sleep. Babies with a tendency toward irregular breathing and apnea experience these episodes during deep sleep. Less deep sleep therefore means less risk.
- Sleep-sharing infants aroused more often and spent more time breastfeeding than did solitary sleepers. Yet the sleep-sharing mothers did not report awakening more frequently.
- Sleep-sharing and breastfeeding infants tended to sleep more often on their backs or sides and less often on their tummies, a factor that could itself lower the SIDS risk, as efforts to increase back-sleeping have indicated. Back-to-sleep campaigns have reduced the risk of SIDS as much as 50 percent over the past ten years in Europe and as much as 30 percent in the United States. Co-sleeping AP mothers instinctively put their babies to sleep on their backs or sides, since this position gives mother and baby better access to one another.

Other AP factors that may reduce the risk of SIDS. Infants who are exposed to the toxins in cigarette smoke, either prenatally or after birth, are at a greater risk of SIDS. AP mothers rarely smoke.

Babywearing may also be a factor in lowering the risk of SIDS. While there is no conclusive research on this yet, consider these findings:

Nurses in neonatal intensive care units have begun using a method of babywearing called kangaroo care, in which the baby is held skin-to-skin against the mother or father's chest. The contact with Mom or Dad, the parent's regular breathing motion, and the heartbeat contribute to a more stable heart rate in the infant, more even breathing, and healthier levels of oxygen in the baby's blood. Kangaroo-care researchers believe that the babywearing parent acts as a regulator of baby's physiology, including reminding baby to breathe. Studies of newborns in the first hours after birth have also shown that mother's body helps regulate her newborn's breathing.

You can see from current research that easy arousability from sleep is a protective mechanism. Sharing sleep helps this happen. It seems that sleeping separately could be not only unnatural for many babies but even dangerous for some. Each year more and more studies are confirming what savvy parents have long suspected: Sharing sleep is not only safe but also healthy for their babies. Thus, I leave it to parents to consider: If there were fewer cribs, would there be fewer crib deaths?

ATTACHMENT TIP
Sleeping *deeper* may not mean sleeping *safer*.

Balance and Boundaries

CENTRAL TO attachment parenting is meeting the needs of your child in all the ways we have described. At the same time, balance and boundaries, concepts that go hand in hand with meeting those needs, are also important. Attachment parenting a baby can make great demands on parents, physically and emotionally. When these demands are high and your ability to cope is low, you can lose your balance, becoming frazzled, overtired, and anxious. You may find it hard to enjoy your baby. Your marriage may suffer from lack of attention. Or you may struggle with how to set boundaries for your toddler. Boundary setting is a natural element of attachment parenting, because it addresses a basic need that children have, too — knowing what the limits are. Attached parents will strive for balance and boundaries for both their children and themselves.

If a mother is feeling out of sync with her baby, she needs to arrange her life so that she can focus more on her baby; the other chapters in this book tell you how to do that. When a mother is feeling overwhelmed by her baby's needs, she must find ways to care for *herself,* so that she can care for her baby. This chapter is

> ### ATTACHMENT TIP
> Setting limits should be easier for AP families than for others. Because you know your child so well, you are more likely to set appropriate boundaries. Because your child trusts you, he is more likely to accept them.

about that side of parenting — balancing baby's needs with mother's needs, and father's as well. When AP gets out of balance, it is no longer true attachment parenting. Mothers burn out, fathers tune out, and babies don't get the happy parents they need, or the boundaries they need.

IS YOUR PARENTING OUT OF BALANCE? — HOW TO TELL

While the definition of "out of balance" will vary from family to family, here are some clues that the way you are meeting your infant's needs may not be as healthy as it could be.

<table>
<tr><td>

ATTACHMENT TIP

If you're worried about getting too attached to your baby, don't. Attachment is healthy, and there's no such thing as being too healthy. Getting the proper balance back in your life is relatively easy. Just back off a bit and pay more attention to your own needs. Not being attached enough, on the other hand, can take years to fix, and you'll feel like you're playing catch-up all the time your child is growing up.

</td></tr>
</table>

"My baby needs me so much I don't have any time for myself."

What's out of balance: On an airplane when flight attendants are explaining emergency procedures, they always tell parents to put their own masks on first and then to assist their children. If Mom isn't getting enough oxygen, she can't help her child. Likewise, if your emotional tank is drained, you can't be as calming and reassuring with your baby as you could be after a refueling. *What your baby needs most is a happy mother.* Mothers forget this when they are trying to take perfect care of their babies.

Solution: Okay, so maybe you don't need a shower every day. But you do need time to yourself, even if it's just fifteen uninterrupted minutes in the bathroom. Be sure to take some time for yourself every day. If baby won't sleep, have Dad take him for a walk while you hit the easy chair or lounge in the bathtub. Take time every day to fill your own emotional tank. (See the related sections Avoiding Mother Burnout, page 112, and The Eleven Commandments for Balanced Attachment Parenting, page 118.)

"I resent my baby's constant demands."

What's out of balance: Resentment and anger are signs that you're being pushed too far. You're giving beyond your boundaries. Perhaps your baby came blessed with a high need level. Perhaps your lack of confidence in your parenting skills makes it difficult for you to be responsive. Maybe you're not getting enough support from the people who care about you.

Resentment is tough on your baby. Children — even babies — are quick to pick up on mother's mood or her attitude. Your sour feelings may make your baby even more demanding and anxious. Sure, AP will s-t-r-e-t-c-h you, but it shouldn't break you.

Solution: Many kids ago we learned a valuable survival principle: IF YOU RESENT IT, CHANGE IT.

You need to find joy in attachment parenting. You're not going to feel happy all day every day, but you should feel good most of the time. You want to mirror positive reflections to your child. Resentment leads to negative reflections. Remember, attachment-parented children, because of their sensitivity, are quick to pick up on your feelings.

Certainly there will be days when baby care feels like a grind, and you don't feel very joyful. That's real life. But remember the Caribbean saying, "Don't worry, be happy." That's the overall impression you want to leave on your baby.

One day five-year-old Matthew was asked to complete a fill-in-the-blanks tribute to his mother. One line read: "I like being with my mother most when _____." He filled in the blank with "she's happy."

So what should you change? There's not too much you can change about your baby, at least not in the short term. Can you lessen the de-

CAN YOU BE TOO ATTACHED?

A therapist once told us: A mother came to me for counseling because she felt she was too attached to her child. I mentioned to her that we don't need to use that term. Attachment is like love. How can there be too much of it? How can you know your baby too well? A mother can't be "too attached." If it's unhealthy, it's not that she loves or understands her baby too much. The problem is elsewhere; maybe she doesn't have good boundaries herself. The answer isn't to become less attached or to put distance between herself and her baby. The answer is to take care of herself better and to understand that the baby doesn't need a perfect AP mom.

For attachment parenting to be good for the whole family, two conditions must be met.

1. Baby needs two connected parents.
2. Baby needs a happy, rested mother.

For parents to be connected, the marriage must be satisfying for both of them. If the marriage is in good shape, the children will do just fine. We have counseled couples whose marriages are falling apart partly because they give so much to their baby that they forget to enjoy one another. In other cases, as Mother becomes more and more involved with the baby, Father withdraws because of his wife's lack of attention.

Unhealthy attachment occurs when your parenting style is no longer an attachment tool, but a control tool. This is marked by signs of a mother who is fulfilling her own needs for attachment at the expense of the baby moving onward. Mothers with a history of forming unhealthy attachments in their own childhood are at greater risk of having attachment problems. Also, a mother who is the product of a detached style of parenting is likely to overcompensate. A red flag goes up if a mother finds it intolerable when her toddler goes through the normal stage of breaking away from her. An appropriately attached mother picks up on the child's clues to separate and encourages that. An inappropriately attached mother gives her own cues of neediness, and the child follows, clinging when he should be separating.

mands on you? Look at other areas of your life. For example, get help with household tasks. Let go of stress at work. Say no to volunteer commitments while your baby is young. Have scrambled eggs and steamed vegetables for dinner instead of a hard-to-fix meal.

Realize that while babies need lots of attention, not all of the attention has to come from Mother. Be willing to let go of the reins a bit in the areas where maybe you've come to feel you're the only one who can do it "right." Have someone else entertain baby so you can do something you enjoy. If Dad is home, don't hover while he plays with your child. Take a walk, or take a bath. Pay a junior high student to come in and play with your baby while you garden or sew or have some uninterrupted time to yourself.

You can also deal with resentment by changing your attitude. Sometimes just acknowledging that you have a very demanding baby eases resentment. Stop wishing that he would sleep through the night; instead be happy that he is so bright and sensitive. Remember that your

HOW TO FIND AN AP THERAPIST

As we have counseled families experiencing difficulties with attachment parenting, we have come to realize how important it is to find the right therapist. We operate on the principle I learned the very first day in medical school: "First, do no harm." A therapist who is working with AP parents should, first of all, not make suggestions that threaten to disrupt the mother-baby attachment. Instead, she should keep you on track to have a healthy relationship with your infant. Here's what to look for and what to avoid:

- Choose a therapist who is an experienced, nurturing parent. You learn things from raising your own child that just can't be taught in psychology classes.
- Choose a therapist who has a lot of experience or even specializes in attachment theory and practice.
- Look for a therapist who takes your child's need level into consideration. You don't want to work with someone who pits you or your husband's needs against your baby's.
- If the advice you're offered doesn't ring true, look for someone else. You are the expert on yourself and your baby.

ATTACHMENT VS. ENMESHMENT

While attachment parenting is healthy parenting that supports and encourages the child toward timely and appropriate independence, enmeshment is a dysfunctional family dynamic in which a parent, usually the mother, smothers the child, keeping him from developing his individual personality because of her own needs. In this case the mother is still functioning at the level of a child in trying to get her needs met by the child — needs that were never met when she was a child. Healthy attachment changes at each stage, as baby becomes more and more mature, and the attachment adjusts itself to meet the needs of the baby, toddler, and preschooler as he grows. Enmeshment occurs when a mother is not able to "let go" and gradually adjust her attachment physically or emotionally. If you are becoming enmeshed rather than attached, seek counseling.

baby is a baby for only a short time. This intense season of your life will fade as your baby grows. Talk to other parents who also have demanding babies. They will be able to listen to your negative feelings better than people who just don't see why you're so overwhelmed by motherhood will. They may also have some ideas on how to find some balance, or perhaps you can brainstorm together.

In the meantime, take life one day at a time, and focus on the moment. If you're awake and nursing in the middle of the night, enjoy the quiet. Gaze at your baby, meditate, think pleasant thoughts. Be careful not to worry or make endless mental lists of all you have to do. Jot things down if you need to have a list — then let go of the tasks until you can actually do something about them. If baby needs to be walked in the baby sling in the afternoon, go outside and enjoy the fall colors or the budding signs of spring. Sing as you walk along. Don't worry about what you "should" be doing instead. You'll get to those things eventually, when baby is less needy or someone else is there to help. What you're doing right now, with and for baby, is more important.

Your child needs a mother who is predominantly happy. If you radiate unhappiness much of the time, your child is likely to take that personally. She may decide that you are unhappy with her, and that feeling may become a part of her personality. If you're dealing with feelings of resentment and anger that are hard for you to fix, consider professional counseling. Discovering where these feelings are coming from and why they are so intense can help you put them to rest.

Shortly after the birth of our eighth child, Martha became overwhelmed with two little ones in diapers and the needs of four other children at home. She reflected stress in her face and didn't often mirror happiness. Fortunately, she recognized what she was projecting to our children. She did not want our children growing up believing that attachment mothering is no fun or that they had caused her to be unhappy. She sought professional help, worked on her inner feelings, and polished her mirror so that the children could see a better image of themselves.

"I feel like an all-night pacifier."

What's out of balance: Some older babies and toddlers love to keep mother's nipple in their mouth and nurse all night long. Some mothers are able to sleep right through this and wake up rested, while others cannot. You know whether this works for you or not. It does not mean you are not an attached mother if you can't handle being literally attached for much of the night. It's one thing to breastfeed in the middle of the night to fill a hungry tummy and give baby a chance to touch base with Mom. It's another thing when you sacrifice your own sleep rather

than deny baby any time sucking at the breast. All-night nursing can lead to sleep deprivation for a mother. If you're tired and crabby from nursing at night, you won't be a very happy mother during the day. If you're beginning to dread going to bed because it's work rather than rest, take it as a sign that you need to make some changes.

Solution: Breastfeeding may be baby's preferred source of nighttime comfort, but it isn't the only choice available. If baby's prolonged sleepy sucking irritates you and keeps you from sleeping, you need to find other ways to comfort your baby while you discourage him from breastfeeding endlessly. For suggestions — from our own experience — on dealing with babies who would suck all night if allowed to, see Night Weaning from the Breast, page 98.

"I need a break, but my baby isn't happy with anyone else."

What's out of balance: Healthy attachment parenting is about bonding, not bondage, yet many stay-at-home mothers in our society find themselves isolated. This problem arises not from the parenting style but from the way the worlds of work and home are separated in our culture. In traditional cultures baby grows up being cared for by aunts and grandmas along with his primary caretaker, his mother. Baby feels comfortable with caregivers besides mother, and mother is surrounded by other adults instead of being stuck at home with an infant whose conversational skills are limited at best.

Solution: Give your baby opportunities to become comfortable with other caregivers. When Grandma comes over for a visit, go to another part of the house and do something for yourself while Grandma plays with baby. If you don't have family nearby, look for an adoptive grandma or a friend who is sensitive to babies and enjoys them.

Get involved in an attachment-parenting support group. (See the list of resources, page 177.) You'll meet women who share your mothering style and who can respond to your baby in a sensitive way. You'll get a break from being on your own, and you may be able to work out some shared childcare arrangements. A weekly playgroup with AP-minded friends was a sanity saver for Martha with several of our little ones, and it resulted in some wonderful long-term friendships for both the children and the moms.

With our fifth child, Erin, I was feeling the need for support. I made friends with another mother, Nancy, who had a child Erin's age. Her child, like Erin, had a high level of need, and we responded to our babies in similar ways. We hung out together (sometimes several times a week), shared our joys and trials, even cooked and cleaned together, and would often trade childcare. When she and her husband needed a night out, I would care for her child, and vice versa. Because Nancy was a naturally nurturing person and very much into attachment parenting, I knew that Erin's needs were being met while I was away meeting my own needs and the needs of my marriage.

"My husband wants his wife back."

What is out of balance: If almost all of your energy is going to your baby and very little toward your marriage (after the first several months), your family is out of balance. Your relationship with your husband will likely deteriorate, and in the years to come, this will affect your child.

Solution: Give your husband his wife back. Romance doesn't have to end when a baby enters your life. There are many ways to recon-

nect with your husband. Some are as simple as finding fifteen or twenty minutes every day to talk with one another about topics other than parenting and running the household. Invite your husband to take a walk with you after work and use this time to listen and share with one another. (Put baby in the sling and he will soon be asleep.) At bedtime, place baby in his crib for the first part of the night once you've nursed him into a sound sleep, so that you and your husband can enjoy some time alone. Leave baby with a sensitive caregiver and go out for lunch or dinner. Find ways to let your husband know that you are thinking about him, even when you're busy with the baby.

Don't shut your husband out of parenting. Ask for his help, and then step back and get out of his way. Explain to your husband that if he shares in the baby care and some household chores, you'll have some energy left over for him later.

A child learns many relationship skills from watching her parents handle problems. Remember, you are raising someone's future husband or wife. You want to provide good models for your children to follow. You don't stop being marriage partners when you become parents.

"Attachment parenting is simply not working."

What is out of balance: Attachment parenting works well for most families most of the time. If it's not working well for you, there may be other challenges and issues getting in the way.

Solution: Get professional help.

Perhaps you need help with learning how to take care of yourself. Are you carrying baggage from your past into your parenting, and does that baggage need to be unloaded? For example, a woman who had a troubled relationship with her own mother may try to "fix" her feelings of being unloved by trying to be the perfect mother to her own children. Women with a history of sexual abuse may find it difficult to practice some of the Baby B's and should consider counseling. If your marriage was shaky going into the pregnancy, or if you or your husband were not really ready for the demands of parenthood, both of you will benefit from marriage counseling. These are tough issues that need professional help from a therapist, particularly one knowledgeable about attachment theory and attachment parenting.

AVOIDING MOTHER BURNOUT

Burnout is a state of emotional exhaustion. A mother feels burned out when she has been out of balance for too long. With so much energy draining out of her, she reaches a point where she feels she has nothing left to give. Yet her baby continues to need her, and she has to go on coping. She becomes unhappy, angry, and tired. She questions her ability to take care of her baby and blames herself for not enjoying motherhood.

Women who are the most highly motivated to be good mothers are most at risk for burnout. You have to be committed to parenting and working hard at it in order to burn out. Mother burnout can be one of the side effects of attachment parenting, especially in families where there is a high-need baby.

Burnout happens when mothers, fathers, and babies get out of balance and stay out of balance for too long. The problem is usually not with attachment parenting itself. We believe that there is a law of demand and supply in attachment parenting. The baby may be demanding, but responding to the baby's needs helps parents get the energy and resources they need

to survive and thrive. Loving and connecting with your own baby can be a source of emotional healing for parents whose relationship with their own parents was not a close one. However, a number of factors can tip the attachment balance toward burnout, such as a high-need baby, an unsupportive environment, mother's or father's personal challenges, outside pressures, or unrealistic expectations for parenting.

We once gave a talk in Australia and used the term "immersion mothering" instead of attachment parenting. A wise grandmother in the audience later reminded us that "immersion" means getting in over your head. We dropped that term.

Modern mothers are expected to do it all: keep a perfect house, raise intelligent and creative children, provide their husbands with companionship and sex, and have a stimulating life of their own on the job or elsewhere. A new mother who tries to live up to this image of Supermom is headed for trouble. Learning how to be your baby's mother is a more-than-full-time job. When too many other demands are placed on a mother, giving her more to do and less time to care for herself, she is in danger of burnout.

Feeling tired is unavoidable when you're a new parent, and there will be days when you wonder if you're cut out for mothering. Burnout, however, is not an inevitable part of attachment parenting. Here are some tips on surviving and thriving as a mother while avoiding burnout.

Do what you can to get your relationship with your baby off to a good start. Being separated from your baby after birth or struggling with breastfeeding problems makes it more difficult to get a good start at parenting. If you are reading this book before your baby is born, take

BABY BREAKS

Sometimes while caring for my baby, I wish someone would care for me that way.

Remember this Sears survival tip for attachment parenting: *What your baby needs most is a happy, rested mother.* Attachment-parenting mothers whom we have counseled often relate how they feel "touched out." They spend so much time giving high-touch mothering to their infants that they have little time left for themselves as persons and mates. Try these baby-break ideas:

Take a walk. In addition to wearing your baby for a daily walk, take a walk by yourself now and then while Dad plays with baby.

Take a shower. One of the first questions Martha asks a mother during a "burnout" counseling session is how many days it has been since she took a shower. Even if your baby fusses, if you need or want to take a shower, do so. Place your infant on the floor in an infant seat and let her watch you. Oftentimes, the noise of the running water and any humorous antics you can do, such as singing in the shower, will calm your baby. Other times you can shower with baby if she likes it, or get into the tub together for "hydro-therapy" on a fussy day.

Nap-nurse. During those frequent high-need days, such as when a baby goes through a growth spurt and wants to marathon-nurse all day and all night, it helps to pick out a couple of times during the day that you are the most tired and lie down with your baby. While it's tempting to use baby's nap time to "finally get something done," resist this temptation and nap with baby.

Hire help. If your spouse isn't able to pitch in during the day with your toddler, hire a teen to come in for an hour or two at least once a week. Go do something just for yourself, even if it is only taking a soak in the tub and listening to music, getting some outdoor exercise, going to a spa, or going shopping.

Enjoy your hobby. If you had a special interest that was temporarily put on hold before baby came, resume it.

Take a class. Enroll in a dance class, jazzercise, aerobics, or a night class on a topic you've always wanted to learn about, or one to further your education. This is not a Mommy and me class, it's something just for Mommy, while your infant has some "Daddy and me" time at home.

Get social. Contact other new mothers, perhaps those you met in your childbirth class or through La Leche League, and enjoy a weekly lunch together. Younger babies go along easily, and older babies can be watched by a shared baby-sitter at someone's home.

Be spiritual. While motherhood is often a spiritually renewing experience, many new parents get so overwhelmed during the high-maintenance stage of the early months that they forget to take good spiritual care of themselves. Frequent mini-breaks with a few minutes of prayer or meditation will help give you that inner peace that both you and your baby need.

Go to the beauty salon. Indulge yourself with a new hairstyle. Or enjoy a luxurious manicure and pedicure — something you may not have time to do for yourself at home.

Get some rest. Don't always feel obligated to go out and do something when you get a baby break. Sometimes just shutting the bedroom door and getting some much-needed sleep (without interruption) can be just what the doctor ordered. Or relax with a good book. Write a letter, send out some e-mails, or call a friend and have a pleasant phone visit.

time now to make careful plans for the birth and the first days of your baby's life. Take a good childbirth class and attend La Leche League meetings to learn about breastfeeding. (Two excellent resources for preparing for your baby's birth are our *Birth Book* and *Pregnancy Book*.) If you are reading this book after your baby is born and still feeling the emotional after-effects of a less-than-ideal start with your baby, it's time to let go. Tell yourself that you did the best you could at the time with the information you had. Then concentrate on the attachment that you are now building with your baby.

Ignore negative advisers. Lots of people will tell you how to parent your baby, and their insistence that what you are doing is wrong can undermine your self-confidence. Don't argue with them. Don't spend a lot of time thinking about their advice. Remind yourself that you have good reasons for choosing the attachment-parenting path and that you are the expert on your baby.

Get Dad involved. I have never seen a case of mother burnout in a family where the father is actively involved in parenting and in caring for the new mother. Some dads are good at this

right from the start. Others need encouragement. Mothers can help their husbands by stating clearly and calmly what their own needs are. Men can't guess what it is women want from them, because most men are not as intuitive about other people's needs as women are. Whether it's dishes in the sink or a crying baby that needs attention, mothers have to ask. If a mother has trouble asking, it's a red flag that some counseling is needed. She may have a severe tendency toward perfectionism, thinking she's the only one who can do things right. Or, if she's struggling with depression after the birth, she may be having trouble communicating her needs.

Don't hover when Dad is caring for baby. Dad has to learn on his own how to soothe baby's cries and play with a happy baby. If Mom is there, supervising every burp, pat, and tickle, Dad won't learn to be a confident baby tender. Use this opportunity to take time for yourself. Go for a walk, do some shopping, or read a book in a far corner of the house. Dad and baby will be fine.

Father and Mother must work together to meet the baby's and the family's needs. This is especially true when they have a baby with a difficult temperament or special needs. If Mother is doing all the childcare, Father can become very hesitant about handling the fussy baby. If all of Mother's energy goes to the baby, Dad may resent being left out in the cold. He may immerse himself in work or other commitments outside the family. Mom then burns out, the marriage gets shaky, and the baby's relationship with both his parents is at risk.

Dr. Bill's father-to-father advice: Attachment parenting works best when husbands are sensitive to their wives' needs. Ask your wife what you can do for her, and then insist that she relax while you take care of dinner, the baby, the preschooler, or whatever. Mothers find it hard to ask for help because part of them feels that they should be able to do it all — though, of course, this is an unrealistic expectation. Very few women discuss their ambivalent feelings about motherhood with their husbands. There are at least two reasons for this. First, women have a tremendous emotional investment in maintaining a perfect-mother image in their spouse's eyes. Second, they know all too well that men want to rush in and "fix" things, and mothers don't want to be bombarded with suggestions for change when all they really want is someone to listen to them.

Minimize outside pressures. Learning how to care for and respond to your baby is a big project. The first year of your baby's life is not a good time to tackle other projects, such as remodeling, moving, or changing jobs (unless it's scaling down to a less demanding job). If there are other problems in your life competing for your attention, such as financial pressures, a parent who is ill, or a demanding toddler, do whatever you can to get help. Reduce your stress level as much as possible, so that all your energy can be channeled to your baby and to the other people in your family. A toddler or preschooler may need a lot of focused attention

from you, but he does not really *need* you to sew an elaborate costume or host a birthday party for twenty.

Set priorities. When you're in the middle of a bad day, still in your nightgown at two o'clock, crossing a sticky kitchen floor to get to the rocking chair to nurse your baby for the third time since noon, you may feel as if you're getting nothing done. You may also wonder what to do next, once baby has calmed down and you get a moment. Having a clear sense of your priorities helps. How do you this? Here are some tips:

- *Put people before things.* This little saying has helped many a mother get through a week when the baby is sick and she is cranky and the mess in the house is growing by leaps and bounds. People's needs are most important: Baby needs comforting, Mom needs a few moments to relax, Dad needs someone to talk to. Everybody needs something to eat, so scraping together some dinner is important — though there's no need for it to be elaborate.
- *Make lists.* Make a list of all the things you need to do, and then evaluate it critically. Assign priority levels: one star, two stars, and three stars. Do the most important things, and don't worry about the rest. Figure out which tasks on your list can be done by other people — your husband, a neighbor, Grandma, or a friend. Then make lists for them. There are very few jobs that have to be done by your baby's mother — and the ones that do, such as nursing, comforting, and carrying, are the ones that should get your attention.
- *Break jobs down to a manageable size.* When your baby is nursing a dozen times a day and needs a clean diaper at least that often, you

don't get long stretches of time in which to accomplish things. When you make lists of what to do, be sure that the items on the list are small ones. That way you can have the satisfaction of crossing several things off the list each day (even if you're only crossing off parts of a larger job).

- *Learn to say no.* A new baby is a good excuse for saying no to outside commitments: "No, I'm sorry, I don't have time to make cookies for the bake sale. We have a new baby," or, "No, I can't join the club this year. I'm staying home most evenings to be with my husband and our baby." Say no to demands you make on yourself as well: "No, I don't have to think about redecorating the living room this year. This is my time to enjoy my baby."

Take time for yourself every day. If this weren't so important, we wouldn't say it as often as we do. You can't be a good mother to your baby unless you are taking good care of yourself. *It's your job to take care of yourself.* Remember that when you care for yourself, you are caring for your baby's mother, and this is an important way to be sure that your baby will get everything he needs. Use baby's nap time to do something you enjoy, something that recharges your spirit. Give Dad a chance to take care of baby daily, while you go for a walk or soak in the tub. Read a good book while baby nurses. Rent your favorite video and stay up late to watch it. (Take a nap with baby the next day to catch up on your sleep.) Buy your favorite healthy foods at the grocery store and look forward to lunchtime. Be good to yourself, because you are very important to your baby.

Get out and get going. Don't let yourself feel trapped at home alone. Get out and go places with baby. Even a trip to the grocery store is in-

teresting if you bring baby along. Go to the park, the library, the neighborhood coffee shop. Go places where you can meet other mothers. Being at home with a baby all day is hard if you don't have other adults to talk with.

Let go of perfectionism. AP parents set high goals for themselves. They want their child to have the best of parents, and they want to do everything "right." This just isn't possible. Nobody has that kind of control over themselves or their family life.

Enjoy the moment. Attachment parenting brings rewards that make you want to give more to your baby and that make it easier for you to do so, but you have to be able to recognize them when they come. This means that when you are nursing your baby in the middle of the night, or walking your baby to sleep at bedtime, don't think about what isn't getting done or fret about sleep deprivation. Instead, appreciate the feeling of relaxation that washes over you as baby relaxes in your arms.

REKINDLING THE FLAME

If you know exactly what we mean when we describe mother burnout, you need to know that it isn't a permanent condition. You can recover from burnout and rekindle your passion for

---

ATTACHMENT TIP

There is no such person as a perfect parent, and certainly this book was not written by perfect parents. Do the best you can with the resources you have. That's all your child will ever expect.

motherhood. If you use what you've learned about yourself to look at your life differently, you can avoid getting burned out again.

A realistic appraisal of what life is like with a new baby is a good first step in the process of recovering from mother burnout. Babies need lots of care. They are unpredictable, and you can forget about schedules and sleeping through the night. Most important is to understand what *your* baby is like, and that your baby is different from the model babies you read about in books. Your job is to respond to *your* baby — not to turn him into the baby in the book.

Another lesson to learn as you recover from burnout is what you need to do in order to cope with the needs of your baby. Just as babies' temperaments vary, so also do mothers' personalities. If you are an impatient person, you're going to have a harder time dealing with a high-need baby than would a woman who is more laid-back and easygoing. You may have to make a great effort to reduce the stress in other areas of your life so that the patience you do have is saved for your baby. If you are someone who is quick to care for the needs of others but less mindful of your own, you need to learn to identify your own needs and find ways to meet them.

All of the suggestions listed above under Avoiding Mother Burnout will also help you reorganize and regroup, so that you can come back from burnout and once again be an effective and happy mother to your baby. Above all, don't be too hard on yourself. You're the only mother your baby knows, and you are exactly the mother your baby needs.

STICK WITH ATTACHMENT PARENTING

Critics of attachment parenting are quick to point out that they have seen mothers worn to

---

THE PARENTING PILL

Certainly, there is no pill that a parent can take that guarantees satisfied parents and emotionally healthy children. But attachment parenting comes close. Suppose AP came in a pill. The package insert would read something like this:

Purpose: To help you become an expert in your child and to increase your chances of rearing an emotionally healthy adult.

Directions: Take as often as needed and for as long as needed.

Side effects: It may seem hard at first, may derail career tracks, and if you overdose, it may lead to sleepless nights and mother- and marriage burnout. To minimize side effects, be sure to take the dosage that is right for your child, yourselves, and your family.

---

a complete frazzle by the demands of their babies. If you are approaching burnout or are wondering if you are "too attached" to your baby, you may also have some doubts about attachment parenting. In fact, parenting advice that promises to get baby on a schedule may be looking pretty good to you. However, if you have the kind of demanding baby that is pushing you toward the edge of burnout, you can bet that you have the kind of baby who will not do well with a more rigid style of parenting.

Keep in mind that balance is a very important part of attachment parenting. If mother is burning out, something somewhere is out of balance. Figure out what it is and what you need to do to improve the situation. One adjustment you may have to make is to change your belief that it is up to you, Mom, to stop baby's cries. Baby's cries need a response, but

THE ELEVEN COMMANDMENTS FOR BALANCED ATTACHMENT PARENTING

I.   THOU SHALT TAKE CARE OF THYSELF.

II.   THOU SHALT HONOR THY HUSBAND WITH HIS SHARE OF THE ATTACHMENT PARENTING.

III. THOU SHALT AVOID THE PROPHETS OF BAD BABY ADVICE.

IV.   THOU SHALT SURROUND THYSELF WITH HELPFUL AND SUPPORTIVE FRIENDS.

V.   THOU SHALT HAVE HELP AT HOME.

VI.   THOU SHALT GET TO KNOW THY BABY.

VII. THOU SHALT GIVE CHILDREN WHAT THEY NEED, NOT WHAT THEY WANT.

VIII. THOU SHALT SLEEP WHEN BABY SLEEPS.

IX.   THOU SHALT GROOM AND ADORN THYSELF.

X.   THOU SHALT HEAL THY PAST

XI.   THOU SHALT REALIZE THOU ART NOT PERFECT.

sometimes you won't be able to find the right response. Many times, to give Mother a break, someone else — usually Dad — can take a turn at comforting and soothing baby. Attachment parenting is designed to make you comfortable with meeting your baby's needs, not anxious about baby's every move. Mothering is not very satisfying when you're constantly worrying about doing it "right." With time, attachment parenting will increase your patience and make you a more giving person. It will give you more confidence in yourself and in your ability to be not a perfect mother, but a good one.

Beware of Baby Trainers

HAVE YOU HEARD THESE?

"Let your baby cry it out."

"Don't carry her so much, you're spoiling her!"

"You'd better get him on a schedule."

"He's controlling you."

"You'll be sorry. She'll never get out of your bed."

"What, you're still nursing!"

Few parents escape their baby's first year without somebody sending one or more of these dire warnings in their direction. These misguided comments come from self-proclaimed experts in baby rearing who are everywhere. They appear at parties and at family gatherings. They write for magazines and even teach parenting classes. They may have no credentials and no children, or they may be professionals who should know better. We call them the baby trainers, because their approach to parenting is similar to the way you might train a pet. They seem to be more interested in showing you how to get baby to fit conveniently into your life than they are in showing you how to raise a happy, healthy, well-balanced human being. And your desire to do the best for your baby or your fear that you might be

harming your baby by responding so sensitively can make you vulnerable to their baby-training advice. "Beware of baby trainers" is another Baby B of attachment parenting.

The basic difference between the BT's and the AP's (baby trainers and attachment parents) is the attitude toward crying. To a BT, a baby's cry is an annoying, inconvenient habit, which must be broken to help baby fit more conveniently into the adult environment. To an AP parent, a baby's cry is a language to be listened to.

Some AP mothers can easily ignore baby-training advice. For others, especially first-time moms whose confidence is a bit shaky, the pronouncements from the baby trainers plant seeds of doubt. They wonder if they really are doing the best thing for their babies and for themselves.

Don't worry if you number yourself among the less confident. Every mother has days when she wonders whether her parenting choices are going to pay off. Every mother has days when it looks like putting baby down in his crib and walking away might be a reasonable thing to do. Your love for your child and your desire to give her the very best make you vulnerable. When someone suggests that your parenting style may actually be harming your baby, this naturally undermines your confidence. The more you learn about attachment parenting, the more you'll understand what's wrong with the baby-training approach to parenting.

WHAT'S WRONG WITH BABY TRAINING?

You can approach the subject of baby training through the eyes of a scientist, through the eyes of a mother, or through the eyes of any ordinary human being blessed with common sense. No matter which approach you take, you'll find reasons why baby training just doesn't make sense as a way to nurture human infants.

SCIENCE SAYS:
Good Science Backs AP

As you will see throughout this book, there is essentially no research supporting the advice of the baby trainers.

What Mom's biology says. Baby training is not in tune with a mother's biology, particularly a lactating mother's biology. And since babies were designed to be breastfed, the way lactation works tells us something about how best to meet baby's needs. The hormones needed to produce and release milk, prolactin and oxytocin, are se-

---

PROFILE OF A BABY TRAINER

Most official baby trainers (BT's) are authoritarian males, so caught up in their role as advice giver that they ignore scientific evidence that shows they may be wrong. Some baby trainers even discount science altogether, rather than hold their own advice up to any scientific standard.

In contrast to uncredentialed BT's, other advocates of baby training are psychologists or pediatricians with lofty degrees and academic appointments in high places. They are so removed from what babies and mothers are really like that their advice fails to reflect the realities of day-to-day parenting. Their advice is based on the kinds of situations they see in their practice, which are often the more difficult and unusual problems. They tend to discount realities that can't be measured, such as mother's intuition and maternal

sensitivity. They approach baby care as a science rather than an art and think of a baby as a project rather than a person. And, like good scientists, they expect babies to follow the predictable rules the trainers set up.

BT's have zero tolerance for differences in personalities and are quick to discount differences in maternal sensitivities and infant need levels. The one-size-fits-all approach seems more scientific to them. As the history of parenting shows us, baby training is likely to go in and out of popularity during the next century, as it has during the past. The best we can hope for is to build up parental sensitivity to the point where parents will carry neither attachment parenting nor baby training to the extreme but instead learn a proper balance in both.

creted when baby nurses at the breast. But these hormones have a very short biological half-life, which means they clear quickly from the body, often within minutes. The natural conclusion is that frequent breastfeeding is necessary to keep hormone levels high. Parenting at a distance and on a strict schedule, as baby trainers advise, is not the way humans are designed to nurture their young. The fact that human milk is quickly digested is another indication that mothers and babies should be near each other. Mother's hormones are telling her to stay close, and baby's tiny tummy makes him want to have his mother handy.

What happens when a mother ignores her biological signals? Either the body stops signaling (that is, stops producing milk), or she becomes desensitized to the signal. This is one way baby training "works." It promotes insensitivity. Ignore those signals long enough and you lose your ability to interpret them. Then you have to rely on schedules and outside advisers to know what to do with your baby.

I heard the baby next door crying. Her own mother didn't.

What Mother's sensitivity says. The more a mother responds to her biological signals, the more she learns to rely on them and to trust them, and the better they work for her. Attachment parenting teaches a mother to rely on her inner wisdom, and gives her lots of rewards for doing so. Baby training tells a mom to rely on a book or a schedule or on the baby trainer's word. It completely bypasses this complex system that parents can use to really know and understand their child.

If we had to pick one word that sums up attachment parenting, it would be *sensitivity.* Sen-

sitivity means you have a feel for your baby (can sense his needs) and that you trust those feelings. Sensitivity helps you understand your child, anticipate her actions and reactions, and appropriately meet her needs.

If there's one word that characterizes baby training, it would be *insensitivity.* Baby training puts mother and baby at a distance, with the result that mother loses her sensitivity — that gut feeling for her baby's needs. Insensitivity leads to mutual lack of trust. Baby does not trust that caregivers will meet her needs. Mother no longer trusts herself to understand and meet baby's needs.

How quickly a mother can become insensitive to her baby following baby-training classes was brought home to me one day as I was examining a newborn at a two-week well-baby checkup. During the pre-exam chat, I was answering the new mother's questions. Midway through our dialogue, the baby started crying. Mother continued asking questions, seemingly oblivious to her baby's cry. My heart rate was going up, and I was becoming anxious, yet the mother didn't acknowledge the baby's cry and kept relating to me. Finally, I advised her in a tone of voice somewhere between advising and pleading, "It's okay. Go ahead and pick up your baby. We can talk while you nurse her." As she looked at her watch, she replied, "No, it's not time for her feeding yet." This mother had been so indoctrinated in baby-training class that she had already desensitized herself to the cues of this tiny baby. It took a while to get her back on track.

What common sense says. It's interesting that traditional cultures, which are not blessed with baby furniture, infant formula, and advice books for parents, don't even have a word in their language for *spoiling*. When mothers from non-Western cultures are told about spoiling and not giving in to their babies, they shun these ideas as nonsense. Responding to baby's needs makes sense. Everyone is happier when mother and baby can relax and enjoy each other.

Use your common sense to help you think like a baby, and you'll see the truth in the following observations about attachment parenting. (We include a translation into more psychologically correct language for those who need it.)

Pick up a baby when she's young, and she'll get down more easily when she is older.

Translation: Early dependence fosters later independence.

Listen to a baby when he's young, and he'll listen to you when he's older.

Translation: Trust fosters communication.

You can put your time in at one end of your child's life or at the other.

Translation: A convenient baby may well become an inconvenient teenager.

DOES BABY TRAINING REALLY WORK?

"But it works," insist the baby trainers. Does it really? That depends on what you mean by *works*. Ignoring baby's cries will eventually shut them down. Stop listening to a baby's cues and the baby will stop signaling. That's a no-brainer. But look beyond the immediate results. What does a baby really learn in the long run from this detachment advice? Baby learns that his cues have no effect on his parents. They have no value, and it follows that he himself has no value. After all, nobody listens to him. All that this training has taught baby is that he can't communicate with his parents.

How a baby handles this discovery depends upon his personality. A persistent personality type will continue to cry and fuss louder and more forcibly, in hopes of breaking through the barriers set up by her parents. She becomes clingy and anxious and expends lots of energy trying to stay near her parents and control them. She is anything but independent. The infant with a more laid-back personality adapts more easily to his parents' lack of responsiveness. He simply gives up and becomes apathetic. He becomes a "good baby," one who conveniently fits into the dictated schedule, sleeps through the night, and generally is "less of a bother." This is the baby about whom BT's say, "It works!" But parents pay a price. This child doesn't trust, doesn't feel. He shuts down.

Here's a story from my practice that happened during the writing of this book. Jim and Karen were new parents who carried their three-month-old daughter, Jessica, into the exam room for her checkup. When they walked into my office, Jessica was strapped in her car seat, and they put her down on the floor a few feet away as we began to chat. They had some questions for me, and as we talked, I noticed that they focused all their attention on me and seldom turned toward their baby. They didn't make eye contact with her or try to engage her in any way during our conversation.

As my interview with the parents continued, I realized that there was a lot of distance between these parents and their baby. The father, as if wearing a badge of parental accomplishment, proudly exclaimed, "Notice how good she is. She sleeps right through the night!" But it seemed to me that something was wrong. I put Jessica on the scale and noticed that she had not gained any weight since her checkup a month earlier. As I held her, I observed that her muscle tone was as limp as her apathetic personality. She made little attempt to sustain eye contact with me, and she didn't make a peep.

The more I examined Jessica, the more I was sure that she was a baby experiencing what I call the shutdown syndrome. (See the box on page 126 for more on this syndrome.) This "good baby" was in reality failing to thrive. I asked the parents about their caregiving practices. They had been feeding Jessica on a three- to four-hour schedule, leaving her alone in her crib much of the time, and letting her cry at night until she gave up and slept. They weren't carrying her very much and weren't giving her very much of themselves.

"Where did you get this advice?" I inquired.

"In a parenting class at our church," they volunteered.

These were loving parents, but they were new to babies and vulnerable. They sincerely wanted to do the best for their baby, but they had fallen into the wrong crowd. I advised them of the dangers of a detached parenting style and gave them tips on how to help Jessica thrive.

Two weeks later the parents brought Jessica in for another checkup. She had already gained a pound! She seemed more animated and looked at her parents and me during the examination. She even fussed a bit when we put her down in the infant seat, so her mother picked her up and put her in the baby sling. The parents were delighted with their changed little girl and were well on their way to becoming attached. A month later I got a thank-you note from them: "Jessica is doing great. Thank you so much for steering us in the right direction. We certainly hadn't meant to do anything that would harm our baby." Jessica continues to thrive on attachment parenting, though I doubt she is as "good" as she once was.

Not all babies react to baby training as dramatically as Jessica did. They may not actually stop growing or be diagnosed with failure to thrive, but they may fail to thrive in a different sense. Thriving means more than just getting bigger. It means optimal all-round development — physically, intellectually, emotionally, and spiritually. This can't happen when Mom and Dad are denying baby what he needs most: their dependable presence.

Parents who use baby-training techniques may fail to thrive as well. Thriving as a parent means that you know your baby, are sensitive to her signals, anticipate her needs, and give appropriate responses. The ultimate in thriving is to enjoy living with your child and to find this relationship fulfilling. Baby training gets in the way of this goal. You lose the ability to read your child (making discipline more difficult), lose trust in yourself, and feel less adequate and, therefore, less fulfilled as a person.

My son went through a spurt of tantrums at around twelve months, and my first response to that was what every parenting book said to do: ignore the tantrums. But that never felt right to me, and it rarely worked. After discussing it with some AP friends, I learned to recognize those tantrums for what they were — overwhelming emotions. I realized that it was okay for me to listen to him, talk to him, and try to give a name to his feelings. I wasn't "giving in," as many critical parents tried to convince me. It worked like a charm. I basically learned to help him work through his tantrums rather than ignore them.

WHY IS BABY TRAINING SO POPULAR?

What makes parents fall for the baby-training advice? Why do they let someone else's rules and schedules override their own knowledge of their baby? There's plenty of better parenting

BEWARE OF BABY MAGAZINES

I have written articles for a lot of baby magazines, and I've discussed parenting philosophy with many editors and publishers. Most parenting magazines give at least equal attention to attachment parenting and baby training. But the fact still remains that baby training sells. A feature about baby-training classes recently even made the front page of the *Wall Street Journal.*

While the best baby magazines offer a balance of parenting styles, many strive to be "parent centered," because that's the way you sell magazines. Parents devour articles with titles such as "Five Ways to Get Your Baby on a Schedule" and "Ten Ways to Get Your Baby to Sleep Through the Night." Here is an excerpt from an article in the May 2000 issue of *Parents* magazine entitled "Teach Your Baby to Sleep in Just Seven Days": "Bedtime sins even smart parents commit: 1. Nursing your baby to sleep. 2. Rocking him to sleep . . ."

Since when is it a sin to nurse or rock your baby to sleep? It's sad but true: Baby training sells.

advice available in bookstores, on the Web, from various AP organizations, and, best of all, from more experienced parents. So why does baby training continue to thrive?

Baby training sells. While there are certainly millions of parents who just don't feel right about the baby-training approach to parenting, there is a large market for advice that promises to make babies fit conveniently into a parent's lifestyle. Baby training gains credibility from the case histories of satisfied parents who swear that getting their baby's crying under control saved their sanity — and their marriage. It's hard being a parent, and baby training promises to make life easier. Who wouldn't want to be able to count on an uninterrupted night's sleep?

In our culture, most adults become parents without having had much experience taking care of babies and young children. As result, they don't have much confidence, so they go looking for advice. Attachment parenting, with its "trust your instinct" message, may be less appealing than parenting methods that come with specific directions and timetables. We are a goal-oriented society. Quick results — or at least the promise of them — are what sells.

Baby training is PC — parent centered. New parents who go looking for advice will encounter baby-training ideas everywhere, and this approach appeals to many of them because it's parent centered. It allows mother and father to schedule their time with their baby in the same way they plan when they will do chores. It makes baby fit into parents' lives, so that parents don't have to change. We've heard these infants dubbed "daily planner babies."

Baby trainers believe that attachment parenting is too infant centered. What parents need, they claim, is a more parent-centered approach. After all, grown-ups should not have to answer to the whims of an infant. Nor, they say, should the baby be making the decisions in the family. These indictments of attachment parenting capitalize on stories of attached mothers who can't ever say no to their infants, sacrificing even their own well-being. Attachment parenting needs to be balanced, we agree, and the parenting style we advocate suggests you make decisions based on what works well for the whole family. This is not the same as letting your baby run your life, but baby trainers find it easier to describe it this way than to understand the complexities of infant cues and parent responses.

Baby training is based on a misperception of the parent-child relationship. It presumes that newborns enter the world out to control their parents, and that if you don't take control first, baby will seize the reins and drive the carriage. Baby training sets up an adversarial relationship between parent and child. This isn't healthy. You shouldn't have to choose between infant centered and parent centered. Family life is not a contest that someone has to win and someone has to lose. In families, the goal is that everybody wins.

Think of the AP family as the *us generation.* This means, for example, that the baby of attached parents is likely to go along when the parents travel to Hawaii. They might bring her because she is still breastfeeding or because they simply enjoy being with baby. A trained baby, on the other hand, is likely to stay home with a sub while her parents escape on vacation. Baby training makes it possible for parents to do this, but think of the cost.

HANDLING CRITICISM

When you become a parent, you also become a target for criticism. When you are practicing a parenting style that is different from what your friends and family are used to, you'll get lots of advice, some of which can make you worry about the wisdom of your choices and shake your confidence as a parent. Nothing divides friends and relatives like opinions about parenting. Here are some suggestions for handling advice from critics and feeling more confident with your own choices.

"What! You're still nursing?"
"Let him cry it out."
"You're spoiling her."
"He's controlling you."
"You hold her too much."
"Get her on a schedule"

BEWARE OF BABY TRAINERS

Surround yourself with AP parents. Join an AP support group (see the list of resources, page 177) or La Leche League (see page 63), and develop friendships with like-minded parents. Seek advice from veteran parents who not only share your views but whose kids you like. These are the people you can share your parenting struggles with. They'll sympathize with what you're going through without trying to win you over to an approach you don't care to try.

Don't set yourself up. If you're seeking support for your parenting choices, or if you just need to complain, be selective about whom you talk to. If you are struggling with a high-need baby, stay away from mothers of "good babies" who eat every four hours and sleep through the night. You won't get the empathy you're seeking. Instead you'll be told to stop spoiling your baby and put him down in the crib to cry, advice you don't want to hear. You'll end up feeling that your baby is fussing because there is something

THE SHUTDOWN SYNDROME

Throughout our thirty years of working with parents and babies, we have grown to appreciate the correlation between how well children thrive (emotionally and physically) and the style of parenting they receive.

"You're spoiling that baby!" First-time parents Linda and Norm brought their four-month-old high-need baby, Heather, into my office for consultation because Heather had stopped growing. Heather had previously been a happy baby, thriving on a full dose of attachment parenting. She was carried many hours a day in a baby sling, her cries were given a prompt and nurturant response, she was breastfed on cue, and she was literally in physical touch with one of her parents most of the day. The whole family was thriving, and this style of parenting was working for them. Enter the baby trainers. Well-meaning friends convinced these parents that they were spoiling their baby, that she was manipulating them, and that Heather would grow up to be a clingy, dependent child.

Parents lost trust. Like many first-time parents, Norm and Linda lost confidence in what they were doing, yielded to peer pressure, and adopted a more restrained and distant style of parenting. They let Heather cry herself to sleep, scheduled her feedings, and out of fear of spoiling they didn't carry her as much. Over the next two months Heather went from being happy and engaged to sad and withdrawn. Her weight leveled off, and she went from the top of the growth chart to the bottom. Heather was no longer thriving, and neither were her parents.

Baby lost trust. After two months of no growth, Heather was labeled by her doctor "failure to thrive" and was about to undergo an extensive medical workup. When the parents consulted me for a second opinion, I diagnosed shutdown syndrome. I explained that Heather had been thriving because of their responsive style of parenting. Because of their parenting, Heather had trusted that her needs would be met, and her overall physiology had been organized. In thinking they were doing the best for their infant, these parents unknowingly pulled the attachment plug on Heather, and the connection that had caused her to thrive was gone. A sort of baby depression resulted, and her physiological systems slowed down. I advised the parents to return to their previous high-touch attachment style of parenting — to carry her a lot, breastfeed her on cue, and respond sensitively to her cries by day and night. Within a month Heather was again thriving.

Babies thrive when nurtured. We believe every baby has a critical level of need for touch and nurturing in order to thrive. We believe that babies have the ability to teach their parents what level of parenting they need. It's up to the parents to listen, and it's up to professionals to support the parents' confidence and not undermine it by advising a more distant style of parenting, such as "let your baby cry it out" or "you've got to put him down more." Only the baby knows his or her level of need, and the parents are the ones who are best able to read their baby's language.

Babies who are "trained" not to express their needs may appear to be docile, compliant, or "good babies." These babies could in fact be depressed babies who are shutting down the expression of their needs, and they may become children who don't ever speak up to get their needs met and eventually adults with the highest needs.

wrong with your baby or your parenting. (Keep in mind also that these mothers are probably stretching the truth a bit about their babies' good behavior.) Instead, seek out experienced parents who have survived and thrived with a high-need baby. These are the ones who are most likely to give you empathy and useful advice.

Try to choose an AP-friendly health-care provider. If, because of your insurance plan, you don't have that luxury, set some ground rules on your first doctor visit. Let your health-care provider know what you are doing and that it is working for you. If he or she gives you detachment advice, such as, "It's time you got him out of your bed," simply let it pass, or respond, "We'll work on it." Then go home and keep doing what you are doing.

Dr. Bill notes: There are three questions you should never ask your doctor: Where should my baby sleep? How long should my baby nurse? and Should I let my baby cry? These are parenting questions that are best addressed to veteran AP parents. You can be sure your doctor learned nothing about these issues in medical school.

Consider the source. Criticism from your parents or in-laws can be a delicate problem, as can criticism from anyone whose opinion you value. Feelings run deep, especially between mother and daughter, and gaining your parents' approval of your parenting style may mean a lot to you. It helps to put yourself in your mother's place and realize that she may think you are criticizing her when you make choices different from the ones she made. Remind yourself that she did the best she could given the information available to her. Your mother (or mother-in-law) means well. What you perceive as criticism is motivated by love and a desire to pass on experiences that she feels will help you and your children. Be careful not to imply that you are doing a better job than your own mother did. Don't be surprised if your parents don't buy AP. It's not because they're against it; they probably don't understand it. If you think it would be helpful, share information with them and explain why you care for your baby in the way you do. But don't argue or try to prove that you're right. When you anticipate a disagreement, the best course is to avoid the issue and steer the conversation toward a more neutral topic.

When someone with little experience and fewer credentials criticizes your parenting style, ignore it. It's a waste of energy to even get into a discussion. This is especially true if you run into hard-core baby trainers who are so completely certain of their own parenting philosophies that they cannot have an open mind about anyone else's.

I've sometimes found that admitting doubts to someone who doesn't agree with me can turn that person into an ally and draw us closer. The other

ATTACHMENT GRANDPARENTING

Grandparents may be less than enthusiastic or even critical of attachment parenting. Go easy on them. Remember, they grew up in a different era. They did the best they could with the advice and information they had, and now it's your turn. You can make your own decisions about your parenting style without having to prove your parents wrong or make them feel guilty about mistakes they made. In fact, a simple statement like "I think I turned out pretty well" will help to ease any tension between you and your parents over how you are raising your child. Assume that grandparents mean well when they make statements such as, "Maybe he's not getting enough milk," or "What, you're still nursing!," or "She'll never get out of your bed." Don't let anyone derail your confidence. You can offer a brief explanation of your choices, without becoming defensive or starting an argument.

Let grandparents help. Instead of focusing on differences in your parenting style, rely on your parents and your in-laws for help when you need it. Grandparents, like you, love your child, and they often can see needs that you don't see. If Grandmother offers to baby-sit so "you two can have a night out," take her up on it, yet let Grandma know you expect baby's cries to be attended to. A wise grandmother realizes that many first-time attachment parents fail to take care of themselves while taking care of their baby. Grandparents can be very important attachment figures for babies and children. I remember the day a child walked into my office sporting a T-shirt that read, "Mom's having a bad day. Call 1-800-Grandma."

Let your child be the best testimony. Your child will eventually be your best advertisement. Once grandparents see the loving, caring, sensitive, and well-disciplined person their grandchild is becoming, you will win them over without having to say a word.

My mother-in-law was watching how I attachment-parented her grandson. She said, "I can see what I did wrong with his Dad when I watch how you parent Jacob. I ignored my child for fear of spoiling. He went through so much pain as an adult."

◆ ◆ ◆

I trust that when my children are grown, some of what they have learned at home will stick with them, and they will nurture my grandchildren as lovingly as they are cared for now.

person can see that I'm not really a know-it-all. I'm just trying to do my best, like every other mother. When someone feels that you need her emotionally, even a little, she is far more accepting of the things you do.

◆ ◆ ◆

My child is now seven years old, and she is a wonderful, bright, sensitive, and empathic person. Sleeping with her helped me be able to keep my milk supply up, even though I worked as a pediatrician three days a week. We slept with her, and I breastfed her until three years of age. I believe I have had less criticism regarding my views on attachment parenting due to the fact that I am a pediatrician and child-development specialist.

Stay positive. People are more likely to suggest you change your parenting style if they sense that you are frustrated and unhappy. If they perceive that you're happy with your parenting style and with your child, they're likely to back off. A simple statement, such as "It's working for me," puts you in a strong position and fends off unwanted opinions.

How you talk about your child is also important. Use this strategy called framing. If your toddler is going through one of those high-need, energetic stages, and your critic shakes his head and says, "He sure is demanding," turn the comment around: "Yes, he has such a strong personality and really knows what he needs." When someone says, "She sure does get into a lot of trouble," come back with, "Yes, she is bright and curious."

Humor helps. Humor disarms a critic. Use it to slow the momentum of a heavy conversation that may not be going in the direction you want. If someone criticizes you by saying, "You're still nursing!" come back with, "Yes, but I'm sure she'll wean before she starts college."

Critics usually back off once they see that you are confident enough about what you are doing to make jokes.

Use the doctor as a scapegoat. To preserve family friendships, I often advise parents to use my advice as a way to get their mother or mother-in-law off their case. For example, if your in-laws are shocked about your baby sleeping in your bed, just say, "My doctor advised me to do this." Even if your doctor is not an advocate of co-sleeping, you can feel you are telling the truth if you just think of me, Dr. Bill, as your second doctor. Of all the Baby B's, extended nursing and having baby in your bed are the ones that seem to bring out the most criticism.

Oftentimes your child will be the best advertisement for your parenting choices. Once your critics see that you have a baby who is happy and healthy most of the time, they'll have to acknowledge that something about your parenting is working. When they see the person your child grows up to be, they will be even more impressed.

It's confusing, yet heartwarming, that the very people who were criticizing me in the first couple of years are the ones who are now noticing how bright, intelligent, and compassionate she is.

11

Working and Staying Attached

THE WORKING MOTHER is a fact of modern life, but there's a lot at stake when a mother is making decisions about when and how to return to her job after the birth of her baby. Financial questions, career advancement, job security, personal fulfillment, pensions, and benefits may all factor into the decision. So will the availability of high-quality childcare. The most important issue to consider, however, is attachment — how mother's absence will affect baby's ability to develop trust. It's possible to work outside the home and still be an attached mom, just as it's possible to be home full-time and mother a baby in a way that hinders attachment. Martha has juggled parenting and a career herself over the years, and I have counseled hundreds of working mothers over several decades in my pediatrics practice, so we've seen families solve the attachment-and-working dilemma in lots of different ways, some more successfully than others. Here's what we've learned about working and staying attached.

A TALE OF TWO MOTHERS

Meet Jill and Susan, two mothers who returned to work during their baby's first year of life. As these two mothers went back to the marketplace, one maintained a strong attachment to her baby, and the other didn't.

Susan was a career woman for ten years before becoming pregnant with her first baby. During her pregnancy, she heard two voices within herself debating whether or not she should return to work. Her professional voice reminded her she had worked long years to get this far in her career and that she enjoyed her job and felt fulfilled by what she did. Susan's maternal voice told her that because she had waited so long to have her first baby, she really wanted to be the best mother she could, for her own sake and for her baby.

As the career-versus-mothering debate continued in her head, Susan learned all she could about babies and came to believe that a strong mother-infant attachment was important to her baby and to her own development as a mother. While she still planned to return to work after her baby's birth, Susan decided to give attachment parenting her best effort. After their daughter was born, she and her husband, Bill, practiced the whole attachment-parenting package. Molly was a high-need baby, and both Susan and Bill worked hard at being responsive to her cues. After a month or so of intense baby care, they started to see their investment pay off, as Molly became happier and more predictable. This made them even more aware of what kind of care Molly needed in order to thrive, so Susan decided to ease back into her career, working part-time at first. She increased her time at work slowly, based on her judgment of how much separation Molly could tolerate and how comfortable she herself felt while away from her baby. Susan and Bill also went to great lengths to choose a naturally nurturing person to care for Molly. The substitute caregiver spent two weeks in their home before Susan returned to work, learning how best to care for Molly. This prework tryout period gave Molly the opportunity to get to know the sub gradually with her mother's help. It also helped Susan feel more confident about how her baby would be cared for in her absence.

When Susan returned to work, she brought a breast pump along and used her lunchtime and breaks to pump milk for Molly. This, and the many pictures of Molly on her desk, reminded her of her baby and helped her feel connected, even when the two of them were miles apart. She called home and talked to the caregiver a couple of times a day, often right before it was time to pump milk. On her way home Susan used her cell phone to call the sub to let her know exactly what time she would be home. If Molly was hungry, the caregiver held off giving her a bottle, so that Molly would be eager to nurse when Susan walked in the door. When Susan arrived home, she kicked off her shoes, took Molly in her arms, and headed for the

rocking chair. She got a briefing on the day's events while Molly nursed. The sub left, and Bill came home and started supper. The family shared a relaxing evening, since Bill and Susan drastically cut back on other commitments so that they could devote almost all of their nonworking hours to their baby. At night, Molly slept snuggled next to Mommy and nursed often — though neither mother nor baby fully awakened. On weekends Bill and Susan put Molly in the sling and kept her close while they caught up on errands or shared household tasks.

Despite the time that Susan and Molly are apart, their attachment continues, because Susan and Bill work hard at building and keeping their baby's trust. Susan's strong attachment to Molly in some ways made it more difficult to leave her and go to work, but in other ways it has made it easier. Susan's knowledge of her baby helped her make wise decisions about substitute care, and Molly's strong attachment to her mother made it easier for her to trust the caring woman who nurtures her while Susan is gone. Susan feels more comfortable leaving Molly because she spends so much of her nonworking time continuing to build a strong attachment.

Now meet Jill. Jill loves her job, is fulfilled by it, and never thought of not returning to it after her pregnancy. A week or so after her baby's birth, she was already planning her return to the job. She and her husband led highly organized lives before their baby was born. They had been warned by friends that children would turn their predictable lifestyle upside down, but they were confident that they would be able to fit parenthood into their already busy schedules. Jill breastfed their son, Jason, for the first few weeks after he was born, wanting him to have the many health benefits. But she began to wean him to formula when he was a month old, fearing that he would be so used to her that he wouldn't take a bottle from his baby-sitter. She wanted him on a schedule, as this would be more convenient for the workers in the day-care center she had chosen, and she read a book about sleep training, determined that Jason should sleep through the night so that she could get enough sleep after she returned to work. She tried out all kinds of gadgets that promised to make her baby need her less: swings, recordings of a heartbeat, a crib that rocked all by itself. She was afraid of spoiling her baby with too much attention during her maternity leave and worried that too much attachment would make it more difficult for her to leave Jason when she returned to work. Although Jill and Tom loved their son and wanted the best for him, they vowed not to let Jason control their lives.

By the time Jill returned to work, Jason was on a reasonably predictable three- to four-hour feeding schedule and was sleeping a six- to seven-hour stretch at night. Jill and Tom were quite happy with the way they had been able to fit Jason into their careers. Their lives seemed to fit the plans they had made. In time, though, a distance seemed to develop between the parents and infant. Jill and Tom often chose to go out to dinner and a movie on the weekend, leaving Jason with another sitter. They found the toddler years exhausting; Jason was an impulsive child and rarely heeded his parents' guidance. Jill read books, tried lots of discipline methods, and even sought counseling on how to handle Jason's behavioral problems. She was often mystified by her child, and the conflicts between them made it difficult for her to enjoy motherhood. Because she had worked so hard to avoid becoming too attached to Jason, she didn't

know her child well enough to be an effective parent as her baby grew.

Susan and Jill represent widely contrasting parenting experiences. We've seen working mothers end up at both ends of this spectrum, and at many points in between. From them we've learned that it is possible to build a strong attachment to your baby while working outside the home, but it does take effort and commitment.

I am an attorney for a large corporation. Before my son was born, I decided that I would breast-feed him for at least a year, and I would find a way to do it despite our physical separation. So I rented a breast pump, found a suitably businesslike bag to carry the extras in (bottles, a towel, and so on), and returned to work after four months at home. Now, several months later, my baby's only liquid when I am away from him is still breast milk, expressed every day at the office.

I keep my breast pump out in the open in my office — tubing, bottles, and all. (Everyone understands that I lock my door when I need privacy.) My mostly male colleagues, of all ages, have been curious, but very supportive. In fact, I have had the general counsel of our company come into my office, sit down, and begin a conversation with the pump in plain sight. Although I assumed its presence would be distracting, he has assured me that since he is a grandfather, it does not bother him a bit! One colleague, seeing me with the carrying case in the elevator, asked jokingly if I was carrying a bomb. When I told him what it was, he was more surprised than if I had answered his question with a yes.

My work frequently takes me out of my office. I take the pump with me. I borrow a conference room or another lawyer's office, or any place with some privacy and an electric outlet. Many of the male lawyers I work with have recently had babies, have been through breastfeeding with their wives, and are more than happy to help me out.

My husband is an essential participant in this endeavor. He makes sure the ice pack is frozen so the bottles can be kept cold and that the pump is packed up and in the car in the morning, because I tend to forget things. So far, we haven't missed a day.

The hardest part of going back to work was being so far away from my baby. But by "feeding" him three times a day at the office, he is in my thoughts no matter what. More important, something only I can give him stays at home with him every day, nourishing him even when I can't hold him in my arms. That makes it all worth it.

TEN TIPS FOR WORKING AND STAYING ATTACHED

Spending lots of time together is a prerequisite for attachment. You have to be there when baby gives a cue in order to respond to that cue. When parents' work separates them from baby, it takes more effort to build and maintain a strong attachment. Having that connection to your baby can make it more difficult to leave every day. On the other hand, attachment parenting can make it easier to work and mother your baby. Because you give your baby so much of yourself while you're together, you feel more confident that your baby trusts you, and you really enjoy the time you spend mothering your baby. Here are some tips for keeping your attachment strong before and after your return to your job.

1. Practice full-time AP while you're a full-time mother. Practice as many of the seven

Baby B's as you can as much as you can. Learn to read baby's needs and, by trial and error, learn the appropriate responses. Wear your baby in a sling at least four to five hours a day, sleep with your baby at night, and get deeply attached. The knowledge of your baby that you gain in these early weeks will help you be a more connected parent after you return to work.

In our experience, after a few weeks of intensive attachment parenting, most mothers are so hooked on their baby that they rethink some of the decisions made during pregnancy about working and mothering. Where at first they felt they could work baby into their busy lives, they now feel compelled to reorganize their lives and work schedule around their baby.

I work full-time, but when I'm home, I mother full-time. I've had to give up a lot of just-for-me activities, but these choices are working for our family.

Developing a strong attachment to your baby will prepare you to make wise decisions about substitute caregivers, work schedules, and what you do during the time that you are not working. You will be surprised what you're willing to do in order to stay attached to your baby. The breast pump that seemed so intimidating a few weeks ago becomes your link to your baby while you're on the job. You discover that the best way to relax after work is to spend time "doing nothing" with baby. You may even make different decisions about your career, cutting back on your hours or looking for a more family-friendly position.

2. Plan ahead, but not too far ahead. Don't dwell on W Day, the day you'll need to return to work. If you are constantly thinking about how

CHOOSING AP CAREGIVERS

When I chose a nanny for my children, I made sure that she was affectionate, connecting, and an appropriately responsive person.

Attachment parenting raises your standards in selecting substitute care for your baby. Once you realize how valuable is the bond you've formed, you will naturally do your best not to let anything weaken it. Because AP is now part of your life, if and when you need to leave your baby, you will want to continue this attachment, not only because you need the reassurance that in your absence your baby is being attachment-parented, but also because a consistent style of care is less confusing for your baby. Also, expect your AP baby to have high standards for a sub. Here are some tips for finding an AP caregiver:

Value your first impressions. First by phone and then face-to-face, impress upon your prospective sub the importance of her nurturing your baby the way you want your baby cared for. But don't get too specific. Find out her own nurturing values before you reveal yours, so that she doesn't simply parrot what you want to hear.

Does she AP her own children? If she has children, go through the Baby B's to find out how many of these she has practiced herself, especially babywearing, breastfeeding, and giving a nurturant response to a baby's cries.

Ask probing questions. "What will you do when my baby cries?" "How will you comfort her?" "How do you feel about spoiling?"

"How will you put my baby down to sleep?" While you listen to her answers, try to determine if she is basically a nurturing, sensitive, and responsive person, and if your mind-sets match. Get a feel for her knowledge of infants in general, such as by asking her, "What do you feel a baby at this age needs most?"

Listen for AP clues. Hopefully, she will ask you to describe your baby — his temperament, his particular needs, and what works and what doesn't work with him. Watch how she interacts with your baby during the interview. Is her behavior forced or natural? Watch how your baby interacts with her. Remember, AP infants usually show a stranger discernment, so don't rush the attachment between your baby and the sub. Simply relate to the caregiver during your interview. If your infant perceives that she is okay to you, then she is okay to baby. As you are relating to the prospective caregiver, your baby is probably getting a feel for whether she's a Mom-approved person.

Of course, besides AP-specific questions, you want to go through a standard list for interviewing caregivers, such as health and safety concerns, smoking, whether she has had CPR training (ask to see the certificate), driving ability, accident prevention, and so on.

It's wise to have your caregiver and baby spend some time together with you present. This gradual acquaintance not only helps baby and sub get acquainted with each other, but it allows you to model for the caregiver how you want your baby cared for. Also, leave your baby gradually, in small intervals of increasing duration. It's unlikely that you're going to be able to jump right into an eight-hour-a-day, forty-hour-a-week work schedule without a protest from your baby.

Show and tell. If you have a feeling that your sub is basically a nurturing person, tell her exactly how you want your baby mothered. You know what works and what doesn't, and she needs to know this. Tell her you don't belong to the cry-it-out crowd, and you expect your baby's cries to be responded to in a nurturing way. Tell her that your baby is used to being carried a lot in a sling and show her how to use the sling. If your baby is used to being nursed off to sleep, show her alternatives. Your caregiver can't breastfeed your infant off to sleep, but she can still nurse her to sleep. Remember, *nursing* means comforting, not only breastfeeding. So, any nurturing caregiver can nurse a baby to sleep. Tell her you want her to rock and sing your baby to sleep and to even lie next to her as she falls asleep, if that is necessary. Tell her about the nap-inducing trick of wearing down in a sling, where you wear your baby around in a sling as naptime nears and then ease her out of the sling into the crib. (For more information see Babywearing for Subs, page 79.)

The sling is the best contraption I've ever used. I carry my baby in it to work, around the house, and to "reattach" when I pick her up at day care.

Reconnect. When you pick your baby up at day care, enjoy a bit of cuddle time or sit and nurse your baby for a while, as the caregiver briefs you on the day's events.

Once you've made your choice, go through a trial period to see if you, baby, and your sub fit. Here's how to tell:

- *Use baby as a barometer.* If after a week or two of the usual getting acquainted your baby becomes clingy, angry, aggressive, or wakeful, or his attachment spark diminishes, either there's a baby-caregiver mismatch or you need to reassess the timing and extent of your returning to work, or both.
- *Use the caregiver as a barometer.* Is she enjoying your baby? Or does she seem frazzled, irritable, intense, and anxious to leave as soon as you return?
- *Make spot checks.* Occasionally arrive unannounced, either a bit early or on your lunch break.
- In the case of one-on-one baby care, if your sub takes baby to a play group you've gotten involved in, ask the other mothers to comment on her care.

In a nutshell, in making a final choice, ask yourself, "Are the impressions that my baby gets from this person ones I want my baby to learn?" Is she a person you want your baby to form an attachment to?

you will manage to leave your baby, you run the risk of keeping yourself from getting attached to your baby. Mothers sometimes do this subcon-sciously. They don't allow themselves to get really involved with their babies as a way of protecting themselves from the pain of separating. The

Working and parenting.

problem is that this withholding of affection and responsiveness can have long-term effects on the mother-child relationship. Make the most of your maternity leave. Don't let the worry about returning to work rob you of the joys of weeks or months of full-time mothering. Keep in mind, too, that the best way to prepare your baby for the time when you will be separated is to build a strong trusting relationship now.

3. Get an AP-friendly sub. When interviewing a prospective childcare provider, if she is a mother herself, inquire about whether and to what extent she practices attachment parenting. Does she seem to be a nurturing person? Ask open-ended questions, such as, "What will you do when my baby cries?" Look for an answer that reveals sensitivity toward babies, something like, "I would pick her up," or, "I just can't stand to let a baby cry. They seem so helpless." Ask her how she would feel about wearing your baby around in a sling for part of the day. What kind of impressions will this person make with your baby? Is this person comfortable with attachment parenting? Ask her how she feels about "spoiling." This will tell you if she is a baby-trainer at heart, or someone who values the concept of attachment.

A substitute caregiver is a very important part of your baby's life. Your baby needs to be able to trust this person and even love her. Is this person's life stable and predictable? Will she still be part of your life a year from now? Once you find the right caregiver, compliment and compensate her well.

Your return to work will be easier on you and on baby if your sub also uses the Baby B's of attachment parenting. A sitter, of course, can't breastfeed and won't bring the same commitment to attachment parenting that you do. But her time with your baby will be easier and more enjoyable if she responds to your baby in ways similar to yours. This is why it's good to have a "show-and-tell time" with your sub before you return to work. This might be several hours, a few days, or even a few weeks in which your baby's caregiver shadows you, watching and learning about how your baby likes to be cared for. Teach your sub how to wear your baby in a sling. This familiar place and posture will help baby adapt better to his mother being away, since he'll be contained in his favorite soft little home.

We have assumed in this discussion of working and attachment parenting that your baby will be cared for either in your home or in a family day-care situation. We believe that this is better for babies than a day-care center, where many babies are cared for in one room by a revolving staff of caregivers with varying degrees of commitment to their jobs. Babies need consistent responses from a single caregiver, not a new person every six weeks. Day care in your home or in a sitter's home is more like being cared for by a parent, as long as the caregiver doesn't take care of too many children at once. An on-site day-care center at your office is worth checking out, however, since the disadvantages may be offset by the proximity. With baby close by, you'll be able to reconnect several times throughout the day.

4. Continue breastfeeding. Giving your baby your milk is a very important way of staying attached to your baby after returning to work. You are the only one who can breastfeed your baby, and continuing to breastfeed will remind you and baby that the relationship between you is unique and special. Pumping at work to maintain your milk production and to supply milk for your baby while you're apart is challenging, but you're rewarded with the ease and convenience of breastfeeding while you and baby are together. Continuing to breastfeed, including pumping at work, also keeps the levels of those maternal-attachment hormones high. Even leaking at work — a bit of an inconvenience should it occur — helps to remind you that you are a mother and that your baby needs you. Breastfeeding is a wonderful way to reconnect with your infant once you get home, and nursing at night makes up for touch time lost during the day. Breastfeeding also saves you money, and keeps you from missing work. Studies show that mothers who breastfeed miss fewer work days, since most breastfed infants are sick less often than formula-fed babies.

My two-year old has a reputation for being bright, affectionate, empathic, independent, adventurous, curious, fearless, secure, and happy, with a great sense of humor. He is comfortable everywhere he goes. I am convinced that these attributes are the result of attachment parenting. For instance, his request to "rock and nurse" when I come home from work in the middle of the afternoon not only affords him an opportunity to reconnect with me, but also gives me a time to relax and let go. Whatever mental/psychological benefit he is getting during this time is what truly motivates me to continue breastfeeding. I wonder how many other active, healthy two-year-old children spend quiet time doing absolutely nothing. There must be a connection between his having time to reflect while nursing and his readiness for learning and mastering all the amazingly complex bits of information continuously coming his way.

5. Plan a happy departure and a happy reunion. Feed your baby before you go to work in the morning. Have your sub encourage your infant to take a mid- to late-afternoon nap, so that baby is well rested for time together in the evening. Instruct your caregiver to try not to feed baby within the hour before you return, so that he is eager to nurse when you arrive. (Call ahead and let your caregiver know when to expect you.) When you arrive home, make reconnecting with your baby your top priority. Chores and dinner preparations can wait. Get comfortable, take the phone off the hook, and settle down with baby in your favorite nursing chair, with relaxing music playing in the background and a healthy snack on the table next to you. Let the cares of your day melt away, and focus on your baby. If you are breastfeeding, the relaxing effects of the hormones released during the feeding will help you unwind from the tensions of the day. If you are bottle-feeding, you won't get the hormonal boost, but you'll still enjoy relaxing with your baby and reentering full-time mothering.

Nursing my baby as soon as I get home from work helps me relax and unwind. It's better than a cocktail.

6. Think of baby while at work. Don't build a wall between your work life and your family. Talk to your baby's caregiver once or twice a day by phone to find out how your baby is doing. Let your baby hear your voice on the phone. Display baby pictures prominently at your work station and talk about your baby around the office water cooler. Babies are every bit as important as Monday Night Football or the latest office gossip. If you're breastfeeding, don't be annoyed by inconvenient letdowns or leaking. Let these and your regular pumping schedule remind you of your baby.

You'll run into people who advise you to shut out thoughts of your baby during the time you're at work. They may advise you not to show pictures of your baby or even let on that you have another life as a mother. After all, if you are thinking about your baby, how can you be concentrating 100 percent on your work? The baby-training philosophy will show up at work as well, in the guise of advisers who warn you against feeling guilty about being away from your baby. There isn't an attached mom in the world who won't have some guilty feelings about leaving her baby. The very sensitivity that you've built up through attachment parenting will leave you feeling somewhat uneasy about being away from your baby. That's normal and healthy, and it's those feelings that motivate you to work so hard at staying attached, even while you're away from your baby. Don't buy into the idea of shutting out thoughts of your baby for eight hours a day. This is the beginning of a de-sensitizing process that will eventually put you at an emotional distance from your baby.

7. Share sleep with your baby. Bedding with your baby is a particularly valuable Baby B for working mothers, for lots of reasons. Most important is that sleep sharing allows you to reconnect with your infant at night. The physical contact helps you make up for missed touch time during the day.

Sleeping with your baby also makes breast-feeding easier. Smart breastfed babies make up for missed daytime feedings by nursing often at night. Sleep sharing makes it possible to nurse your baby frequently at night without completely waking up. This keeps mothers from becoming sleep deprived. Sleep sharing while breastfeeding helps to boost your milk supply, which is especially important for mothers who have a hard time pumping enough milk while they're away from baby.

Studies have found an increased incidence of sleeping difficulties in children of mothers who work outside the home. Sharing sleep with your baby offsets this tendency. Your presence helps to regulate baby's sleep and reassure him that even though there has been a change in daytime caregiving arrangements, nighttime is still "Mommy and me" time.

Babies, especially AP babies, have a way of extracting what they need from their parents, whether the parents like it or not. Watch out for this scenario. You pick your baby up at the caregiver's around 6 P.M., and the baby-sitter exclaims, "My, what a good baby. She slept all afternoon." You get home, and that daytime sleeper turns into a night owl. This mismatch is exhausting. Baby is tuning out the baby-sitter during the day and saving his energy for you at night. The problem is that when you go back to work, you usually need extra sleep. Nestling baby in bed next to you can help you get it. Telling the baby-sitter to place a time limit on naps will also be helpful. Even infants who previously slept well solo may need to nestle next to mother at night after she returns to work.

As a working mom, I get my full dose of my baby each day by sharing sleep.

8. Wear your baby. When you are home with your baby, spend time with your baby. Put baby in the baby sling while you fix dinner, sort mail, or do laundry. Wear your baby on weekends while you clean the house, take a walk, or go out to dinner. If you and your baby must be apart during your working hours, make sure that you are together the rest of the time. Baby-wearing naturally includes baby in your adult activities and reminds you that baby is happiest in your arms. Babywearing will also help you enjoy special moments between just baby and you — a walk outside at bedtime or even in the early morning before it's time to go to work. Both parents can take advantage of this way to stay in touch with baby.

9. Care-share. The increased involvement of fathers has been one of the better by-products of having mothers in the workplace. Honor your husband with his share of baby care, day and night. If today's mother is expected to share the breadwinning, today's father should be expected to share the childcare. It's easier for a baby to accept care by Dad after Mom returns to work if Dad has been involved in babywearing, diaper changing, comforting, soothing, and putting baby to sleep right from the start. Sharing the care starting at birth makes it easier to share the care once you return to work. (For attachment-fathering tips, see chapter 12.)

10. Search for an AP-friendly job. If possible, choose employment that allows you maximum time to mother. This is a time to be open to making changes in the amount of time and energy you devote to your career. You have only so much to give, and you want to be sure your baby gets what he needs. Here are some suggestions for reshaping your working life to accommodate your baby better:

• Work out a schedule with your employer that allows you to work part-time, work from home, or work flexible hours. In some workplaces these options aren't possible, but many smart companies realize that helping employees meet family needs is good business. Happier workers are more productive and less likely to go searching for a new job.

• If your company has a good on-site day care, consider using it. When baby is close by, you can drop in during the day to breastfeed and

reconnect. If on-site day care is not available, consider teaming up with other parents to ask your employer to provide this benefit.

• If you're job hunting, look close to home. Shortening your commute shortens the time in which you are away from your baby. You may be able to go home for lunch or nursing breaks, or your caregiver may be able to bring your baby to you. Another way to keep baby closer is to look for childcare near your workplace rather than near your home. Unless your baby hates car rides or public transportation, you and baby can commute together.

• If you have the type of employment that allows you to bring your baby to the workplace, by all means do it. This may work out well, at least during the first six months. (For suggestions, see Work and Wear, page 79.)

• Consider starting a home business. Many women use the time when their children are small to reevaluate their goals and start a new career. You may be able to free-lance or work from home in your profession. Or start something new.

Being true to yourself and to your baby is a balancing act. Ideally, you want to experience satisfaction at home and at work. Realistically, you may not be able to have everything you want from both worlds, at least not all at once. As one mother put it: "Full-time mothering was too much for me; full-time working was too much for my baby. So I cut back to part-time."

Babies teach parents to be more realistic about their time and their abilities. This is one of the things you gain from being an attached parent. Listen to that wisdom as you make decisions about how your baby and your career fit together.

Lily, a mother in our practice, was a perfectionist, and she got a lot of strokes from her achievements at work. She had a corner office, a title on the door, respect from her colleagues, a fat paycheck, and a bunch of perks that fed her ego. Lily was blessed with a high-need baby, and these challenging babies have a way of derailing even the best-laid career plans. Realizing that because of her perfectionist tendencies she couldn't do her best at both jobs, Lily took a leave of absence and became a full-time mother until her baby was two years of age. When she and her husband attended various social functions, most of the other women she met were juggling careers and motherhood. When she was asked the inevitable question "And what do you do?" she proudly responded, "I'm a specialist in early-childhood education."

When I'm dying, I won't be thinking about the corporate jets I flew on or the high-rise office I occupied. I'll think of the children I loved and the effect my parenting had on them.

HOW A BABY CAN CHANGE A MOTHER'S CAREER PLANS

By now you've probably realized that we use our own children and our pediatrics practice as a sort of laboratory for learning more about real-life parenting. I have learned a lot over the years from women who have come up with their own solutions to the career-versus-motherhood dilemma. When they ask me for advice or information about going back to work, I never hesitate to urge them to get deeply attached to their babies during those first weeks of life. Everything we know about mothers and babies tells us that this is critically important to baby's health, happiness, and development. I'm often impressed by what these mothers are willing to do to continue that attachment once it's established.

Couples often come in to talk to me during pregnancy, as part of the process of choosing a pediatrician for their new baby. Mothers frequently mention that they plan to go back to work a few weeks or a few months after baby is born, and they ask for suggestions about how to make this plan work. I point out that one of the dangers of combining working and motherhood is distancing, where mother doesn't let herself become too emotionally involved with her baby because of how much it might then hurt to leave baby with a caregiver and return to work. I tell mothers that the way to prevent distancing is to practice attachment parenting to the max in the early weeks. This means no bottles, no pacifiers, no substitute care to come between mother and baby. I tell them, "You might as well enjoy some full-time mothering while you can, since these six weeks of maternity leave may be the only time in your life that you have so much time to devote to your child." Here's what happens to these mothers after a couple of months of super-intense attachment parenting:

The two become one. Mothers now think of their baby as a part of their lives. Whereas before, they considered returning to work as the usual and normal thing to do, they now realize that it will be difficult to leave baby with another caregiver. In fact, it feels as if they are being asked to leave a part of themselves behind when they go to work.

Mothers look for ways to step off their career track. They procrastinate about going back to work and come up with various ploys for extending their maternity leave. I sometimes help them with a few tricks of my own. When I sense that a mother is grasping for some excuse to delay returning to work, I'll ask her if she would like a medical release to extend her leave. Here is Dr. Bill's standard letter: "Because Mrs. Smith's baby is allergic to formula, it is medically necessary to extend her maternity leave so she can safely meet her baby's nutritional needs."

Lest you think that this is a little medical white lie, I should inform you that the statement above is technically correct for any baby, at least in the first six months. At this age, infants' intestines are allergic to any food other than human milk, even though sometimes the allergic reaction is only microscopic and not enough to bother a baby. If our society as a whole had a better grasp of the concept of human milk for human babies, it would be assumed that a breastfeeding mother should not be separated from her baby.

Lifestyle changes. Because they get so hooked on their baby, these mothers make changes in their lifestyles and in their career ambitions. Some start successful Internet businesses, which allow them to work out of their homes. Some change jobs to accommodate their baby's needs. Some decide to work part-time or negotiate flex-time arrangements with their employers. Some go into battle to change corporate maternity-leave policies and make their workplace more parent-friendly. When it comes time to choose a substitute caregiver, these parents grill prospective sitters and keep looking until they find the right one. Some mothers never do go back to work and revise the family financial plans to make this possible.

What happened to these mothers? After a month or two of attachment parenting, these mothers developed a relationship with their babies that brought out the lioness in them. They were willing to do everything possible to protect this relationship. Such is the power that a baby has over a sensitive mother. The closeness between mother and baby taught these women lessons they could not have learned from a book. Baby showed mother how important she was.

I left a promising academic career to stay home when Victor was born, feeling that my career as a mother was even more promising.

Attachment Fathering

MOST OF THE BABY B'S seem more about the close physical relationship between a mother and her infant. Where does this leave Father? How does a dad get attached to his baby? Don't make the mistake of thinking that attachment parenting is just for mothers. Dads who think this way miss out on one of life's most important experiences, one that challenges fathers to grow, mature, and put love into action. Becoming a father brings out unique nurturing skills — skills you probably didn't even know that you had. Dads can't breastfeed, but they can use all the rest of the Baby B's to get to know their child well from day one. Everyone benefits when fathers are involved with their babies.

Even a dad who has never been interested in babies before can become a baby enthusiast when he has one of his own. Dads learn to care for babies the same way new mothers do — with hands-on experimentation. You can't wait until your son is old enough to throw a football to become an involved father. If you want him to enjoy playing catch with you when he's ten, you have to start enjoying him when he's a baby. (The same goes for girls, including the part where they'll need a baseball glove.) Babies know right from the start that fathers are different, and a baby whose father spends lots of time with her will appreciate that difference.

When Dad is involved, the whole family functions better. Attachment fathering makes attachment mothering easier. Dad's knowledge of his baby helps him understand how important Mother is to baby, and this motivates him to create a supportive environment that allows Mother to devote her energy to the baby. An attached father also is ready to take a baby handoff from Mom when she is tired or needs a break. When both parents share the baby duties, mothers are able to steer clear of burnout. Both parents thrive, and so does their marriage.

I couldn't have survived without the help of my husband.

◆ ◆ ◆

Attachment parenting has allowed his sweet, nurturing side to dominate over his macho, strict disciplinarian side. How could he be any other way? Sharing our bed with our babies and carrying them around in slings has really created a sweet, caring father who is committed to raising them in an atmosphere of love and trust.

143

MY STORY: HOW I BECAME AN ATTACHED DAD

Dads, let me share with you how I blew it with our first three babies. Our first two came while I was in pediatrics training, and the third as I was getting a practice started. At that time, I put my career ahead of everything. I believed that earning a good living was important to my family, and I thought that I would find most of my personal fulfillment in the practice of pediatrics. I grew up without a father and had no model of what it meant to be an involved father. I left the parenting to Martha — after all, she was good at it! When the boys were older, I thought, we could toss a football around, and talk baseball together during the World Series. And when my sons needed words of wisdom, I would be there to provide them.

Put children before career. I was wrong about postponing my involvement with my kids. Even as toddlers and preschoolers, my children needed me, not my resume. This finally became clear to me when I was offered the position of chief resident of pediatrics at Toronto's Hospital for Sick Children, the largest children's hospital in the world. This was a very prestigious position, one that would assure me lots of great job offers in the years to come. But it also meant I would have to work weekends, evenings — all the time — taking care of other people's children and not seeing my own. I realized that this was not the life I wanted for my family. So I turned down the job, found a less demanding position elsewhere, and looked for ways to enjoy the time I now had available to spend with Martha and our two sons. We went camping a lot. We took up sailing. I got to know and enjoy our two boys, Bob and Jim, and managed to convince Martha to have another baby, our son Peter. I was more involved this time, but my education as a father was far from complete.

A child teaches an old dad new tricks. Then came our first daughter, Hayden, whose birth would change my life and whose personality inspired us to coin the term *high-need baby*. This bundle of energy came wired differently from our other children. She was not happy unless she was in our arms. She breastfed often and was on an unpredictable schedule. She cried when she was put down. Martha, a skilled baby tender, was exhausted from the effort it took to be Hayden's loving mother. I had no choice about becoming a dad who carried, walked, and comforted his baby. If Hayden was not in Martha's arms, she was in mine. On days when she nursed constantly, I had to take over with the boys when I got home from work. As I became more sensitive to her needs, Hayden grew to trust me, and Martha felt more comfortable about leaving Hayden in my care.

Martha and I got through Hayden's baby days by working together. I realized that I had reached a new level of sensitivity and that this demanding little girl had taught me a great deal. This newfound sensitivity carried over into my relations with all my children and with my wife. Our family was functioning better than it ever had, and I was a wiser disciplinarian. Instead of being a distant dad who dispensed punishment and life advice from the safety of his den, I had learned to really know my children, especially Hayden, and as a result, I knew how to help them behave better. I realized that you can't set limits for a child based on abstract ideas. You have to know the child well, and the child has to know and trust you if she is going to behave as you wish her to.

Bonded from birth. We had four more children after Hayden — Erin, Matthew, Stephen, and Lauren. Each one has been a growing experience for me. With Matthew in particular I made an effort to be all that I could be as a father, since we believed at the time that he would be our last baby. Or maybe I felt so close to him because I caught him as he was being born. (Martha had a fast labor, and our birth attendant didn't get there in time.) Matthew may not remember that first touch from my quivering hands, but it's a moment I will never forget. I wouldn't trade it for a chance to be the quarterback at the Super Bowl.

Father nursing. With Matthew, I discovered the joys of father nursing. Martha would breast-feed Matthew, and I would hold him or carry him around in a baby sling after feedings. Why it took me six children to discover this kind of closeness I don't know. (I hope my readers try this with baby number one!) Matthew knew that I was not Mom but another person who loved him and with whom he could feel content.

Matthew thrived on that difference. He liked being in my presence as well as in Martha's. My newly discovered aptitude for baby comforting was also good for Martha. She became more comfortable releasing him to me, and with more time for herself, she was more relaxed and better able to care for the rest of the family. She liked watching me with Matthew — and she knew that my tenderness as a father would spill over into tenderness toward her. Even our sex life improved.

During Matthew's first year, I moved my pediatrics practice into our remodeled garage ("Dr. Bill's Garage and Body Shop" to my teenage patients). I took "baby breaks" during the day and was able to spend a lot of time with him. After a year, I closed my home office and moved into a nearby medical building. But even though I worked outside the home, I was still hooked on fathering. My attachment to Matthew and the rest of the family acted like a strong rubber band. It stretched enough for me to go to work, to teach, and to write. But it always pulled me back home. Also, I was careful not to stretch it so far that it would weaken or break.

From "Dada" to "Daddy" to "Dad." Matt and I are still incredibly close. As he has moved

---

ATTACHMENT TIP

Watching a man nurture a baby really turns a woman on.

from one stage to another, I have encountered new challenges — coaching Little League, planning activities for a den of Cub Scouts, and the like. I wouldn't have found the time for these volunteer activities if they hadn't mattered to Matthew, but I've learned a lot and have become a more patient, more balanced person from these experiences.

After Matthew, we added two more children to the Sears family pack. But my kids are not finished with me yet. My eight children are always teaching me to be a better person and a better father — because I'm there for them. Attachment fathering pays off.

During the writing of this book, I had my first opportunity to play the role of father of the bride. Our high-need baby, Hayden, grew up, and, true to form, honored us with a high-cost wedding. As I walked her down the aisle and later danced with her to the tune of "Daddy's Little Girl," I flashed back to those hours she spent in my arms as a fussy baby. I remembered the nights in our bed, the time spent at Martha's breast, and all the years of high-need parenting she required of us. Here she was now, a beautiful, confident, and compassionate young woman of whom I was so proud. It was a great feeling!

NINE ATTACHMENT TIPS FOR FATHERS

Becoming attached isn't something that happens to you. It's something you do. I've learned from my own journey into attachment parenting and from what other fathers have told me that the more you put into fatherhood, the more you get out of it. Here are some attachment tips to help you get connected to your baby. Challenge yourself to put these into play,

and reap the rewards in the months and years to come.

1. Start Early

Fathering begins before birth. Fathers don't have the physical experience of pregnancy to help them get used to the idea of having a baby around, but they can still use these nine months to get the connection started.

A custom Martha and I enjoyed during "our" pregnancies was the nightly ritual we called laying on of hands. Each night before going to bed I would put my hand on what we affectionately called the bulge, and I would talk to our baby: "Hi. This is your daddy. I love you and I'm looking forward to seeing you." At first you may feel a little bit foolish talking to someone you can't see, but the more you do it, the more it will seem as if your baby is really listening to you (as, in fact, she is). We know that babies can hear sounds in the womb, and some prenatal researchers believe that babies can hear Father's voice better than Mother's because low-pitched sounds travel more easily through the amniotic fluid. Studies have shown that babies whose fathers talked to them before birth are more interested in their fathers' voices soon after birth. Babies have been known to turn their head and look around the delivery room, searching for the source when they hear Dad's voice soon after birth. It's as if baby is saying, "I know you."

As you place your hands on your baby and touch your wife's body, appreciate the little one growing inside her. Picturing your baby as she grows will help you feel pregnant, too. (One of the meanings of the word *pregnant* is full; a father can indeed feel full of love for his growing child.) If you can, accompany your wife on prenatal visits, where you can listen to your baby's

ATTACHMENT FATHERING AND THE BABY B'S

Here's how Dad can be involved in each of the seven attachment tools.

Baby B's	What Father Can Do
1. Birth Bonding	Share the bonding time with your wife; stroke your infant, talk to him, and gaze into his face. If a medical complication separates mother and baby, stay with baby and give him father contact during the first hours of his life. (See Father-Newborn Bonding, page 49.)
2. Breastfeeding	*Nursing* means comforting, not only breastfeeding. A father can nurse his baby using other comforting techniques. Father can also nurture the mother to make it easier for her to breastfeed.
3. Babywearing	Babywearing promotes father-infant bonding and gets baby used to hanging around with Dad.
4. Bedding close to baby	Support your wife by being open to this style of nighttime parenting. If it's working, avoid putting pressure on your wife to wean baby from breast or bed.
5. Belief in signal value of cries	Avoid the "fear of spoiling" mind-set. Develop unique ways of responding to baby's cries, such as the warm fuzzy and the neck nestle (page 149).
6. Balance and Boundaries	Remember, an AP mom is at high risk for giving out. She needs her mate to give to her and share the childcare.
7. Beware of baby trainers	Protect your wife from advisers who undermine her confidence. Trust and support her maternal instinct.

heartbeat or see that tiny body on the ultrasound screen.

The laying on of hands is as important to your wife as it is to you. Women experience a lot of emotional upheaval during pregnancy. They worry about whether they'll be a good mother and about how motherhood will change their life. When you lay a warm hand on your wife's pregnant belly, you are not only affirming your commitment to the new baby, you are telling her that you will be there to help her care for

this child you have made together. It might seem like a small thing, or something that goes without saying, but your wife will treasure this regular reassurance of your love and commitment. Martha once told me, "Every night I look forward to this special dialogue between you and our baby. Every time you embrace our baby, I feel you embrace me, too. I feel your commitment to both of us." Repeating this ritual nightly will strengthen your commitment to being a good husband and father.

I'm hooked. I was so used to putting my hands on our baby and talking to our baby before his birth that now that he's born I can't go to sleep at night until I lay my hand on his warm little head and reaffirm my commitment to him as a father.

2. Bond with Your Newborn

Father is more than a spectator at birth. Although early bonding research focused primarily on maternal behavior, researchers have also studied fathers' first encounters with their newborns. Fathers' reactions have been described with the term *engrossment.* A fathers who holds his newborn baby, stares into his eyes, strokes his skin, and talks to him gets hooked. Dr. Martin Greenberg, in his book *The Birth of a Father,* says that these fathers feel more important in their baby's lives and have a stronger identity as a parent. This leads them to be more involved in their baby's care. They can be just as nurturing and capable as mothers. The earlier they start, the more competent they feel. Newborns have an incredible ability to draw parents magnetlike toward them. Get in there and get your hands on your baby, so that baby can work her magic on you.

3. Take Paternity Leave

Everyone knows about maternity leave, but few realize the importance of dads not hurrying back to work so soon after baby is born. Take as much time off as you can, so that you can care for your wife and get to know your baby in a relaxed way. You need more than a few days to get connected. The busywork of your job will still be there when you get back, but your baby is a newborn for only a few short weeks. If you can, when your baby is small, limit the amount of extra work you do. Cut back on evening meetings and out-of-town travel. Both your wife and your baby need your presence and support during the first year. Now is a good time to get in the habit of taking your family's needs into account when you plan your work schedule.

4. Keep in Touch

You get to know another adult by talking together and by sharing experiences. You get to know babies by holding them — and by sharing experiences. A baby's language is made up of sounds and movement, grimaces, and body tension and relaxation. When you hold your baby in your arms or wear your baby in a baby sling, you tune in to all these subtle means of communication. The more you share this experience of closeness, the better you and baby will understand one another.

The warm fuzzy. Skin-to-skin contact feels good to baby and to dads, especially in the early months. Try the warm fuzzy to help your baby drift off to sleep. Drape your diaper-clad baby over your bare chest with his ear near your heart. You can do this while lying down or while relaxing in your favorite recliner. Your heartbeat, the rise and fall of your chest as you breathe, and the warm air from your nose moving over baby's scalp will soothe baby and lull him into a sound sleep. The skin contact makes this position feel extra good. Baby will enjoy this masculine alternative to mother's breast. Dads are different — but baby will learn that's okay.

The neck nestle. Another favorite position of dads and babies is the neck nestle. Hold baby against your chest with his head snuggled in under your chin. His head will rest against your larynx, and baby will feel comforting vibrations

The warm fuzzy.

as you talk or sing in a low voice. Dads excel at comforting baby in this position, since the male voice is lower and the vibrations that make the sound are stronger. This is no time to imitate the three tenors or to sing rock and roll in a screeching falsetto. Sing "Ol' Man River," or another tune that rumbles in the throat and chest. Or make up your own words and music. It doesn't have to be fancy. Here's a lyric that worked for me:

Go to sleep, go to sleep
Go to sleep my little baby.
Go to sleep, go to sleep
Go to sleep, my little girl.

Baby will enjoy the repetitive words, the music, and the gentle rumbling beneath your Adam's apple.

Start at the bottom. Most men realize that to climb the corporate ladder they have to start at the bottom. Attachment fathering works the same way. Baby's bottom is your entrance point.

The neck nestle.

So why should Dad get stuck with the dirty work? Because diapering is yet another way to interact with your baby and get to know her better. After all, it's the nitty-gritty shared experiences of life that draw a family together. If you want to know your child well, you've got to be around for more than just playtime. And besides, changing baby, bathing baby, and dressing baby all present opportunities for play and interaction. Do the math: during the first two to three years, your baby will need around five thousand diaper changes. If you do even 20 percent of these diaper changes, that's a thousand chances to interact with your baby. Your newborn won't know if you can't tell the back of the diaper from the front, but she will recognize that she is being handled gently and with love. Starting at the bottom, literally, helps you work your way into your child's affections and establish yourself in an executive, in-charge position.

5. Get Moving

Baby slings aren't just for mothers. Slings work for dads, too (and if you don't like the floral print on your wife's sling, get one of your own in a more masculine color or design). Using a baby sling to carry your baby gets you in the mind-set that baby belongs wherever you are. Put baby in the sling and go for a walk when you get home from work. You'll be able to unwind, and Mom will get a much-needed break. Or get up early in the morning and snuggle baby into the sling while you make breakfast and read the paper. Our nine-month-old Matthew was so accustomed to his daily time in the sling with me that all I had to do was say the word *go*, and Matthew would crawl over to the door where the sling was hanging and reach up

for it. I'd put the sling on, put him in it, and off we'd go for a daily "Daddy and me" stroll on the beach.

When your baby is tiny, use the sling to help you support her in the neck nestle position (see page 149). With baby snuggled close to you, you can sing and sway or dance her into a sound sleep while continuing to watch the football game on television. The familiarity of the baby sling combined with the comfort of the neck nestle can make Dad a hero during baby's dinner hour fussiness (what we call happy hour) or when it's time to get the reluctant sleeper to bed. Not only will you get connected to your baby, you will also win points with your wife.

6. Be Supportive

Most new mothers do not have a lot of confidence in their own baby-tending wisdom. They may put a lot of energy into appearing to be self-assured, but underneath, they are not so sure. Because they love their babies and are trying so hard to do what's right, they are very vulnerable. Conflicting advice can undermine the confidence of even the best of mothers. One of your most important jobs as a dad is to support your wife's mothering. Fend off preachers of bad baby advice.

If you sense that outside advice is upsetting your wife even a little, put a stop to it, even if the baby-raising tips come from your own mother. It's easier to do this if you yourself have a strong commitment to attachment parenting. But even if you have a few doubts, stick with your wife's instincts. There are times in parenting when dads have to trust mothers. Mother is the one with the close biological relationship to your child. Don't get in the way as she listens and responds to your baby's needs. If you trust her, she will trust herself more, and everyone will be happier. Remembering to say things like "I think that you are just the mother our baby needs" will pay off. Your child will have a better mother, and you will have a happier wife.

Even though I can't breastfeed our baby, I can do a lot to make it easier for my wife to breastfeed more successfully.

7. Stretch Yourself

Whether it's mastering the art of diapering, understanding toddler language, or soothing a fussy baby in the middle of the night, being a dad means you have to stretch and grow. Be open to trying new things for the sake of your child. Mothers may provide much of the security and reassurance children need; dads can bring novelty and fun. Become involved in your child's activities. Don't be a distant dad — get down on the floor and play. Sometimes take the lead and suggest new games, but be sure to spend lots of time letting your child lead the activities. When you take time to play what your preschooler wants to play, you build his self-esteem and let him know that you love him no matter what.

As your children get older, you can know and enjoy them more by getting involved with their sports teams, scouting programs, school activities — the possibilities are endless. Volunteer to coach your child's favorite sport, or try a stint as scoutmaster. You don't have to be an expert, you just have to be there and be willing to learn. You're smarter and more skilled than the kids you're leading (well, most of them). I remember coaching Matthew's soccer team when he was six. I knew nothing about soccer and didn't think I liked the sport, but Matthew

didn't know that. All he knew was that his dad cared enough to get involved. Years later, I coached eight-year-old Lauren's soccer team at a time when some distance had developed between us. All those practices and games gave us an opportunity to reconnect.

You will learn a lot about kids in general and your child in particular when you get involved with coaching and other activities. Realize that most other parents who volunteer for these positions don't know any more about what they're doing than you do. As a scoutmaster, I learned a valuable principle in childcare: KISMIF — keep it simple, make it fun.

8. Know Your Child

In order to guide and discipline your children, you have to know them. And to know them, you have to be involved in their care. All of the attachment tips outlined above are aimed at helping you know your child better. As you open yourself to your baby and respond sensitively to baby's language, you will begin to identify what makes your baby happy and what is hard for her. As you support your wife's mothering, you'll gain insights from her into what makes your child tick. Knowing your child well is not a difficult goal to attain. You just have to listen and respond (and perhaps let go of a few preconceived notions about babies sleeping through the night or playing quietly alone in their cribs).

If you let this openness and knowledge of your child develop, you will be able to discipline your child in a way that is sensitive and intuitive. You will have fewer struggles, fewer occasions when you lock horns. You will know how to motivate your child to do what you want him to do. You'll also learn to recognize what your child is capable of doing, and what you cannot expect him to do yet.

I can guide our children effectively because I know them. They obey me because they trust me. My own experience as a dad and a pediatrician has convinced me that many fathers have a tough time with discipline because they are not connected to their kids. Their children may obey them out of duty or fear, but these kids are not becoming self-disciplined individuals. If you want your children to internalize your values, you have to know and respect what is going on inside them. This process begins already in the first year of life, as you listen and respond to baby cries.

9. Remember That Fathering Matters

Mothers and fathers parent differently, and our children profit from that difference. Fathers are not mere pinch hitters, a second-best substitute for mother, not even in the early days when mother has comforting breasts and father has only a bony shoulder. There is nothing optional about father involvement. Studies have shown that much about the way children turn out depends on Dad, for better or for worse. In the first year of your child's life, when baby has an intense attachment to mother, it can be easy to forget this.

In my pediatrics practice I meet older fathers who come in with their wives for well-baby checkups. These are men on their second marriages, and many express regrets that they were not more involved in the lives of their older children. Now at midlife, with their priorities in order, they want to spend more time with their children from their first marriage, but these children don't have time for them. Now, with new babies, they are determined not to miss

anything, because they know they need this solid foundation to carry them through the years ahead. Take your cue from these dads and plan now to have no regrets later. Kids pass through each stage only once.

WHERE'S DAD?

The plight of the working mother gets lots of attention, but what about the working father? Most men must be away from their children for forty hours or more each week to keep a roof over the family's head and food on the table. Being a good provider is important, but so is staying connected to your kids. Juggling all it takes to achieve both these goals is a challenge.

For me, this challenge takes the form of balancing the time I spend with the children in my home and the time I spend writing books and taking care of the children in my practice. I love doing them all, and being available is an important part of being both a pediatrician and a father. I spent a year working out of a pediatrics office in my home. I let my children know that I was moving my office into our home so that I could be closer to them, although I also impressed upon them that while I was there, I would be working, not playing. What a revelation! I realized that traveling to my job every day may have been exhausting, but it was also therapeutic. I missed the camaraderie of the office. My social world had become just my family. Discovering just how important the social interactions of the workplace were to me helped me understand the adjustment women go through when they leave a career behind to stay home alone with a baby all day long. This experience also helped me recognize what a temptation it is for a father to escape into his job and

LET DADS LEARN TO BE DADS

Mothers, remember that men may not learn to read baby's signals as quickly or as instinctively as women do. Give your husband time and space to learn how to comfort and care for your baby. Picture this scenario: You're in the other room, and Dad is looking after baby. Baby starts to fuss and then to cry. You wait for a minute, hoping Dad can solve baby's problem, but as the cry escalates, you rush in and offer a stream of advice, even as you are preparing to rescue the fussy baby from fumbling Daddy. You may have the best of intentions, but stop and consider what kind of messages you are sending. You've let your husband know that you think he's inept — a belief he may share, though he doesn't benefit from having you point it out to him. And you give your baby the message that there really is something to be anxious about when he's in Dad's care. Instead of rushing in, hold your hormones a bit and give Daddy and baby a few minutes to work things out. Get yourself out of earshot if that's what it takes.

Whenever you can, set up Dad and baby to succeed at being happy with one another. Leave baby in Dad's care after a good feeding and at a time of day when baby is generally in a good mood. Get out of the house and let Dad and baby have some time together. Take a walk, or go shopping. If you let Dad know that you believe he can care for "your" baby, he'll live up to your expectations. Dads can come up with unique and interesting comforting measures in a pinch.

put less effort into home life than into his career.

Staying Connected While Apart

It is important for your child to know where your priorities are. Even though you may need to work away from home, your child should understand that your home is more important. Being absent by necessity is pardonable; being absent by choice is not. Here are some ways to keep your connection to your family strong, even when you are apart:

- When you're away from home, take time to think about your kids. Carry pictures, display them on your desk at work, and show them to your colleagues.

- Call home during the day and talk to your wife (or your baby's caregiver) about what baby is doing.

- Incorporate your children into your work life instead of maintaining a wall between job and family. Bring your children to visit your workplace if possible. Let them see where you go every day and tell them about what you do there.

- Let your child see your accomplishments or watch you at work. Seeing this other side of you is valuable for your child. You are forming her ideas about work and helping her to know you better.

- If possible, take an older child along on a business trip. This is a great use of your frequent-flier miles, and it can be lots of fun for both of you. Children behave well when presented with the challenge of traveling with Dad. I often took one of my kids along when

I had to make a television appearance. Visiting a TV studio was an enlightening experience for them.

- When you get home at night, leave the job behind. Use your commute time to shift from being an employee to being a dad. When you walk in the door, focus on your family.

It's unfortunate that the years when children are young are often the same years when fathers feel they must give 110 percent to their job in order to build a career. Remember, though, that ten years from now, there will still be career opportunities open to you. They may not be the same opportunities, but there will be some. Your baby, however, will be a baby no longer.

When Dad is on the road. Staying connected is even more difficult when Dad travels. It is especially challenging for dads in the military or in other jobs that keep them away from home for a long time. One of the side effects of the attachment style of fathering is that both father and child feel the loss when they are apart. A baby who is very attached to Dad is likely to protest when the object of his attachment goes away. Parents notice effects like these when Dad is away:

- Baby's sleep patterns may change. Night waking may be more frequent, and getting settled may be once again more difficult.

- Baby has more fussy periods, and younger children may have more tantrums or angry outbursts. Because Dad's absence changes the whole structure of their world, baby's behavior may be tense and less organized.

- When dad's away, kids may stray. Discipline problems often surface when Dad travels. Many children test Father-imposed limits when only Mother is there to enforce them. High-need or impulsive children who are attached to their fathers are particularly prone to these separation behaviors.

- Mother acts differently, especially in a home where attachment parenting is practiced. Then the child gets a double whammy! Father is not there, and baby feels his absence. Mother, in reacting to her husband's absence, may seem "not all there," too.

- Children's moods change. They swing from quiet withdrawal to impulsive belligerence. This is especially true of young children, who may not understand what's happening. As one two-year-old declared to his mother after being away from Dad for over a week on a vacation trip with Grandma, "Not see Daddy ever again." They were going back home in two days, but to this little one it seemed as if his life had changed forever.

Don't be disturbed if your baby or small child gives you the cold shoulder when you return. This is only temporary. It takes time for baby to get over the confusion and anger associated with your absence and to adjust to your return. The first time I experienced this reaction I was devastated. I walked in the door after being away for several days, and instead of a "happy to see me" reaction, our one-year-old acted as if he couldn't care less. After a while I picked him up and walked with him and began to sing his favorite song. He perked up, and we were finally reunited. After a separation — even one that's only the length of a workday — you may have to woo your baby back into trusting you.

Phone home. Parenting is ideally a two-person job. If you travel a lot, keep in touch. Your wife needs your support and affection even when you are gone. Phone your family frequently and talk to everyone. Let your children know you miss them and love them. Even a baby can respond to hearing Dad's voice over the phone. Tell your kids what you are doing, and when you'll be home, and be sure to listen patiently as they tell you about themselves. You might consider taking your family with you when you travel. Babies are very portable and travel very easily. Home to a tiny baby is where Mom and Dad are, whether it's your house or a distant hotel room.

When I had to travel when our infants were young, I would leave behind an 8 x 10 photo of me that Martha put next to the bed. When baby awoke in the morning he would see Mommy — and me. You can also make tapes for your children to play while you're gone. Sing a favorite song or tell a story. Nowadays, with computers and e-mail, there's no excuse for not staying in touch with your family. You can send messages, pictures, even recordings instantly. Be creative and use all your fancy business-communication devices to stay in touch with the people who are most important to you.

FATHER FEELINGS ABOUT MOTHER-INFANT ATTACHMENT

"All she does is nurse." "She's too attached." "That baby is hanging on her all day, and now she wants to sleep with the baby." "We need to get away together, alone." "We haven't made love for weeks." These are actual statements from dads who truly care about their wives and babies. Yet they are feeling left out, confused, and lonely. Fathers who don't yet understand AP can identify with these emotions, since they are a common part of the new father experience. It's perfectly normal to want more of your wife's attention than you are getting. It's also normal and healthy for her to be so intensely involved with your baby. But since your feelings and your wife's seem to be headed into conflict, take them as a sign that some adjustments need to be made. Babies need parents who are happy.

The hormonal changes a woman goes through after birth explain why mothers are so attached to their babies and apparently uninterested in their mates. Before pregnancy, women's hormonal cycles prompt them to be interested in sex. This, after all, is how eggs get fertilized. After the baby is born, maternal hormones take over, since nature is now interested in making sure that this little baby gets the care she needs to survive. Mothers enjoy breastfeeding and caring for their babies.

Much of the energy that your wife previously directed toward you has been redirected toward your baby, as a result of your wife's instinctual urge to mother. Her body is telling her that she should focus on the little one in her arms. During the time that this infant is exclusively nursing, your wife will most likely be infertile (nature's way of pointing out that another baby too soon would hurt this one's chances to survive and thrive). Because she is not ovulating, she may have little interest in sex.

Some mothers, for all kinds of reasons, react more strongly than others to what's going on inside of them hormonally. If your wife seems totally involved with the baby, don't panic. This does not mean that your infant has taken your place in your wife's affections or that you must compete with baby for her attention. It simply means you have to wait. This is your wife's season to master mothering. She is loving you by loving and caring for your child. In time, her focus will return to you, and if you are an involved and supportive father in the early

WHEN FATHER AND MOTHER DON'T AGREE

I'm using attachment parenting with my three-month-old baby. Baby is happy, and so am I, but my husband is sure I'm spoiling our son. He wants our child to be more independent so we can go out more often.

Attachment parenting works best when both parents agree that it is best for baby. Disagreements about parenting style can cause problems in a marriage and create distance between husband and wife.

If your husband feels this way, you need to talk with him to find out why. Perhaps the way you are mothering your baby is unfamiliar to him. He may come from a family where babies were left in cribs to cry. His friends or his own family may be telling him that you are spoiling your baby. Or he simply may not understand that your baby will become more independent as he grows up.

Explain to your husband why you are practicing attachment parenting. You know best which of the many benefits will appeal to him. Reassure him that the high-maintenance baby stage does not last forever. Above all, let your husband know that he is very important to your baby, and encourage him to get in on the babywearing and the responding to baby's cries. You want attachment parenting to feel right to him, too.

Finally, husbands often criticize attachment parenting when they are feeling left out. Attached mothers can be so busy with their babies that they inadvertently leave Dad to watch from the sidelines. You can do something about this situation. Talk to your husband and tell him that you have not lost interest in him. Think of ways that you can show him your affection, and make these a priority every day. Share with him how tired you feel, and suggest ways for him to share in the baby care and household routine, so that you can have energy left over for your life as a couple.

Finding time and opportunity to enjoy one another's company can be difficult when there are babies and small children in the family. Here are some tried-and-true suggestions from couples who have been there:

- Try a little romance. Believe it or not, men are pushovers for candlelit dinners and soft music. You can do this at home after baby is asleep. If you create the right atmosphere, even sharing a take-out pizza can be romantic.
- Go for a drive together during baby's naptime. Baby will fall asleep in the car seat, and the two of you can talk without interruption.
- Seize any opportunity to share quality time. If baby wakes both of you in the middle of the night, cuddle up and have a conversation while you nurse baby back to sleep. Then . . . who knows?
- Attached babies are wonderfully portable. Head for your favorite restaurant with baby in the baby sling. You can discreetly nurse baby to sleep, and then linger over dinner.
- Consider a night out alone together. It's okay to leave your baby with a sensitive caregiver occasionally. Or perhaps you're more comfortable leaving baby in the morning or afternoon, when he's in a better mood. Go out for breakfast together, or see an early movie.

Dr. Bill notes: One time a couple came in for counseling because Mom was so attached to baby that the couple's attachment was weakening. When I advised that they have a night out to themselves, Mother looked at me like I was speaking a foreign language, while Dad gave me an enthusiastic "Yes!"

What children need most is two happy parents. If Mom and Dad aren't doing well as a couple, this unhappiness filters down to the kids. Sometimes you may have to say no or wait to your baby (once you're past those early months), so that you can say yes to your relationship with your spouse. It's okay not to be a 100 percent perfect attachment parent.

If your parenting style is causing serious problems in your marriage — problems that the two of you can't seem to resolve — consider counseling. You may need the help of a professional in finding ways to meet your individual needs and each other's needs, as well as those of your baby.

months, her energy will probably turn your way sooner.

One of the other reasons that mothers seem to tune out fathers in the early weeks is fatigue. By the time a woman cares for her baby and does what's necessary to keep the household running, she wants nothing more than to sleep, or to have some time to herself with no demands placed on her.

My need for sleep is greater than his need for sex.

If you do what you can to lighten her load, she'll have more energy for you. Do you want her to clean up the kitchen after baby is in bed? Or do you want her to spend that time with you? If you prefer option two, then you would be wise to clean the kitchen yourself as she nurses baby down to sleep. Helping out in whatever way you can will stimulate your wife's interest in you.

On those seemingly rare occasions in the early months when the two of you manage to connect sexually, you'll find that sex is not the same as it was before baby. You may be holding your wife's body in your arms, but part of her mind is monitoring baby. It seems, too, that baby checks in on his parents as well. Many couples are certain that their infant has a built-in romance alarm. Mom and Dad finally find a time to get together, and no sooner do things start to heat up than baby awakens, cries, and needs a response. This may not kill the mood for you, Dad, but it will instantly kick your wife from lover mode into mother mode. You can't compete, and you're better off not trying. Don't get angry. Instead reassure your wife that you agree that baby's needs come first. Go retrieve your baby and give her to Mom to nurse. Then snuggle in with mother and baby. You and your wife might not get back to making love that night (although you never know), but your tender concern will earn you points that you can cash in later.

Nothing matures a man like becoming a father. Fatherhood forces you to put someone else's needs first on a regular basis. You learn to accept delayed gratification. You become more disciplined yourself in order to guide your children well. Above all, becoming an attached father will make you more sensitive to your children, to your wife, and to others as well.

For mothers only. Remember, Mom, that while your hormones are changed by birth and motherhood, your partner's are not. You may have little interest in sex in the months after baby is born, but your husband needs reassurance that you still care about him. He can't know how you feel unless you tell him. Be sure to convey to your husband that your lack of interest in sex during those early months is no reflection on your love for him. Then, when you can, make an effort to rekindle the romance. Here's how one mother in our practice balanced her attachment to her baby and her attachment to her husband.

Susan and her husband were blessed with a high-need baby who awakened frequently at night. Because Dad needed his sleep, he moved out of the bedroom when baby was about one month old and spent most nights on the living room couch. Susan recognized that everyone had nighttime needs, so she would occasionally tiptoe into the living room and surprise her husband after baby had fallen into a deep sleep. These midnight visits did wonders to help Dad accept Susan's attached nighttime parenting.

Attachment Parenting in Special Situations

NOT ALL FAMILIES MATCH the middle-class stereotype of two parents married to each other, with 1.8 healthy, above-average biological children, a comfortable income, and a three-bedroom house in the suburbs. You don't have to fit the stereotype to practice attachment parenting. In fact, if you have a child with special needs, or if you yourself are facing out-of-the-ordinary challenges, you will find attachment parenting especially valuable. When life is not going according to plan, you need all the tools you can muster to stay sane yourself and to give your baby what he or she needs. The Baby B's will help you become such an expert in your baby that you will be able intuitively to match your parenting to the need level of your baby.

SINGLE AND ATTACHED

Being a single parent means you put in double duty. True, attachment parenting is more challenging when going at it solo, but when the sole responsibility for your child rests on you, anything that makes parenting easier in the long run will be especially valuable in your life. At-

tachment parenting can give you the self-confidence and discernment you need to make good decisions for your child. The extra sensitivity and wisdom that you gain from AP should make single parenting much easier as your child gets older.

In the early months, even in the early years, AP may seem more difficult for a single parent. With two parents in the home, there's somebody there to fill in when you need a break. Without that backup person, a parent has to work harder, since she's on call nearly all the time. Yet the first commandment for attachment parenting still applies: What your baby needs most is a happy, rested mother. This caveat is even more important for the single parent, especially if you're dealing with divorce or separation. Giving all to your child and having no time for yourself will quickly lead to burnout. Here are some suggestions for keeping your life in balance as a single, attached parent:

Realize you can't do AP alone. If you're practicing AP, don't do it as a *single* parent — that is, one who is completely alone. You may be a single parent, but you're not a superparent, nor should you expect to be. As the saying goes, it takes a village to raise a child. You need people behind you, around you, supporting you. (Even two-parent households need support.) Connect with single-parent support groups, relatives, friends — any nurturing person who can lend you a helping hand. Form friendships with other AP single moms so that you can share childcare, ideas, and late-night phone calls when you really need to talk.

Reserve time for adult company. Doing it all, all by yourself, all the time is what makes you frazzle and burn out. Some mothers try to make up for their baby's not having an involved father by being both mother and father. Their entire world revolves around baby, but they often end up not being able to function very well as adults. Again, remind yourself that what your baby needs most is a happy mother.

Work around your baby. Being a single parent will slow down your career. You can't be all things to your employer and all things to your baby, and the investment in your baby must be made now. Your career can wait. If possible, arrange your job around your child instead of making your child fit the demands of your employment. At least for the first year, see if you can work out of your home as much as possible. Of, if you can, take your baby to work with you. (See Work and Wear, page 79.) If you must work out of the home, look for a breastfeeding-friendly workplace, such as one with on-site day care, a lactation room for pumping, or other perks that make it easier for you to stay connected even while you and baby are apart.

My daughter is only a newborn. Right now my life is my child. I know I'm going to need to go back to work soon, but I'll cross that bridge when I come to it.

ADOPTION

When our eighth child, Lauren, came into our family as a newborn by adoption, we wanted her to have the benefits of attachment parenting. (We don't tag her "our adopted daughter." Adoption is not part of who she is; it only explains how she came to be in our family.) Just because she was adopted didn't mean she should be deprived of the attachment a baby continues to experience with her mother after birth. Attachment parenting is especially valuable for infants who come into your family by adoption because it helps you build your relationship with your baby on every level.

Adopting mothers often wonder if they will be able to feel as close to their adopted baby as they would to a biological child. They wonder what they are missing by not having the biological experience of pregnancy and birth. In our experience, adopting parents are so thrilled to have a baby, one they've waited so long for, that compensating for this biologically different start is not difficult. In fact, we find that most adopting parents naturally practice varying degrees of attachment parenting because they are so eager to get to know their baby physically as well as emotionally. Try these attachment tips:

Bond with your baby prenatally. If you are planning an open adoption, get involved in the birth mother's pregnancy. Communicate with her about how she is doing and how baby is growing. Perhaps you can see an ultrasound picture of your baby. Prenatal bonding is a bit risky emotionally, because there is always the chance of a last-minute change of heart by the birth mother. But establishing a relationship with her and caring deeply for your baby-to-be can also be very satisfying.

Be present at the birth or shortly after. You can ask to be present at the birth and bond with your baby as soon as possible. Whether this is possible will depend on the situation. With the birth mother's permission and an okay from the medical personnel, hold your baby immediately after birth and follow the bonding tips listed in chapter 4. As much as possible stay with your baby in the hospital, and sleep in a nearby hotel. Certainly, ask to give your newborn most of her feedings. Sit and hold her in a rocking chair and give her lots of skin-to-skin contact throughout the day. Again, this can be emotionally risky, since there's always a chance that the birth mother may change her mind about the adoption, but you may decide that the rewards outweigh the risks.

Practice the Baby B's. Babywearing and bed sharing are two attachment tools that will give you lots of time to build your relationship with your baby through physical contact. Bottle-feed your baby with the same nurturing sensitivity that you would use to breastfeed. Or consider breastfeeding.

Yes, you can breastfeed a baby who is not biologically yours. Where there's a will, there's a way. Even without a prior pregnancy, nipple stimulation can cause your body to produce milk. Mothers who breastfeed adopted babies use a combination of mechanical pumping, the baby's own sucking, and sometimes lactation-stimulating medications to bring in a milk supply. They also use a device called a nursing supplementer to give their babies supplementary milk at their breast. The supplementer holds formula or pumped human milk, which is delivered to baby through a thin tube taped to mother's nipple. Martha breastfed our daughter, Lauren, for ten months, and we have

counseled many adopting and attachment-parenting mothers in our practice.

The most important piece of advice we give an adopting mother who wishes to breastfeed is to enjoy the closeness that comes with the act of feeding. Don't obsess over the number of ounces of milk you produce; the amount at the start is likely to be precious little. Most adopting mothers are able to supply some, but not all, of baby's nourishment at the breast. What they find most satisfying about nursing an adopted baby is the physical closeness. For step-by-step tips on breastfeeding the adopted baby see our *Breastfeeding Book*.

If you have adopted an older baby, it is possible to undertake catch-up attachment parenting. Most of the Baby B's of attachment parenting can be instituted anytime during the first year. Don't worry about the attachment your baby may have "missed" in foster care. Infants are extremely resilient. What you do now will have farther-reaching effects than what may not have happened in baby's first few months. As soon as your baby comes into your home, begin using the Baby B's of babywearing, bed sharing, and belief in your baby's cries. The more your baby is physically and emotionally connected to you, the sooner he will become attached to you, and you to him. If you know when you will be receiving your baby and are simply playing the legal waiting game while baby is in foster care, see if you can't get the foster parent to practice some attachment parenting. Better for baby to become attached to the foster parent and then have to shift that attachment to you than for him not to become attached to anyone in those early weeks.

We believe attachment parenting is even more important for adopted babies, since adopted children can carry feelings of rejection deep inside them. A close and trusting relationship with their parents helps them overcome their feelings of loss related to their birth mother. When our daughter Lauren was seven years old, she asked us why her birth mom didn't love her. We reassured her that her birth mom did indeed love her; and because she loved her, she chose adoption. She loved her so much that she realized she couldn't give Lauren the life she wanted her to have. Did this resolve Lauren's puzzlement about her birth mother? Not completely. We know this question will come up again. We realize that the best we can do is give Lauren high doses of attachment parenting as "preventive medicine," so that she has the resources and self-confidence she'll need to come to terms with the feelings of loss that are likely to surface periodically throughout her life.

Because attachment-parented children become so sensitive and caring, they may do even more soul searching about their birth mother than other adopted kids do. Try not to take this personally. Children who are adopted search for roots, not for different parents. When they feel very secure with their own parents, it may be even easier for them to express their need (if they have that need) to find out more about the parents they lost. Try not to take statements like "You're not my real mother" personally. While statements like this may hurt, they simply reflect a deeply caring child who is working through a bit of normal confusion. You know what's really in your child's heart.

My husband and I became foster parents almost seven years ago. We take babies in when they are two days old and keep them from two weeks to three months. Children raised in foster homes are at high risk for having attachment problems later on, so it's important that they begin life with some attachment roots. I wear each of these babies in a sling for the greater part of each day, taking them *everywhere with me. Every single one of these babies has loved the sling! And my foster babies are always complimented on their good behavior. I also sleep in close proximity to these babies. A portable crib set up next to our bed lets me respond to their needs quickly and throughout the night. Though I breastfed my two birth children, I discovered early on that it really wasn't difficult to comfort a baby without nursing. I guess I develop harmony with these babies, and by holding them and talking to them, I am able to calm them down. We keep in touch with most of our twenty-six babies. How are they doing? They all appear to be doing great with no evident attachment disorders!*

ATTACHMENT PARENTING THE HIGH-NEED CHILD

You can often spot high-need babies right at birth. They come out, look up, and start to wail, announcing to the world, "I am *not* an average child, and I need above-average parenting. If you give it to me, we're going to get along fine. If you don't, we're in for trouble." They then latch on to the breast and don't let go of Mom until sometime, it seems, after their first birthday.

High-need infants crave physical contact. They are in arms, at breast, in your bed, take-along babies for whom crib is a four-letter word. They look upon strollers as miniature versions of a paddy wagon, and they don't take kindly to substitute care. Fortunately, high-need babies are also bright, energetic, and as much a joy as they are a trial.

We didn't know high-need babies existed until we had one. The parenting that had worked for our first three children simply wasn't enough for Hayden. We had to hold her constantly. She nursed frequently around the clock. Martha was

PROFILE OF A HIGH-NEED BABY

Over the twenty years since we came up with the term *high-need baby* we have met many of these challenging children and counseled their parents. From our gallery of these children, we have compiled a profile of a high-need baby. While all babies show some of these features some of the time, high-need babies have most of these features most of the time. A word of caution: The personality traits are descriptive only and should not be judged as good or bad. We are just trying to describe what these infants are like and introduce you to the style of parenting they need to help them thrive — and help you survive.

- The word *schedule* is not part of the high-need baby's vocabulary. These babies are unpredictable and do not easily settle into a routine, even a flexible routine. They force you to forget any expectations you may have had about living life by the clock.
- High-need babies demand constant physical contact. They cry when they are put down and settle only when they are picked up. Cradles, cribs, swings, and baby seats don't come close to being acceptable substitutes for a parent's arms. Babywearing has been the salvation of many a mother of a high-need baby.
- High-need babies nurse frequently around the clock and suck as much for comfort as for nourishment. Nothing can take the place of Mother's breast. Once you get used to this idea, you'll realize that in nursing, you have the one tool that will calm your little live wire.

- Get a babysitter? Forget it! High-need babies won't settle for substitute care. (As our neighbors and friends realized, everywhere that Bill and Martha went, Hayden was sure to go.) Even Dad may be considered second best, but it's important for him to be involved in baby's care. Without Dad as a backup, Mother will burn out.
- These "Velcro babies" don't like to sleep alone. They share your bed, and they share your sleeping space, as if they were glued to mother's arms and chest. Hayden was the first baby in our family with whom we shared sleep; once we accepted the idea that she would sleep well only in our bed, we were all finally able to get a good night's sleep together.
- High-need babies feel everything more intensely. They cry more loudly and in a way that demands attention. Parents soon learn to respond to these cries quickly, because if they don't, baby becomes inconsolable. A high-need baby will make a more sensitive parent out of you, as long as you are open to the language of his cries.
- High-need babies are constantly in motion. They don't seem to know what it is to be still. As these children grow up, they can learn to channel this tremendous energy into all sorts of activities. While you may expend a lot of energy chasing them around as toddlers, you will also learn to see the world in a new and wondrous way.

High-need infants are incredibly demanding. The challenge for parents is to learn to see this as a good thing. The traits that make these children so exhausting as infants and toddlers have a positive side to them. These children are alert, busy, determined, and interested in everything as preschoolers. By the time they are teens, you'll see them as enthusiastic, passionate, and resourceful individuals. You'll also find that the way you have responded to their needs over the years has taught them to be compassionate and empathic.

exhausted, as she struggled to give Hayden what she seemed to need so urgently. Friends advised us, "You're spoiling her!" "You're carrying her too much." "Just let her cry." "She's manipulating you." If Hayden had been our first baby, we might have believed them and disregarded our own perception of Hayden's personality. But she was our fourth child, and by that time we felt we had a handle on what babies needed. We were confident enough to know that it wasn't our fault she fussed. She and all the other high-need babies fuss because of temperament. High-need babies need more of everything: more touch, more nursing, more sleep-sharing, more carrying. They are very sensitive little individuals who depend on their parents to help them cope with their environment. They simply can't wind down by themselves.

There really wasn't a proper term for explaining Hayden to friends and family. We didn't like calling her difficult or fussy, because these descriptions were too negative for someone we were beginning to see as such a positive little person. These labels suggested that something might have been wrong with our baby or with us. We found ourselves explaining Hayden's behavior and our parenting style by saying, "She just has high needs." So eventually we came up with the term *high-need baby.*

When I began using this term in my pediatrics practice, I knew that I had found the right way to describe the experience we shared with other parents of challenging babies. Whenever new parents came into my office desperate to know what to do about their fussy baby, I would say, "Oh, you have a high-need baby!" As I explained what I meant, I could see hope and understanding reflected on their faces. They had been told so many things about their baby that were negative and critical. Finally, someone had something positive and useful to say that helped them understand their baby better.

Actually, the description *high-need baby* says it all. It's a positive, uplifting, and accurate term. The answer to what to do about this baby lies in the term itself: If your baby has high needs, then your job as a parent is to go ahead and take care of those needs. Don't try to make them go away. Don't apologize to others for the way you are parenting your baby. Attachment parenting is exactly what your baby needs. For more about the challenges of parenting the high-need child, see our *Fussy Baby Book.*

ATTACHMENT PARENTING A CHILD WITH SPECIAL NEEDS

Regardless of what kind of special needs your infant or child has — whether physical, mental, behavioral, or a learning disability — one thing is certain: Attachment parenting will help both you and your child cope. How you care for a special-needs child affects how that child learns to handle his problems and challenges. Attachment parenting will also help you know your child and see the world from his point of view, which can be more difficult when a child is somehow "different."

Parenting a child with a disability can be tremendously rewarding and will force you to grow in ways you never imagined. When our seventh child, Stephen, was born with Down syndrome, we knew he was a special child who would need a special kind of parenting. We knew his cues and language skills would be more challenging, and we imagined he would have more medical problems. So we needed to learn to be even keener observers. Here's where attachment parenting really shines. It's like having an extra radar system or sixth sense to read the needs of your child and respond appropriately. Martha breastfed Stephen for three and a half years, and I wore Stephen in a baby sling many hours a day. He weaned from our bed at three and a half years. Attachment parenting has helped us help Stephen be all that he can be.

Focusing on building a healthy attachment to your child can heal the hurts you may feel and help you enjoy your child's many positive qualities. Attachment parenting may even lessen the degree of the disability. The benefits AP brings to other babies will work for your child as well. Particularly when a child has ongoing health problems, the parents' ability to judge when something is wrong is critical to getting good care.

Challenges to attachment parenting. When you have a child with special needs, you often find you need expert advice, whether it's on health problems, infant-stimulation techniques, teaching methods for school-age children, or behavioral strategies. It's up to you, as the expert in your child, to filter this advice through your own sense of what will and won't work for your family. This isn't always easy, especially when you're worried about your child and unsure about what is best. Some of what you hear from others will be helpful information that you can use, along with what you know about your child, to make his life and yours better. Some of what you hear may be advice that does not feel right to you. Attachment parenting will help you know which advice is good to follow and which is better to disregard.

It's harder to keep your balance as an attachment parent when your child has special needs. Love for your child and the desire to "fix" what's wrong compels you to put all your energy into taking care of your child's needs. Meanwhile, you neglect your own needs, and you may also neglect your spouse and your other children. There comes a time when you have to back off a bit. Take the "Caribbean approach," as hard as it may seem: "Don't worry, be happy." The best you can do for your child is to enjoy her for who she is. This is far more important than fixing her problems. Loving her and being happy with her is your main job as a parent.

ATTACHMENT PARENTING MULTIPLES

Can you practice attachment parenting if you have twins, triplets, or more? Absolutely! However, each one of the Baby B's requires double the commitment — and yields double the rewards.

Many multiple require extra medical care after birth. Even though your babies are likely to need multiple doctors and nurses for a few days after birth, Mom and Dad are valuable members of the medical team. Don't let yourselves be displaced even though because of medical complications the ideal birth-bonding experience may not be possible.

Remember, as we have often said, the term *nursing* means comforting, not just breastfeeding. While Dad can't breastfeed, there are many ways he can help Mom breastfeed better. While Mother breastfeeds one baby, Father can "nurse" the other by holding, rocking, and wearing. As one proud father of twins in my practice said to me on their one-week checkup: "Our babies have two mothers — she's the milk mother, and I'm the hairy mother." The babies enjoyed lying on Dad's chest in the warm fuzzy position.

Try these tips for attachment parenting more than one baby.

Hire a lactation consultant. While mothers of singles may consider hiring a lactation consultant as a luxury, with mothers of multiples it's a must. Within a few days after birth, have at least one hands-on session of positioning and latch-on instructions from a lactation consultant who has experience teaching breastfeeding of multiples.

Teach both babies to latch on. In the first week or so, breastfeed your babies one at a time so you can give each one individual attention to learn how to latch on efficiently. Typically one infant learns latch-on a lot more quickly than the other one, and sometimes one twin is much smaller than the other and requires more milk for catch-up growth.

Switch babies from one breast to the other. If one baby is more efficient at breastfeeding than the other, by switching them from one breast to the other, both of your breasts will receive equal stimulation from sucking.

Learn to breastfeed both babies at the same time. Once both babies learn to latch on well, try breastfeeding both at the same time for many of the feedings. There will be times when you want to give each baby individual attention for breastfeeding and times when you will find it easier to nurse them both at the same time. As a double perk, feeding two babies at the same time is likely to give your milk-making and mothering hormones a double boost.

Nap-nurse. Master the art of nursing both babies while lying down. Cradle a baby in each arm, with both of their bodies on top of yours and their knees meeting at the center. Place your arm under each baby and prop them up by placing a pillow under each one of your arms. The double shot of the relaxing hormones will also help you nap.

Develop a feeding routine that works for you and your babies. The typical "demand feeding" or "cue feeding" may be best for breastfeeding one baby, but realistically, this may be too tiring for most mothers of multiples. Keep working at establishing a breastfeeding routine that works for you and your babies, always keeping in mind that a physically and emotionally drained mother (and a sleep-deprived mother) is not what your babies need.

Prepare a nursing station. This may be an easy chair or a big recliner with large armrests that allow you to support both babies while feeding them. Place a table nearby with your favorite music and nutritious beverages and snacks. Enjoy listening to soothing sounds and nibble while you nurse.

Doubleteam at night. Bedding close to both babies allow for easier breastfeeding. Some parents do fine with both babies in bed, while others find it easier to have both of them in a co-sleeper next to their bed. (Twins often sleep better nestled side by side. After all, they have been womb mates for a long time.) If your babies are sleeping across the room or in a different room from you, let Dad (the father nurser) get up and bring them to you for breastfeeding and then return the babies back to their bed. That way you don't have to leave your nest and further disturb your sleep.

Wear both babies. As you learned in chapter 6, carried babies cry less and grow better. Double this for twins, since one crying baby can set off the other. Get two baby slings, one for Mom and one for Dad, and take family walks together. This outdoor exercise is good for mind and body.

Balance your needs and your babies' needs. One of the often forgotten Baby B's of attachment parenting is balance — knowing when to say yes and when to say no. Double this precaution for twins. Realize that you can't give 200 percent, and there may be times when you don't have the time and energy to practice all of the Baby B's. Remember the sign I put up for Martha on our bathroom mirror: "Each day remember what our baby needs most is a happy, rested mother." Put up two signs for twins.

Realize that you are only human. You can't possibly calm three crying babies with one set of arms, for example. There are times when one baby may need to wait while the more needy one is attended to, and there may be days when even mothers who are committed to 100 percent breastfeeding realize that they have not failed attachment parenting if their babies get an occasional bottle from another caregiver. Just do the best you can.

Double your household help. While all new parents should have household help, with multiples it's a must and not a luxury. At least in the first six months, get help with all the household chores that drain your energy from your babies, so that you can do what no one else can do as well — mother your infants.

Double your support and resources. Take advantage of the experience of parents who have survived and thrived with multiples. Try to surround yourself with other AP parents of multiples, since you may find that some organizations are not as knowledgeable about attachment parenting as others are. See the list of resources on page 177.

Attachment Testimonials

CONCEPTS SUCH as being in harmony with your baby, mutual trust, and sensitivity are hard to describe on paper, but seeing them in action will inspire you to develop these qualities in your own relationship with your child. If you're practicing attachment parenting, support from more experienced parents is invaluable. Watching them interact with their children gives you a model to follow and also reassures new parents that they are on the right path.

We can't package live, experienced parents in this book, but we can give you the next best thing: stories that attached parents have shared with us. We hope that as you read the testimonials in this chapter, you will see something of yourself somewhere and find the support you need to trust your own intuition as you build your own attachment.

COULD A MOTHER *NOT* WANT THIS?

I never intended to be a parent. My teaching career was on a roll, I owned five horses, all needing constant attention, my husband and I were in the process of building a house and

horse barns, and I wanted to get my writing career back on track.

Three months into this process, I discovered I was pregnant. Actually I was quite happy about it. Like all expectant mothers, I had dreams of the nursery and the crib and the matching decor. I had illusions of a cooing baby playing quietly in her crib as I went about my daily life undisturbed. I was ready to hand her off to my husband or mother while I spent my evenings training horses. Maternity leave would be a paid vacation.

Then Bridget arrived.

In an instant I questioned every plan I had ever had about being a parent — and a mother. How could I ever leave my baby? What sort of absurd idea did I have in the first place about putting her in a dark room all by herself at night? A stroller? I wanted to be close to my baby all the time. Hence, an AP mother was born — without even knowing there was such a term as *attachment parenting* or even a Dr. Sears!

I love breastfeeding — even in the middle of the night. Unless you've been there, there are no words to describe the incredible closeness and bond between a mother and a nursing child.

How many times have I had women tell me that they nursed for only a month and then stopped because they just didn't like it? How often have I encountered the looks of disbelief when I venture forth my intention to nurse Bridget for at least a year? I cannot fathom wanting to give up something that no one but a breastfeeding mother can experience. I look down at my three-month-old daughter as I sit here typing one-handed. She is nestled against me nursing, with one hand softly caressing the exposed skin of my upper breast. She frequently breaks away to glance up at me, eyes shining as she smiles wide with unabashed contentment and love. How could a mother *not* want this?

And how could a mother not want the first image of each day to be the shining, happy face of her baby? The highlight of my mornings is to find Bridget already awake and eagerly anticipating her mommy's first stirrings. We meet face to face, and her tiny features crinkle with joy. She wriggles excitedly as she cuddles up and buries her little fists in my hair. If ever I could have only one memory to take with me on this long road of life, Bridget's morning welcomings are all I would need.

On outings I wear my baby in a sling as one might wear a fine fashion accessory — proudly. People are intrigued and often comment about the baby in the kangaroo pouch. They want to ask questions. "How old is she?" "How does she sit in there?" And most commonly, "Where did you get that thing? I wish I had had one when my baby was little. Your daughter looks so happy!" Yes, she is happy. She is close to me while safely interacting with the world. Of course, she can't say these things; instead, she smiles broadly and excitedly shakes her chicken rattle. I think it's unfortunate that a sling is foreign to so many people. But having it makes me accessible, and that accessibility provides me the opportunity to show people a positive way of parenting that is so common in most parts of the world yet so absent in the hands-off world of parenting in America.

I suppose, by definition, I am an attached mommy. But I wouldn't describe myself that way. Instead, I'd say I am in love. I am wildly, passionately, and head-over-heels in love with a three-month-old baby named Bridget Genevieve.

WHAT IS A GOOD BABY?

The first few weeks after Isabel's birth, I kept trying to put her down for naps and at night without me, just to allow myself time to eat, take a shower, or write a thank-you note. I had read about wearing your baby and about sleep sharing and had been very impressed by these concepts. But I did not know how to wear Isabel, and I was insecure about sleeping with her. I was surrounded by well-meaning relatives who knew only about the "putting baby down" method of parenting. My mother kept wanting to take Isabel for rides in her stroller, and my mother-in-law kept trying to lay her down on the couch or in her stroller outside. She said to me once, "I thought she might be getting tired of being held."

At her one-month checkup I told Dr. Sears that Isabel would not lie down without me. He laughed and said, "Sure, she knows what's good." It began to dawn on me: This man really believes this stuff; he really believes in keeping your baby just as close as you can. As for my complaint that I could not get anything done and that I was exhausted, he suggested that I lie down with her twice a day for naps. He added that over time I would learn how to do things with her in the sling.

With our new regimen of naps together, walks in the sling, and sleep sharing at night, Isabel calmed down considerably. Each week she seemed a little more peaceful, more alert and happy. At two months old, she still liked being held most of the time, but she rarely fussed. Now she only cries at night when she's ready for bed. When I place her on the bed and then lie down next to her, fiddling with my clothes to offer her the breast, she gets this big, sloppy grin on her face. She is joyous, and I know, "Yeah, this is the right thing."

It seems that when I try to limit what I give Isabel, whether because I'm distracted or tired or out of some vague sense that perhaps so much indulgence is not good, baby care becomes more difficult. Isabel is unhappy, and I feel put upon. When I allow Isabel to be physically close to me and allow my own body to be her comfort and home, she becomes calmer and easier to care for. She relates to me more, and I feel more connected to her.

People on the street ask me, "Is she a good baby?" I find this question perplexing. By this they mean, "Does she sleep through the night?" and "Does she let you lay her down?" I never know what to answer, because if Isabel were sleeping alone, or left alone much, I'm sure she would not be a "good baby." Her world would be chaotic and painful. She would kick and scream bloody murder. She would not be the contented and delighted baby she is now. So I will have to keep thinking about how to answer that question.

A GIFT FOR DAD

My wife and I have been attachment parenting our son for all of his nearly four years of life. But true confessions here: I was a detached dad from Conor's birth until he was about three months old. The responsibility of fatherhood hit me over the head like a ton of wet diapers. Conor was beautiful, but he was also colicky, was only happy with his mom (I told myself), needed to be carried all the time, wouldn't sleep alone, wouldn't sleep much at all, and needed someone, it seemed, every moment of the day and night. He was the epitome of the high-need baby. So I did what guys know how to do best: I went into escape mode. "Let's face it," I would assure myself, "Mom does it best."

I remember one day very well when Conor was about three months old. It was a turning point for me, a threshold moment of attachment parenting. It was time for my wife to return to work, so I was on duty. (We had arranged our working lives to avoid day care.) Conor was inconsolable. He had been crying his eyes out for fifteen minutes, his little body shuddering, his face soaked in tears. I thought I was going to have a nervous breakdown. Instead, I put him in his bouncy chair, smiled into his eyes, and started bouncing him. For some reason, it worked. He suddenly stopped crying, and the most beautiful smile I had ever seen spread over his glistening face. This smile was for me and me alone. He had offered me a gift of himself — the only thing a little baby has to give. The years following that moment have been filled with opening Conor's gifts to me. Sometimes they're wrapped in that tough packing tape; other times it's just cellophane. And sometime I'm all thumbs. But every time, the gift is worth the effort.

WORKING AND STAYING ATTACHED

I am a university professor. I worked hard to complete my doctoral degree and hoped to complete it quickly so that I would still be young enough to have a family. I did not realize then how strongly I would feel about attachment parenting and the benefits my baby and I would enjoy from being together for so much of his young life.

My university provides for three weeks of maternity leave. Even before my son was born, I knew this was not enough time. Fortunately, my husband, who is in the same field as I am, agreed to cover my courses for about six weeks after our son was born. Still, I was working, preparing classes, grading papers, and completing articles for publication during most of this time — all the while breastfeeding my son, holding him, and carrying him in a sling.

After six weeks at home, it was time to return to the classroom. I was very concerned that I would find myself swept up in the routine and that I would miss precious moments with my son while finding it difficult to pump milk for him and keep everything going. Since I could not leave my job to stay at home with my son, I decided instead to try bringing him with me.

Much to my surprise, everyone in my department was very helpful. I moved to a bigger office. My mother agreed to come with me and the baby, to care for him while I was teaching or meeting with students.

My mother and my son had a wonderful time together. I reminded her frequently she was there to make it possible for my son to be with his mama whenever he felt he needed her. So, with no pacifiers or other distractions, my son and I were together whenever either one of us felt a need for the other. When he wanted to nurse, he came with me to class, nursing in a sling as I taught. I remember after a meeting with the chair of the department, a secretary stepped up to me to get a close peek at the baby. As she peered over my shoulder, she said suddenly and quietly, "Is he eating?" When I nodded, she left the room, and when she saw me later, she asked with great interest, "How did you *do* that? I thought he was sleeping!" I told her that nursing clothes had come a long way since she had breastfed her own children a generation earlier.

My son came with me to work for the first eighteen months of his life. For the last six months of this period, as he was beginning to walk and my mother found it hard to keep up with him, my husband rearranged his schedule so that he could come to work with us. In the last few months, they found wonderful activities to share at home while I taught. I am currently working as much as possible from home. I am also taking advantage of technology, using cyberspace as an extension of my classroom, so I can keep in touch with my students and their needs throughout the semester. If this arrangement does not work well in the next few years, I can always work at a virtual university until my son is older!

SENSITIVE NIGHT WEANING

Although I became a parent only twenty-one months ago, I had worked with young people for most my life and felt confident that I could raise a child in a humane and respectful way. Our daughter, Amae, has been treated as a full member of this family since birth. We have always spoken to her as though she could understand everything we said, telling her gently what was going to happen next. She was walked for hours in a sling by both my husband and me, nursed on cue day and night, and always slept with one or both of us. We felt we were doing everything right.

What we didn't anticipate and weren't prepared for was sleep deprivation. Amae is a very aware, very wise, very connected child who had woken and nursed every two hours since birth. I could count on one hand the nights I had had more than four hours of sleep in a row, and the nights I had awakened more frequently — like every twenty minutes — were much more common. This incredible, lovable child often woke from deep sleep screaming or crying, leaving us with raw nerves. She had cranky, sometimes very depressed parents. Our family learned the hard way that you cannot make anyone sleep.

We tried everything we could think of: a calm predictable bedtime routine; visits to various doctors; voracious reading on the subject. The answers were all the same: Amae was healthy, and she just needed to cry it out. We were unwilling to do this, but our family life was disintegrating into chaos.

In a tearful conversation, my husband suggested we try to night-wean — that is, not allow Amae to nurse at night. He would sleep with Amae, while I slept in another room. I felt heartbroken. I was worried that somehow this change would hurt Amae. Mostly, I hated that we would be abandoning the style of parenting we believed in passionately.

Over the days that followed, I began to think that there must be a way to go about this that would be consistent with our commitment to attachment parenting. We came up with the following plan:

1. We would write a book for Amae to help her prepare for the change.
2. We would read the book several days in a row before we began our new nighttime routine.
3. If at the end of a week Amae was showing any worrisome changes in her daytime personality, we would stop and try something different.
4. My husband would talk gently with Amae at night, repeating soothing words and offering choices.
5. When the alarm went off in the morning, I would go in and nurse Amae.

We wrote the book, and I drew illustrations. We read it to Amae during the day rather than at bedtime, so that she wouldn't associate the stress with going to sleep. Amae cried when we read the book, but she had both of us there, acknowledging her feelings in a calm, no-pressure atmosphere. We felt this helped her prepare emotionally for the change, and we believe she did most of her crying about it while we were all together reading the book.

When we embarked on our first no-nursing night, Amae cried on and off for fifteen minutes while her Dada spoke softly to her; then she draped herself over him and fell asleep. She quickly began sleeping longer stretches — six to eight continuous hours without waking. She now sleeps until 8:00, where before she would wake at 5:30 or 6:00. We are down to one, maybe two night wakings, which are very peaceful. Amae laughs when she hears the alarm go off, says "Nurse!" when she sees me, then does just that before falling back asleep.

UNDERSTANDING "CRIES"

Now that Michael is nearly three and a half years old, we are seeing the results of early attachment parenting in how easy it is to discipline him. We knew in those early days that the way we cared for Michael would pay off. We just didn't know exactly how much.

When "we" were pregnant with Michael, we were elated. Because I was exposed to DES when my mother was pregnant, I was at high risk for infertility, miscarriage, early labor, and other problems. So to hear that a baby was coming was such a miracle! I bonded with him during my pregnancy. My husband spoke nightly to my bulging abdomen, as if the baby were right in his arms. Many times when I told him that the baby was pressing on a nerve, he would say, "Baby, please move. You're getting on Mommy's nerves." Every time my husband spoke to the baby, the baby would respond by moving. We were amazed at how aware Michael was of his father's presence even then. He also moved to music, especially Handel's *Messiah*. (He still loves music and even plays guitar.)

Michael was born a few weeks premature. I had an emergency cesarean due to a breech presentation and early labor. Because I couldn't hold him by myself right away, my husband nestled Michael's head into my shoulder and then kissed and hugged him while talking to him as he had when I was pregnant. Once we were home, he told me: "You take care of the baby, and I'll take care of you." He already felt so close to Michael that he ended up taking care of both of us. He changed diapers and walked baby through the house. (I almost had to push him out the door to get him to go back to work.)

Because Michael was so sleepy and immature, breastfeeding was difficult. A lot of people suggested "everyone would understand if we gave up," but we refused. I worked with a professional lactation consultant, and with the relentless support of my husband, we succeeded. (We even won an essay contest with a description of our incredible against-all-odds breastfeeding experience.)

It was my husband who insisted we respond to Michael's cries at night. We would always go to him, but my heart would ache when I would put him back in the crib and he would cry. Something didn't feel right, but I didn't know what to do. Child psychology courses I had taken in college and various reading materials had stressed the need for baby to learn independence and self-comforting skills. My husband saw things more clearly than I did and said that was ridiculous. He was the one who said, "Let him sleep with us." We did (supported by the advice in Dr. Sears's books, of course!).

When I think back, I remember how even when Michael was in the bassinet by our bed, I longed to have him closer. It was absurd, but I would sleep with my arm (aching) over the edge of the bassinet around him all night to let him know I was right there, although it never occurred to me to put him in bed next to me.

People were amazed at how well rested we all were. Amazingly, we sold my parents on the idea of sharing sleep, and they were never critical, perhaps because they had never read anything at all on the subject. They simply saw how secure Michael was.

Our son's first year felt like Parenting 101: the basics. Just as you need some math classes before you can take physics, we are finding that the foundation of attachment parenting in infancy prepared us for Parenting 102, the second year, and Parenting 103, the third. If we hadn't learned to know Michael in infancy, we would be failing desperately. There are always new issues as he grows, new "cries" of frustration and growth.

Here's an example. One night my husband returned home late from work, as he had all week. We put on one of Michael's favorite videos, *The Sound of Music*, and sat down to watch it together. Michael is incredibly communicative for a three-year-old, with an extensive vocabulary. However, there are days when he can't seem to say what he needs and wants to say.

After a few minutes of the movie, Michael said angrily, "Turn it off!" We were surprised and said, "But you love this music. What's wrong?" He replied, "Turn it off!" He proceeded to toss some toys around. I suggested, "Why don't you go on the couch and sit with Daddy to watch the movie." He said, "No, I don't want a Daddy." My husband and I looked at each other puzzled. We knew we had to find out what this irrational, yet substantial, "cry" meant. If we continued to watch the movie, we would selfishly be ignoring what Michael was trying to tell us. And because we know him, we knew his behavior was more than him just wanting his way. We had to respond to him, not to his words. But we were getting frustrated. Suddenly we both noticed that Michael was on the verge of a tantrum. He was lying next to my husband on the floor, kicking the couch, as if wanting Dad to tell him to stop (anything to get Dad's attention). So, my husband said, "How would you like to help Daddy calibrate his level?" (My husband's work is with tools.) Michael's whole face lit up. I said, "I thought you didn't want a daddy." He replied, "I do want a daddy. I want my daddy to be with me." My husband had worked late every night that week, and this was the first night he had come home when Michael was still awake. How could Michael possibly say, "Excuse me, Daddy, would you mind watching the movie another time? I haven't seen you all week and I really need some time with you." Michael knew that sitting next to his dad on the couch wouldn't give him the one-on-one time that he so longed for.

We were amazed at how the evening changed because we invested time in "responding to his cries." Had we not looked beyond Michael's behavior that night (and many times since), we would have failed to communicate to him how much we care.

COMPASSION FOR OTHERS

My ten-year-old son, John, went with me as part of a community-outreach program to visit a geriatric home. We had made Valentines to give to the elderly people who lived there. When we were there, I noticed that John seemed to be able to relate better than the other kids to the people he met. Most kids were taken aback by the older peoples' disabilities and frailties and found it hard to see beyond this. John, on the other hand, showed a great deal of compassion for them. He went out of his way to help the older people, for example, by reaching out and helping them with walking. He showed that he was paying attention to the human beings inside these aging bodies. Later, he spoke about what a wonderful heart one of these patients had, how kind another was, and how another one had such a great sense of humor. The disabled physical forms did not seem to bother him or take up his attention, whereas that was what most of the other kids talked about. They were stuck on the outside appearance and couldn't see beyond this to appreciate what was going on inside of these people.

I attribute John's compassion to my attachment-parenting practices. I'm grateful for having the opportunity to guide him in establishing values and having compassion for others.

WHEN BABIES WITH TEETH NURSE AND SIXTEEN-YEAR-OLDS DRIVE

Imagine my surprise to find I'm suddenly the shortest member of my family! My three breast-fed babies have disappeared, and in their place I find three independent adults (well, three almost adults: one out of college, one in college, and one still at home in high school). My oldest is an artist and a teacher, living many miles from home, successfully patching together an assortment of jobs to support himself while pursuing the creative urges that many in my generation set aside when we reached what we thought was the age of adult responsibility. Number two, my only daughter, is finishing up a semester in London, where she learned she can navigate the Tube, shop for and cook a three-course dinner for four, and plan a spur-of-the-moment weekend in Paris all on her own, without Mom to hold her hand. But it's my youngest I want to talk about, Mr. fifteen-year-old six-foot-tall high school student. I may have to stand on tippie-toes to kiss him now, but he'll always be my baby — the one who shared my bed, who nursed past age three, who benefited from all my trial-and-error experiences mothering his older siblings, the last warm bundle to hold my nipple so gently between his teeth as he paused from nursing to smile up at me.

Recently David's school had a program for sophomores and their parents to prepare us for the fast-approaching moment when our kids will be driving, age sixteen in this state. The program was mandatory. David didn't want to go, and to tell the truth, neither did I, having been through this twice before with no problems. But I believe in obeying the rules, so that's how I found myself sitting next to fidgety David in the auditorium one Wednesday evening, listening to a "family educator," a well-intentioned young woman who isn't yet a mother, telling us that she'd brought us together to address our fears about our children becoming drivers.

But wait. I don't belong here. I'm not afraid. Really. I trust David to drive as carefully as any sixteen-year-old can. I trust him not to drink and drive. I trust him to obey the law. I trusted his big brother and sister before him, and my trust was rewarded with safe driving and responsible, law-abiding behavior. Now I will trust David. But first, I have to trust myself — to know my child and to judge what situations are or are not safe and appropriate for him, just as I once trusted myself to know when he was ready for weaning, for potty training, for nursery school, for riding a bike. If I don't think he's ready for the responsibility of driving, I won't take him for the test. When I decide he's ready, and he passes the test, I'll gladly hand over the keys, trusting him to live up to my expectations.

And that's when I started thinking about nursing, right there in the high school auditorium, surrounded by blue-jeaned kids shifting restlessly in their seats, tapping their oversize sneakers, girls flipping back their hair, boys fingering hopefully for stubble on their chins. I knew that it was breastfeeding — and La Leche League in particular — that had prepared me for this moment. Back when I trusted my baby to tell me his needs, and I trusted myself to fulfill his needs — those most basic needs for nourishment and life — I was preparing for the time when I'd have to trust him to grow up, and I'd have to trust myself to let him.

So when the young "family educator" advised us parents to hide the car keys, so that our new drivers wouldn't be tempted to sneak away with the car and break all our rules, I patted David on the knee, and we got up and left. I knew I'd be giving David his own set of car keys as soon as he passed the driving test, just as I'd done for his older brother and sister. Don't get me wrong, I'm not planning to just close my eyes and set him free. It's just that I trust him to know that along with the keys come rules and responsibilities: ask permission before you take the car; tell me where you're going; tell me what time you'll be home; if I say come home sooner, do; if I say don't go, don't; of course, no drinking and driving under the influence or no handing those keys over to any of your friends. Most important: If you're ever in trouble — even if you've broken any of the above rules — call me!

No matter how good a parent you try to be, you never know how things will turn out. You might still end up with children whose problems cause you heartache. But I have to believe that the reason I've been so richly rewarded as I've watched all three of my children grow up is at least in small part because I've always trusted them.

Oh, and by the way, remember all those times I trusted three-year-old David to hold my nipple ever so gently between his teeth while we nursed? Well, he did bite me once, and I used a tip I'd learned from La Leche League: I just hugged him closer, so he had to open his mouth for air. He never bit me again. One more thing. I hope when that "family educator" has children of her own someday, she'll find her way to breastfeeding, and she'll discover — as did I — that we can learn as much from our children as we can teach them as long as we trust them.

Resources

PARENTING AND PEDIATRIC INFORMATION

www.parenting.com An informative Web site on parenting issues. Dr. Bill and Martha Sears answer parenting questions and host frequent chats and workshops.

www.AskDrSears.com A comprehensive Web site on healthcare information for infants and children.

Attachment Parenting International (API) A nonprofit organization networking with parents, professionals, and like-minded organizations around the world. In addition to providing assistance to those forming attachment-parenting support groups, API provides educational materials, research information, and consulting and referral services to promote attachment-parenting concepts. 615-298-4334 or www.attachmentparenting.org

BABY CARRIERS

A soft baby carrier is one of the most useful parenting products you and your baby will enjoy. Consult the following resources for information on sling-type carriers and step-by-step instructions on using a sling.

The Original Baby Sling
800-421-0526 or www.originalbabysling.com or www.nojo.com

Crown Crafts Infant Products
310-763-8100 or www.crowncraftsinfantproducts.com

www.AskDrSears.com Visit our store.

BEDSIDE CO-SLEEPERS

A bedside co-sleeper lets baby and parents sleep close to one another yet still have their own space. This criblike bed safely attaches to the parents' bed.

Arm's Reach Co-Sleeper
800-954-9353 or 818-879-9353 or www.armsreach.com

NURSING CLOTHING AND ACCESSORIES

Motherwear 800-950-2500 or
www.motherwear.com

BREASTFEEDING HELP AND RESOURCES

La Leche League International (LLLI)
800-435-8316 or 847-519-7730 or
www.lalecheleague.org

International Lactation Consultant Association (ILCA)
919-787-5181 or www.ilca.org

Corporate Lactation Program by Medela
800-435-8316 or www.medela.com

ATTACHMENT PARENTING MULTIPLES

National Organization of Mothers of Twins Clubs
877-540-2200 or 615-595-0936 or
www.nomotc.org

National Organization of Fathers of Twins Club
www.nofotc.org

www.twinslist.org A valuable resource with lots of message boards with practical tips.

Mothering Multiples: Breastfeeding and Caring for Twins or More, by Karen Gromada (La Leche League, 1999)

Index

Page numbers in boldface type refer to main discussions.